COGNITIVE NEUROPSYCHOLOGY

Volume 28 • Issues 3 & 4 • May & June 2011

Special Issue: The specialization of function: Cognitive and neural perspectives on modularity
Guest Editors: Bradford Z. Mahon and Jessica F. Cantlon

COGNITIVE NEUROPSYCHOLOGY

Cognitive Neuropsychology aims to promote the investigation of human cognition that is based on neuropsychological methods including brain pathology, recording, stimulation or imaging. The research can involve brain-lesioned or neurologically-intact adults, children or non-human animals as long as it makes an explicit contribution to our understanding of normal human cognitive processes and representations. Cognition is understood broadly to include the domains of perception, attention, planning, language, thinking, memory, and action. The research may, additionally, contribute to issues regarding clinical populations and the neurobiology of cognition.

Cognitive Neuropsychology is currently the only journal in which the focus is the investigation of human cognition informed by neural data.

Cognitive Neuropsychology is of interest to cognitive scientists and neuroscientists, neuropsychologists, neurologists, psycholinguists, speech pathologists, physiotherapists, and psychiatrists.

Notes for contributors are available from the publisher on request and manuscript submission guidelines are given on the inside back cover of most issues. *Cognitive Neuropsychology* now offers an iOpenAccess option for authors. For more information see: http://www.tandf.co.uk/journals/iopenaccess.asp

Subscription information

Cognitive Neuropsychology is published by Psychology Press, an imprint of the Taylor & Francis Group, an Informa business.
New subscriptions and changes of address should be sent to: Psychology Press, c/o T&F Customer Services, Informa UK Ltd, Sheepen Place, Colchester, Essex, CO3 3LP, UK. Telephone: + 44 (0)20 7017 5544; Fax: + 44 (0)20 7017 5198; E-mail: subscriptions@tandf.co.uk

Send change of address notices at least six weeks in advance, and include both old and new addresses.

Subscription rates to Volume 28, 2011 (8 issues) are as follows (prices inclusive of postage and packing):

Institutions (full sub'n):	£1,229.00 (UK)	€1,620.00 (Europe)	$2,036.00 (RoW)
Institutions (online only):	£1,106.00 (UK)	€1,458.00 (Europe)	$1,832.00 (RoW)
Individuals:	£381.00 (UK)	€504.00 (Europe)	$633.00 (RoW)

An institutional subscription to the print edition also includes free access to the online edition for any number of concurrent users across a local area network.

Dollar rate applies to all subscribers outside Europe. Euro rates apply to all subscribers in Europe, except the UK and the Republic of Ireland where the pound sterling rate applies. All subscriptions are payable in advance and all rates include postage. Journals are sent by air to the USA, Canada, Mexico, India, Japan and Australasia. Subscriptions are entered on an annual basis, i.e., January to December. Payment may be made by sterling cheque, dollar cheque, euro cheque, international money order, National Giro or credit cards (Amex, Visa, and Mastercard).

Subscriptions purchased at the personal (print only) rate are strictly for personal, non-commercial use. The reselling of personal subscriptions is prohibited. Personal subscriptions must be purchased with a personal cheque or credit card. Proof of personal status may be requested.

Taylor & Francis has a flexible approach to subscriptions enabling us to match individual libraries' requirements. This journal is available via a traditional institutional subscription (either print with online access, or online only at a discount) or as part of the Behavioral Science Collection or SSH Library. For more information on our sales packages please visit http://www.tandfonline.com/page/librarians

Cognitive Neuropsychology (**USPS 016265**) is published eight times per year (in February, March, May, June, July, September, October, and December), by Psychology Press, 4 Park Square, Milton Park, Abingdon, Oxon OX14 4RN, UK. The 2011 US Institutional subscription price is $2,036.00. Airfreight and mailing in the US by Agent named Air Business Ltd, c/o Worldnet Shipping USA Inc., 155-11 146th Street, Jamaica, New York, NY 11434, USA. Periodicals postage paid at Jamaica, NY 11431, USA. **US Postmaster:** Send address changes to *Cognitive Neuropsychology* (PCGN), C/O Air Business Ltd, 155-11 146th Street, Jamaica, New York, NY 11434, USA.

Copyright: It is a condition of publication that authors vest copyright in their articles, including abstracts, in Taylor & Francis. This enables us to ensure full copyright protection and to disseminate the article, and the journal, to the widest possible readership in print and electronic formats as appropriate. Authors retain many rights under the Taylor & Francis rights policies, which can be found at http://journalauthors.tandf.co.uk/preparation/copyright.asp. Authors are themselves responsible for obtaining permission to reproduce copyright material from other sources.

Disclaimer: Psychology Press makes every effort to ensure the accuracy of all the information (the "Content") contained in its publications. However, Psychology Press and its agents and licensors make no representations or warranties whatsoever as to the accuracy, completeness or suitability for any purpose of the Content and disclaim all such representations and warranties whether express or implied to the maximum extent permitted by law. Any views expressed in this publication are the views of the authors and are not the views of Psychology Press.

Back issues: Taylor & Francis retains a 3-year back issue stock of journals. Older volumes are held by our official stockists: Periodicals Service Company, 11 Main Street, Germantown, NY 12526, USA to whom all orders and enquiries should be addressed. Tel: +1 518 537 4700; Fax: +1 518 537 5899; E-mail: psc@periodicals.com; URL: http://www.periodicals.com/tandf.html

Information about Psychology Press journals and other publications is available from http://www.psypress.com

Go to www.psypress.com/cogneuropsychology for current information about this journal, including how to access the online version or to register for the free online table of contents alerting service.

Cognitive Neuropsychology is covered by the following abstracting, indexing, and citation services: Current Contents (ISI); ASSIA; APA PsycINFO; Sociological Abstracts; Biosciences Information Service; MLA International Bibliography; EMBASE; LLBA; Neuroscience Citation Index (ISI); Research Alerts (ISI); Social SciSearch (ISI); Social Science Citation Index (ISI); Social Services Abstracts; SciSearch (ISI); CDAB; UnCover; Linguistics Abstracts; SCOPUS; MEDLINE.

Typeset in the UK by Techset Composition Limited, Salisbury, Wiltshire. Printed by Hobbs the Printer Ltd, Totton, Hampshire, UK.

This publication has been produced with acid-free paper manufactured to strict environmental standards and with pulp derived from sustainable forests.

COGNITIVE NEUROPSYCHOLOGY, 2011, 28 (3 & 4), 147–155

The specialization of function: Cognitive and neural perspectives

Bradford Z. Mahon[1,2] and Jessica F. Cantlon[1]

[1]Department of Brain and Cognitive Sciences, University of Rochester, Rochester, NY, USA
[2]Department of Neurosurgery, University of Rochester Medical School, Rochester, NY, USA

A unifying theme that cuts across all research areas and techniques in the cognitive and brain sciences is whether there is specialization of function at levels of processing that are "abstracted away" from sensory inputs and motor outputs. Any theory that articulates claims about specialization of function in the mind/brain confronts the following types of interrelated questions, each of which carries with it certain theoretical commitments. What methods are appropriate for decomposing complex cognitive and neural processes into their constituent parts? How do cognitive processes map onto neural processes, and at what resolution are they related? What types of conclusions can be drawn about the structure of mind from dissociations observed at the neural level, and vice versa? The contributions that form this Special Issue of *Cognitive Neuropsychology* represent recent reflections on these and other issues from leading researchers in different areas of the cognitive and brain sciences.

Keywords: Modularity; Additive factors; Brain function; Cognition; Neuropsychology; Functional magnetic resonance imaging.

Functional specialization is a property of biological systems generally. Specialization of function in the human brain is most clear at the periphery of the system at the levels of primary sensory and motor systems. Neuroscientific, psychophysical, and cognitive neuropsychological research over the last half century has demonstrated the existence of cortical maps in primary input and output systems that are organized topographically. Topographic organization—for instance, of eccentricity preferences in early visual cortex—indicates a high degree of specialization of function in the cortical representation of a psychophysical continuum, such as spatial location with respect to the fovea. However, beyond the primary input and output systems there is little agreement as to whether there is specialization of function and, if so, over what cognitive dimensions that specialization should be understood to operate. Perhaps one of the unifying themes that cuts across all research areas and techniques in the cognitive and brain sciences is whether there is specialization of function at levels of processing that are "abstracted away" from sensory inputs and motor outputs.

Correspondence should be addressed to Bradford Z. Mahon, Meliora Hall, Box 270268, University of Rochester, Rochester, NY, USA. (E-mail: mahon@rcbi.rochester.edu).

The authors are grateful to Jorge Almeida, Max Coltheart, Karl Friston, Cathy Price, Brenda Rapp, and Wayne Wu for their comments on an earlier version of this manuscript. J.F.C. was supported by National Institutes of Health (NIH) Grant R01-HD064636 and a grant from the James S. McDonnell Foundation.

http://www.psypress.com/cogneuropsychology

http://dx.doi.org/10.1080/02643294.2011.633504

The contributions that are collected together within this Special Issue of *Cognitive Neuropsychology* represent recent reflections on this issue from leading researchers in different areas of the cognitive and brain sciences.

Cognitive neuropsychology—the method of revealing the organization of the mind from patterns of spared and impaired performance in brain-damaged individuals—has played a central role in the development of claims about the specialization of function in the human brain for well over a century (e.g., since the contributions of Broca and Wernicke). This method is based on the supposition that it is possible to dissociate different components of cognition through damage to the brain, which has led to the interesting consideration of whether the mere fact that the method works implies certain properties about functional specialization in the human brain (e.g., Caramazza, 1992; Coltheart, 1989; Dunn & Kirsner, 2003; Farah & McClelland, 1992; Rapp, 2001; Shallice, 1988). More recently, with the widespread use of functional neuroimaging techniques such as functional magnetic resonance imaging (fMRI), there has been renewed interest in the mapping of cognitive processes onto neural events and substrates (e.g., Coltheart, 2006; Henson, 2006; Poldrack, 2006; Posner, 2003; Uttal, 2011). But even setting aside brain organization, research into the organization of cognitive processes has fuelled intense debates about whether specialized representations should be posited, or whether the empirical phenomena can be explained without assuming specialization of representational content. Connectionist modelling has made a particularly important contribution to these debates, as it can offer existence proofs of why specialized content need not be assumed in order to observe a particular empirical result (McClelland, Rumelhart, et al., 1986; Rumelhart, McClelland, et al., 1986).

The cognitive revolution was founded on the methodological commitment that an adequate explanation of behaviour must make reference to cognitive processes, and that it is possible to understand the structure and content of the mind through experiments that tease apart complex processes into their component parts. Saul Sternberg's contributions to cognitive psychology, from his now classic 1969 theoretical article (Sternberg, 1969a) through to his most recent contribution on this issue (Sternberg, 2011), are some of the most enduring contributions that have been made to the science of the mind. Motivated in part by the early work of F. C. Donders (Donders, 1868), Sternberg's classic studies (Sternberg, 1966, 1969b) introduced the "additive factors approach". In his initial studies, he systematically varied memory load and measured its effect on speed and accuracy of recall in order to assess the cumulative effects of information-processing stages. Subjects were given a list of N numerals to memorize and were then asked whether a test numeral had appeared in the list. Sternberg showed that each additional item in the initial memory set added about 30 to 40 milliseconds to search time, indicating that subjects were engaging in a serial rather than a parallel search. In addition, he showed that the time to respond at test increased linearly with the total size of the memory set, indicating that subjects engage in an exhaustive search, rather than a self-terminating search. Those systematic experimental manipulations provided evidence for cumulative effects of component stages of information processing. More broadly, the introduction of additive factors logic provided a toolbox with which to decompose complex series of cognitive processes into their elementary operations and then to study the content and dynamics of each operation or stage.

We are now at a point where it is possible to direct the insights from many different methods toward a single question of how the mind works—using behavioural performance in normal subjects or individuals with brain damage, neural activation as measured with fMRI, the effects on cognition and neural function of transcranial magnetic stimulation (TMS), neurophysiological recording and stimulation studies in both nonhuman primates and humans, electroencephalography (EEG), magnetoencephalography (MEG), optical imaging, and more. We have the tools to measure and probe the human mind at almost all levels of analysis. However, the strength of our science will not depend on the tools, but on how they are used to develop new ideas and resolve existing issues. This Special Issue of *Cognitive Neuropsychology* is a step in that direction. An element common to all of the papers in this volume, and which distinguishes this group of articles, is the careful scrutiny applied to the role of functional specialization in developing a theory of how the mind/brain works.

The many meanings of "modularity"

Modularity, across the many uses of the term, can be understood as a special case of specialization of function. Hypotheses about cognitive and brain function gain traction when embedded within, or contrasted against, a coherent theoretical framework of modularity. However, there are a number of meanings that have been given to the theoretical term "modularity". In some cases, the different uses of the term "modularity" have led to dichotomies in the cognitive science literature that disappear when the meanings of the word are ironed out. For that reason, we believe it is useful to attempt to (nonexhaustively) lay out some of the more common deployments of the term; this exposition is meant to be purely descriptive and to distinguish different theoretical constructs of modularity. At the broadest level, different notions of modularity can be separated according to whether they are based on a methodological criterion or on properties that a system/process must possess in order to be modular.

1. For Sternberg (2011), a process is modular if it is separately modifiable; in this usage of the term, a module corresponds to a "stage" of processing. Thus, modularity is defined according to a methodological or epistemological criterion. Of course, if a process is observed to be separately modifiable, then within the framework of additive factors logic, certain features of its processing may be inferred. But, for Sternberg (2011), processes that might be hypothesized to have those same processing features, but which could not be demonstrated to be separately modifiable, would not be referred to as modular.

2. An alternative is to define modularity in terms of the properties or characteristics that a process must have in order to be modular. The best known articulation of this view is that developed by Fodor in his monograph "Modularity of Mind" (Fodor, 1983). For Fodor, modules possess some combination, or all, of a set of properties that include information encapsulation, shallow outputs, dedicated neural machinery, a characteristic developmental profile, and being fast, automatic, innate, and domain specific. Of these properties, information encapsulation is, in Fodor's words, "the essence" of modularity. On the basis of that constellation of properties that characterize (putative) modular processes, Fodor hedged (presciently) that modular processes were most likely to be observed at the periphery of the system, in the input and output systems. This is because peripheral processes can operate without access to global information, and so encapsulation would not be a hindrance to their processing (as it would be for more central processes).

Coltheart (2011) provides a direct comparison between what counts as a modular process for Sternberg and what counts as a modular process for Fodor (1983). In many ways, there is very little in common between Fodorian modules and Sternbergean modules, except, perhaps, that both types of modules are domain specific—that is, specialized in their content.

3. Researchers interested in the origins of cognitive and brain processes have tended to emphasize the joint criteria of domain specificity and innateness as defining of the modularity of a process (Cosmides & Tooby, 1994; Pinker, 1997). This research tradition has not emphasized the role of information encapsulation in modularity. Because information encapsulation is not considered a critical "criterion" for modularity of cognitive processes, evolutionary and developmental approaches

have postulated modular processes at all levels of processing. That approach has sparked an interesting discussion of how much of the mind is and is not candidate territory for modular processes (Carruthers, 2005; Fodor, 2000, 2005; Marcus, 2006; Pinker, 1997, 2005a, 2005b; Rabaglia, Marcus, & Lane, 2011). D'Souza and Karmiloff-Smith (2011) argue that those more promiscuous modular theories are challenged by evidence showing deep interactions among all levels of cognitive processes during development.

4. A similar emphasis on domain specificity is advanced within the still narrower construal of modularity by Coltheart, who argues that a "cognitive system is modular when and only when it is domain-specific" (Coltheart, 1999, p. 115; quoted in Coltheart, 2011). This notion of modularity could be considered quite close to Sternbergean modules, as Sternberg (2011) argues that separate modifiability is likely to be implied by domain specificity. However, the important point is that for Sternberg, the modularity of a process is warranted only when it is demonstrated to be separately modifiable; processes that are domain specific but not, for whatever reason, separately modifiable would count as modules for Coltheart but not for Sternberg.

5. A more relaxed construal of modularity has been articulated with respect to patterns of brain activation observed in functional neuroimaging. In the context of neuroimaging work, for instance, Op de Beeck and colleagues (Op de Beeck, Haushofer, & Kanwisher, 2008) have argued that *brain regions* are modular if there is "clustering of selectivity in discrete regions, with clear selectivity discontinuities at the boundaries of these regions" (Op de Beeck et al., 2008, p. 124). Under this approach of defining modularity (i.e., in terms of discontinuities in neural preferences), care must be exercised before concluding that the underlying cognitive processes are also "modular". For instance, if participants are shown different types of stimuli, and one type leads to neural specificity, then it is comfortable to conclude that the underlying cognitive processes are specialized for that type of stimulus. But, as many researchers have noted (see, e.g., Coltheart, 2006, and associated commentaries), this is not enough—it is necessary to dissect out exactly which aspects of the stimulus (and task) the region is responding to and, at that level, design new experiments to establish specificity in the region for that particular stimulus/task component. And even then, issues arise about the way in which cognitive processes (or types) map onto neural processes (or types; see Friston & Price, 2011, and discussion below). The relationship between neural specificity and specificity of the underlying cognitive processes is far from straightforward and is one of the themes that runs throughout the papers of this Special Issue.

6. Another approach for understanding modularity is to abandon "information content" as the primary benchmark of modularity and instead evaluate the modularity of processes in terms of the dynamics of information processing. Within this framework, so-called "modular" processes are counterposed to interactive processes (for cogent discussion on this point, see Coltheart, 2011). In other words, processes are modular if they do not leak or spread activation to other processes before they complete their processing. This deployment of the term "modularity" is prevalent, for instance, in theories of language processing (Levelt, 1999). Pulvermüller contrasts modularity with embodied views of cognition, in stating that "cortical functions might be served by distributed interactive functional systems [i.e., embodied cognition] rather than local encapsulated modules" (Pulvermüller, 2005, p. 576). This version of modularity is somewhat derivative of Sternbergian modularity, in that certain aspects of the dynamics of information exchange are precluded if the processes are modular.

Summary

A number of different meanings, all well defined in their respective contexts, have been given to the term "modularity" (for an overview, see Barrett & Kurzban, 2006). The goal, of course, is not to conclude whether a process is modular for its own sake, but to understand substantive issues such as the dynamics of that process, the nature of its computations, its scope of input and output, the other processes with which it interfaces, its neural implementation, and so on. For instance, if a process were found to be domain specific but not innate (e.g., printed word recognition; Dehaene & Cohen, 2011), then this would raise important questions about how cognitive and neural processes can become tuned in a highly specialized way to a completely learned category (see Plaut & Behrmann, 2011, for a computational model that explores this issue).

Moreover, the degree to which neural reorganization can result in cognitive recovery after impairment to purported modules needs to be reconciled with strong claims of modularity, domain specificity, and innateness. This issue is potentially even more complex when understanding the developmental trajectory of cognitive and neural organization. D'Souza and Karmiloff-Smith (2011) argue that specialization of function in the adult brain represents the "consolidated end state of a developmental process", and so caution must exercised when using adult organization as a model for studying development. These considerations emphasize that an understanding of the origins of (putative) modules can reveal critical aspects of their functional properties as well as their functional interactions within broader cognitive and neural systems (Gallistel, 1993; Hauser, Chomsky, & Fitch, 2002; Karmiloff-Smith, 1992).

Modularity at the cognitive and neural levels

One of the most important issues that runs throughout the cognitive and brain sciences is how cognitive processes relate to brain processes. When a purely psychological theory (a theory that makes no reference to the brain) identifies a specialized cognitive process, should we "expect" there to be a dedicated brain region for that process? What should the grain of our search in the brain be for that process—cellular through to

systems level? Might some well-defined cognitive processes not map one-to-one to brain processes? Perhaps even more difficult is to consider the reverse direction of inference: If a particular brain region is observed to respond to well-defined inputs and to be connected to other regions that also have well-defined stimulus preferences, then what types of inferences are sanctioned about the underlying cognitive processes?

In some ways, the entire enterprise of cognitive neuropsychology validates the idea that modification of the brain can lead to separate modifiability of cognitive processes; a core component of this method is the observation that a cognitive process has been separately modified in a given individual. However, this straightforward paradigm assumption does not carry over into functional neuroimaging. For functional neuroimaging, separate modifiability of neural processes/regions does not ipso facto constitute evidence for separate modifiability of cognitive processes.

Poldrack (2006) and Henson (2006) distinguished two types of inference: reverse inference (Poldrack, 2006) and forward inference (Henson, 2006). Reverse inference is reasoning from some pattern of brain activation to the claim that a given cognitive process is engaged, which Poldrack (2006) formalizes within a framework of Bayesian inference. The strength of reverse inference, as described by Poldrack, increases with the selectivity of the neural response to the putative cognitive process and the strength of prior evidence that the putative cognitive process engages that region (see Yarkoni, Poldrack, Nichols, Van Essen, & Wager, 2011). Forward inference, as defined by Henson (2006), is a way of distinguishing among two cognitive theories that differ in that one theory postulates a cognitive process involved in one experimental condition (A) but not in another condition (B), while the other theory does not postulate a difference in cognitive processes between the two conditions. If the pattern of brain activation differs between the two conditions, then that would constitute, according to forward inference, positive evidence for the theory that states that an additional cognitive process is involved in Condition A. Henson (2011) further considers the nature of the inferences that one might derive when reasoning from observed neural effects to the structure and organization of cognitive processes.

On the other side of this issue is the problem of ascribing highly specific functions to neural processes using functional neuroimaging. As Friston and Price (2011) discuss, the fact that brain regions are shown to be dissociable with functional neuroimaging, and thus have the property of separate modifiability, does not imply one way or the other whether those regions are necessary and/or sufficient for the (putative) underlying cognitive process. There are multiple reasons why. One is that it is very difficult, if not impossible, to study a "part of the brain" in isolation from the network of regions within which that region is embedded (for discussion, see also Rabaglia et al., 2011). A second reason is that there is degeneracy (Price & Friston, 2002) in neural networks (e.g., Edelman, 1978; for discussion and full references see Price & Friston). Quoting from Price and Friston's repositioning of Edelman's definition, degeneracy is "the ability of elements that are structurally different to perform the same function or yield the same output".

At first pass, it would seem to be the case that lesion evidence can ground inferences about the necessity of a given region for a given cognitive process, while functional neuroimaging data can ground inferences about the sufficiency of a given region for a given cognitive process. However, Price and Friston (2002) articulate a strong form of an argument against this, in maintaining that lesion evidence alone cannot ground inferences about necessity. The reason why is that brain lesions may compromise not only the processes that were subserved by the damaged tissue but also processes that are subserved by functionally connected regions (Price, Warburton, Moore, Frackowiak, & Friston, 2001). Price, Friston, and colleagues (Friston & Price, 2011; Price et al., 2001) refer to this property of brain lesions as "dynamic diaschisis". Previous work by those authors (Price et al., 2001) provides an example of dynamic diaschisis in that patients with lesions

to left frontal cortex and expressive but not receptive language impairments show reduced neural responses to printed words in temporal regions that are known to be functionally coupled with the damaged frontal regions. However, this raises the question of whether the fact that lesions induce effects of dynamic diaschisis should reduce confidence in inferences about the necessity of a lesioned area for a given cognitive function that is observed to be impaired. For instance, even though it is the case that neural responses in the temporal lobe are "yoked" in critical ways to processing in the frontal cortex, it may still be the case that the integrity of those frontal regions is necessary for the normal operation of some of the cognitive processes involved in reading. What is clear, however, is that the simple model of "lesions provide a window into which parts of the brain are necessary for which aspects of cognition" will not work, and that these issues must be worked out empirically for each pattern of cognitive/neural dysfunction.

A potentially even more complicated situation arises, according to D'Souza and Karmiloff-Smith (2011), for understanding developmental cognitive impairments. Those authors argue that developmental cognitive impairments may not represent selective impairment to a specialized (read: "modular") process, but rather cascading effects of perturbations early in development that prevent specialization of function from developing. How such "derailed modularization" might affect, through dynamic diaschisis, processing within a broader network of regions represents an important issue for future cognitive neuroscientific research.

In order to understand the significance of dynamic diaschisis, we need a deeper understanding of the relationship between the dynamics of information flow among levels of processing within a cognitive model and interregional connectivity in the brain. This is particularly important because the additive factors method applies to stage models, and different types of (postulated) information exchange among functionally distinct systems (cascaded activation, interactivity) preclude the use of the additive factors approach for dissociating different levels of processing. Turning this around, an important issue is whether neural evidence of interactivity among regions/processes can be counted as evidence against a theory that holds that the different regions subserve distinct stages of processing, where "stage" is understood in the Sternbergean sense. Coltheart (2011) points out that in order for neural evidence of interactivity among regions to count as evidence against a stage model of processing, "one would have to demonstrate that [the function of those] ... pathways in cortex ... is to deliver the type of feedback that [the] model denies". This level of correspondence between neural data and cognitive models represents an important direction for future research.

Rabaglia et al. (2011) also address the degree to which configurations of neural activation can be used to support or reject claims of modularity. They demonstrate that shared neural resources among cognitively distinct tasks can give rise to the well-replicated observation that variation across different tasks is highly correlated within individuals. In other words, even for tasks that would putatively depend on dissociable (read: "modular") systems, such as mathematical versus verbal reasoning, individuals who tend to be good on one task also tend to be good on another task. The authors argue through meta-analytic and computational simulation approaches that constellations of neural overlap vary among combinations of distinct tasks (i.e., there is no common pattern in the overlap of all tasks), and a single domain-general cognitive parameter need not be postulated in order to account for substantial explained variance across different tasks. The authors argue that even if components of a network of regions are shared between two different tasks, that finding may not be problematic for claims of domain specificity or modularity, as different computations may depend on different aspects of a broad network.

The cognitive neuropsychological approach, together with functional neuroimaging methods, offers a vehicle with which to understand not only the brain regions that are involved, but whether their role is sufficient, necessary, or both for executing a given operation. As Friston and Price (2011) emphasize, conducting functional neuroimaging in brain-damaged individuals offers the opportunity to test hypotheses about whether intact abilities in brain-damaged individuals are supported by latent brain networks that are not typically "online" in the normal system because there are other redundant networks that typically carry out the process. As the authors emphasize, a complete treatment of modularity and its role in understanding the brain basis of cognitive processes must account for functional activation in both healthy and damaged brains, as well as behaviour in both healthy and brain-damaged individuals.

This Special Issue of *Cognitive Neuropsychology*

Cognitive Neuropsychology is an excellent venue to host the collective contribution made by the papers gathered together in this volume. The journal has, over the last several decades, come to be aligned with a brand of cognitive research that emphasizes the study of cognition through an analysis of patterns of performance under conditions of brain damage. Under the new leadership of the journal starting in 2010, the journal has broadened its aims to include new methods, while at the same time remaining faithful to the central goal of articulating detailed cognitive theories. The articles collected together within this volume advance our understanding of the roles of modularity and functional specialization in deriving inferences about the structure of the mind from behaviour in normal and brain-damaged individuals, functional neuroimaging, computational modelling, development, and the study of individual differences.

REFERENCES

Barrett, H. C., & Kurzban, R. (2006). Modularity in cognition: Framing the debate. *Psychological Review, 113*, 628–647.

Caramazza, A. (1992). Is cognitive neuropsychology possible? *Journal of Cognitive Neuroscience, 4*, 80–95.

Carruthers, P. (2005). The case of massively modular models of mind. In R. Stainton (Ed.), *Contemporary debates in cognitive science* (pp. 205–225). Oxford, UK: Blackwell.

Coltheart, M. (1989). Cognition and its disorders. *Science, 246,* 827–828.

Coltheart, M. (1999). Modularity and cognition. *Trends in Cognitive Sciences, 3,* 115–120.

Coltheart, M. (2006). What has functional neuroimaging told us about the mind (so far)? *Cortex, 42,* 323–331.

Coltheart, M. (2011). Methods for modular modelling: Additive factors and cognitive neuropsychology. *Cognitive Neuropsychology, 28,* 224–240.

Cosmides, L., & Tooby, J. (1994). *Origins of domain specificity: The evolution of functional organization* (pp. 85–116). Cambridge, UK: Cambridge University Press.

Dehaene, S., & Cohen, L. (2011). The unique role of the visual word form area in reading. *Trends in Cognitive Sciences, 15,* 254–262.

Donders, F. C. (1868/1969). On the speed of mental processes. In W. G. Koster (Ed.), *Attention and Performance II,* (pp. 412–431). *Acta Psychologica, 30,* 276–315. (original work published in 1868).

D'Souza, D., & Karmiloff-Smith, A. (2011). When modularization fails to occur: A developmental perspective. *Cognitive Neuropsychology, 28,* 276–287.

Dunn, J. C., & Kirsner, K. (2003). What can we infer from double dissociations? *Cortex, 39,* 1–7.

Edelman, G. M. (1978). The Mindful Brain. In G. M. Edelman, & V. B. Mountcastle (Eds.), (pp. 51–100). MIT Press.

Farah, M. J., & McClelland, J. L. (1992). Neural network models and cognitive neuropsychology. *Psychiatric Annals, 22,* 148–153.

Fodor, J. (1983). *Modularity of mind.* Cambridge, MA: MIT.

Fodor, J. A. (2000). *The mind doesn't work that way: The scope and limits of computational psychology.* Cambridge, MA: MIT Press.

Fodor, J. A. (2005). Reply to Steven Pinker "So how *does* the mind work?". *Mind & Language, 20,* 25–32.

Friston, K. J., & Price, C. J. (2011). Modules and brain mapping. *Cognitive Neuropsychology, 28,* 241–250.

Gallistel, C. R. (1993). *The organization of learning.* Cambridge, MA: MIT Press.

Hauser, M. D., Chomsky, N., & Fitch, W. T. (2002). The faculty of language: What is it, who has it, and how did it evolve? *Science, 298,* 1569–1579.

Henson, R. N. (2006). Forward inference in functional neuroimaging: Dissociations vs associations. *Trends in Cognitive Science, 10,* 64–69.

Henson, R. N. (2011). How to discover modules in mind and brain: The curse of nonlinearity, and blessing of neuroimaging. A comment on Sternberg (2011). *Cognitive Neuropsychology, 28,* 209–223.

Karmiloff-Smith, A. (1992). *Beyond modularity: A developmental perspective on cognitive science.* Cambridge, MA: MIT Press.

Levelt, W. J. M. (1999). Models of word production. *Trends in Cognitive Sciences, 3,* 223–232.

Marcus, G. F. (2006). Cognitive architecture and descent with modification. *Cognition, 101,* 443–465.

McClelland, J. L., Rumelhart, D. E., & the PDP research group (1986). *Parallel distributed processing: Explorations in the microstructure of cognition* (Vol. II). Cambridge, MA: MIT Press.

Op de Beeck, H. P., Haushofer, J., & Kanwisher, N. G. (2008). Interpreting fMRI data: Maps, modules and dimensions. *Nature Reviews Neuroscience, 9,* 123–135.

Pinker, S. (1997). *How the mind works.* New York: W. W. Norton & Company.

Pinker, S. (2005a). A reply to Jerry Fodor on how the mind works. *Mind & Language, 20,* 33–38.

Pinker, S. (2005b). So how *does* the mind work? *Mind & Language, 20,* 1–24.

Plaut, D. C., & Behrmann, M. (2011). Complementary neural representations for faces and words: A computational perspective. *Cognitive Neuropsychology, 28,* 251–275.

Poldrack, R. A. (2006). Can cognitive processes be inferred from neuroimaging data? *Trends in Cognitive Science, 10,* 59–63.

Posner, M. I. (2003). Imaging a science of mind. *Trends in Cognitive Science, 7,* 450–453.

Price, C. J., & Friston, K. J. (2002). Degeneracy and cognitive anatomy. *Trends in Cognitive Science, 6,* 416–421.

Price, C. J., Warburton, E. A., Moore, C. J., Frackowiak, R. S., & Friston, K. J. (2001). Dynamic diaschisis: Anatomically remote and context-sensitive human brain lesions. *Journal of Cognitive Neuroscience, 13,* 419–429.

Pulvermüller, F. (2005). Brain mechanisms linking language and action. *Nature Reviews Neuroscience, 6,* 576–582.

Rabaglia, C., Marcus, G. F., & Lane, S. P. (2011). What can individual differences tell us about the specialization of function? *Cognitive Neuropsychology, 28,* 288–303.

Rapp, B. (2001). *What deficits reveal about the human mind/brain: A handbook of cognitive neuropsychology*. Philadelphia, PA: Psychology Press.

Rumelhart, D. E., McClelland, J. L., & The PDP Research Group (1986). *Parallel distributed processing: Explorations in the microstructure of cognition* (Vol. I). Cambridge, MA: MIT Press.

Shallice, T. (1988). *From neuropsychology to mental structure*. New York, NY: Cambridge University Press.

Sternberg, S. (1966). High-speed scanning in human memory. *Science, 153,* 652–654.

Sternberg, S. (1969a). The discovery of processing stages: Extensions of Donders' method. In W. G. Koster (Ed.), *Attention and Performance II* (pp. 276–315). *Acta Psychologica, 30,* 276–315.

Sternberg, S. (1969b). Memory-scanning: Mental processes revealed by reaction-time experiments. *American Scientist, 57,* 421–457.

Sternberg, S. (2011). Modular processes in mind and brain. *Cognitive Neuropsychology, 28,* 156–208.

Uttal, W. R. (2011). *Mind and brain: A critical appraisal of cognitive neuroscience*. Cambridge, MA: MIT Press.

Yarkoni, T., Poldrack, R. A., Nichols, T. E., Van Essen, D. C., & Wager, T. D. (2011). Large-scale automated synthesis of human functional neuroimaging data. *Nature Methods, 8,* 665–670.

COGNITIVE NEUROPSYCHOLOGY, 2011, 28 (3 & 4), 156–208

Modular processes in mind and brain

Saul Sternberg

University of Pennsylvania, Philadelphia, PA, USA

One approach to understanding a complex process starts with an attempt to divide it into *modules*: subprocesses that are independent in some sense, and have distinct functions. In this paper, I discuss an approach to the modular decomposition of neural and mental processes. Several examples of process decomposition are presented, together with discussion of inferential requirements. Two examples are of well-established and purely behavioural realizations of the approach (signal detection theory applied to discrimination data; the method of additive factors applied to reaction-time data), and lead to the identification of *mental modules*. Other examples, leading to the identification of *modular neural processes*, use brain measures, including the fMRI signal, the latencies of electrophysiological events, and their amplitudes. Some measures are *pure* (reflecting just one process), while others are *composite*. Two of the examples reveal mental and neural modules that correspond. Attempts to associate brain regions with behaviourally defined processing modules that use a brain manipulation (transcranial magnetic stimulation, TMS) are promising but incomplete. I show why the process-decomposition approach discussed here, in which the criterion for modularity is *separate modifiability*, is superior for modular decomposition to the more frequently used task comparison procedure (often used in cognitive neuropsychology) and to its associated subtraction method. To demonstrate the limitations of task comparison, I describe the erroneous conclusion to which it has led about sleep deprivation, and the interpretive difficulties in a TMS study.

Correspondence should be addressed to Saul Sternberg, University of Pennsylvania, 3401 Walnut Street, C-Wing, Philadelphia, PA 19104, USA. (E-mail: saul@psych.upenn.edu).

For providing unpublished details of their data I thank Brent Alsop, Marinella Cappelletti, Stanislas Dehaene, Russell Epstein, Silke Goebel, John Kounios, Lotfi Merabet, Allen Osman, Alvaro Pascual-Leone, Philippe Pinel, Eric Schumacher, and Fren Smulders. For helpful discussions I thank Geoffrey Aguirre, David Brainard, Russell Epstein, Martha Farah, Joshua Gold, Roy Hamilton, Nancy Kanwisher, John Kounios, David Meyer, Jacob Nachmias, Allen Osman, and Seth Roberts. For helpful comments on the manuscript I thank Jessica Cantlon, Max Coltheart, Stanislas Dehaene, Martha Farah, Silke Goebel, Ronald Knoll, Brad Mahon, David Meyer, Allen Osman, Brenda Rapp, Eric Schumacher, Richard Schweickert, Fren Smulders, Sharon Thompson-Schill, Vincent Walsh, and two anonymous reviewers. For computer support I thank Vincent Hurtubise, Christopher Leary, and Roderick Smith.

Supplementary data (a table of features of the nineteen examples in this article and Sternberg, 2001) is published online alongside this article at: http://dx.doi.org/10.1080/02643294.2011.557231

http://dx.doi.org/10.1080/02643294.2011.557231

TABLE OF CONTENTS

1. MODULES AND MODULARITY

The first step in one approach to understanding a complex process is to attempt to divide it into *modules*: parts that are independent in some sense, and have distinct functions.[1] Early in the last century, scientific psychology, dominated by behaviourism, emphasized the directly observable relations between stimuli and responses, and devoted little effort to describing the perception, memory, and thought processes that intervene. During the second half of the century there was a change in the kinds of questions that psychologists asked and in the acceptable answers. This change was perhaps influenced by the growth of computer science, which persuaded psychologists that programming concepts might be acceptable as precise descriptions of information processing by people as well as by machines. And the software-hardware distinction added legitimacy to theories couched in terms of abstract information-processing operations in the mind rather than only neurophysiological processes in the brain. In the "human information processing" approach, complex activities of perception, decision, and thought, whether conscious or unconscious, came to be conceptualized in terms of functionally distinct and relatively independent ("modular") subprocesses responsible for separate operations such as the input, transformation, storage, retrieval, and comparison of internal representations—modules whose arrangement was expressed in systematic flow charts.[2] Comparing the brain to a digital computer encourages the distinction between processors and the processes they implement. The existence of functionally specialized processors (either localized or distributed) is a sufficient condition but not a necessary one for functionally distinct processes, the concern of the present paper.

The rise in the 1980s of parallel distributed processing might seem to conflict with the idea of modular organization of processes, but it need not: PDP models "do not deny that there is a macrostructure," and are intended to "describe the internal structure of the larger (processing) units" (Rumelhart, McClelland, & the PDP Research Group, 1986, p. 12). Furthermore, even starting with a relatively unstructured neural network, there is reason to believe that over time and with experience it will develop functionally specialized processing modules, and hence, functionally specialized processes (Jacobs & Jordan, 1992; Jacobs, 1999).

Toward the end of the century, it became possible (using fMRI, for example) to measure the human brain in action with previously unattainable spatial resolution. Because functions of the brain are often implemented by specialized neural processors that are anatomically localized, these new measurement methods encouraged scientists to attempt the modular decomposition of complex neural processes, just as they had been doing for complex mental processes.

In the present paper, I describe an approach to the modular decomposition of two kinds of complex process, mental and neural, along with several examples of its application from the psychology and cognitive neuroscience literature. A mental-process module is a part of a process, functionally distinct from other parts, and investigated with behavioural measures. Such modules will be denoted **A**, **B**, etc. A neural-process module is a part of a neural process, functionally

---

[1] A module may itself be composed of modules.

[2] Heuristic arguments for the modular organization of complex biological computations have been advanced by Simon (1962, 2005) and, in his "principle of modular design", by Marr (1976), who argued (p. 485) that "Any large computation should be split up and implemented as a collection of small sub-parts that are as nearly independent of one another as the overall task allows. If a process is not designed in this way, a small change in one place will have consequences in many other places. This means that the process as a whole becomes extremely difficult to debug or to improve, whether by a human designer or in the course of natural evolution, because a small change to improve one part has to be accompanied by many simultaneous compensating changes elsewhere."

distinct from other parts, and investigated with brain measures. Such modules will be denoted $\boldsymbol{\alpha}$, $\boldsymbol{\beta}$, etc.

The important distinction between processes and processors is sometimes overlooked. *Functional* decomposition leads to process*es* that occur over time; their arrangement is described by a flow-chart. In contrast, *structural* decomposition leads to processo*rs* (e.g., as described by Erickson, 2001; Goodale, 1996; Op de Beeck, Haushofer, & Kanwisher, 2008) that are parts of a physical or biological device (such as the brain); their arrangement can sometimes be described by a circuit diagram.[3]

2. THE PROCESS-DECOMPOSITION APPROACH

2.1. Separate modifiability, selective influence, process-specific factors, and functional distinctness

Much thinking by psychologists and brain scientists about the decomposition of complex processes appeals either implicitly or explicitly to *separate modifiability* as a criterion for modularity: Two (sub)processes **A** and **B** of a complex process (mental or neural) are modules if and only if each can be changed independently of the other.[4] One purpose of the present paper is to explicate by example the notion of separate modifiability and the conditions under which one can assert it. To demonstrate separate modifiability of **A** and **B**, we must find an instance of *selective influence*. That is, we must find experimental manipulations (factors) F and G that influence **A** and **B** selectively, i.e., such that **A** is influenced by F but is invariant with respect to G, whereas **B** is influenced by G but is invariant with respect to F.

Often one starts with hypotheses about what the component processes are, and about corresponding *process-specific factors* that are likely to influence them selectively. Alternatively, the selectivity of effects may be discovered in experiments with other goals. Separate modifiability of **A** and **B** is also evidence for their *functional distinctness*; information about what a process does is provided by the sets of factors that do and don't influence it; if two processes have the same function they are likely to be influenced by the same factors.[5] With separate modifiability as the criterion, it should be clear that modularity is a relation between or among processes, not an absolute property of one process.

2.2. Processes and their measures, pure and composite, and combination rules

How do we demonstrate that a process is influenced by a factor, or invariant with respect to it? We know only about one or more hypothesized *measures* M_A of process **A**, not about the process as such. Depending on the available measures, there are two ways to assess separate modifiability of **A** and **B**.

Pure measures. Suppose we have pure measures M_A and M_B of the hypothesized modules: A pure measure of a process is one that reflects changes in that process only. Examples include the durations of two different neural processes (see Section 3), and the discriminability and criterion parameters of signal-detection theory (which reflect sensory and decision processes; see Section 5). To show that F and G influence **A** and **B** selectively, we must demonstrate their selective influence on M_A and M_B. That is, we must show that M_A is influenced by F and invariant with respect to G, and vice versa for M_B.

---

[3] Machamer, Darden, and Craver (2000) distinguish "activities" and "entities".

[4] This criterion for modularity seems to be far weaker than the set of module properties suggested by Fodor (1983), according to whom modules are typically innate, informationally encapsulated, domain specific, "hard-wired", autonomous, and fast. However, domain specificity appears to imply separate modifiability.

[5] Such double dissociation of subprocesses should be distinguished (Sternberg, 2003) from the more familiar double dissociation of tasks (Schmidt & Vorberg, 2006), discussed in Section 9.

Table 1. *Inferential logic for pure measures*

Joint Hypothesis
H1: Processes **A** and **B** are modules (separately modifiable).
H2: M_A, M_B are pure measures of **A, B**.

Prediction
We may be able to find factors F and G that influence M_A (**A**) and M_B(**B**) selectively:
$p_1{:}M_A \leftarrow F$, $\;p_2{:}M_B \nleftarrow F$, $\;p_3{:}M_B \leftarrow G$, $\;p_4{:}M_A \nleftarrow G$.

Alternative Results	
We find factors F, G that influence M_A and M_B selectively.	We fail to find such factors.

Corresponding Inferences	
Support for joint hypothesis $H1 + H2$.	Refutes one/both of *H1*, *H2*, *or* we didn't look enough for F, G.

If F_j has two levels, $j = 1, 2$, the *effect* of F on M_A is a difference:

$$effect(F) = M_A(F_2) - M_A(F_1). \qquad (1)$$

For factors with multiple levels, the effect can be regarded as a vector of differences associated with successive ordered levels. The logic for inferring separate modules when we hypothesize that we have pure measures is shown in Table 1.[6,7] The $\{p_k\}$ are four properties of the data; $M_A \leftarrow F$ should be read as "M_A is influenced by F"; $M_B \nleftarrow F$ should be read as "M_B is not influenced

by F". All four of the requirements are critical; the instances of invariance are meaningful only if we also know that both factors are potent and both measures are sensitive. Unfortunately, it is seldom appreciated that persuasive evidence for invariance cannot depend solely on failure of a significance test of an effect: such a failure could merely reflect variability and low statistical power.[8]

Composite measures. Suppose that instead of pure measures we have a composite measure M_{AB} of the hypothesized modules—a measure to which they both contribute. Examples of possible

---

[6] Adapted from Table 2 of Sternberg (2001) by permission.

[7] When the hypotheses about A and B are sufficiently detailed to specify particular process-specific factors that should influence them selectively, this leads to an alternative formulation of the inferential logic, in which the specification of F and G is included in the joint hypothesis, with the remainder of the reasoning adjusted accordingly. For a discussion of such alternatives, see Sternberg (2001, Section A.2.3).

[8] A common error of interpretation is to assert the nonexistence of an effect or interaction merely because it fails to reach statistical significance. In evaluating a claim that an effect is null, it is crucial to have at least an index of precision (such as a confidence interval) for the size of the effect. One alternative is to apply an *equivalence test* that reverses the asymmetry of the standard significance test (Berger & Hsu, 1996; Rogers, Howard, & Vessey, 1993). In either case we need to specify a critical effect size (depending on what we know and the particular circumstances) such that it is reasonable to treat the observed effect as null if, with high probability, it is less than that critical size. The critical size might be determined by the sizes of effects generated by plausible models. Bayesian methods (e.g., Gallistel, 2009; Rouder, Speckman, Sun, Morey, & Iverson, 2009) provide another alternative, especially if the null is framed as an appropriate interval hypothesis rather than a point hypothesis. An example of suitable caution about inferring a null effect can be found in Ghorashi, Enns, Klein, and Di Lollo (2010).

Table 2. *Inferential logic for a composite measure with summation as the combination rule*

Joint Hypothesis
H1: Processes **A** and **B** are modules (separately modifiable).   *H3:* Contributions u_A, v_B of **A**, **B** to M_{AB} (**A**, **B**) combine by *summation*.

Prediction
We may be able to find factors F and G that influence **A** and **B** selectively: $p'_1 : u_A \leftarrow F, \quad p'_2 : v_B \nleftarrow F, \quad p'_3 : v_B \leftarrow G, \quad p'_4 : u_A \nleftarrow G,$ and jointly influence no other process. If so, their effects on M_{AB} will be *additive*.

Alternative Results	
We find factors F and G with *additive effects* on M_{AB} .	We fail to find such factors.

Corresponding Inferences	
Support for joint hypothesis *H1 + H3*.	Refutes one/both of *H1, H3*, *or* we didn't look enough for F, G.

composite measures are the event-related potential (ERP) at a particular point on the scalp (which may reflect several ERP sources in the brain), and reaction time, RT (which may depend on the durations of more than one process of interest). To support a hypothesis of selective influence in this case, we must also know or have evidence for a *combination rule*—a specification of how the contributions of the modules to the measure combine. With pure measures, factorial experiments (rather than separate experiments for different factors) are desirable, because they provide efficient tests of generality and promote new discoveries at little cost. With a composite measure, factorial experiments are essential, to assess how the effects of the factors combine; unfortunately such experiments are rare, despite their efficiency (Section 12.5).

The logic for inferring separate modules using a hypothesized composite measure when we either know or hypothesize that the combination rule is *summation* is shown in Table 2.[9,10] To understand Table 2, it is important to keep in mind what the effect of a factor is, and what it means for effects of different factors to be *additive*. To simplify the discussion, let us assume that there are two factors, each with just two levels. Let u and v be the contributions of processes **A** and **B** to M_{AB} . If summation is the combination rule, $M_{AB} = u + v$. If **A** and **B** are selectively influenced by factors F and G,

$$M_{AB}(F_j, G_k) = u(F_j) + v(G_k), \qquad (2)$$

where $u(F_j)$ is a function that describes the relation between the level of F and the contribution of **A** to M_{AB}.

---

[9] Adapted from Table 3 of Sternberg (2001) by permission.

[10] Whereas properties $\{p_k\}$ (Table 1) apply to observable quantities, the analogous properties $\{p'_k\}$ (Table 2) apply to contributions to a composite measure that are not directly observable.

Now in general, we work with averages rather than individual values of M_{AB}, and we regard u, v, and M_{AB} as random rather than deterministic variables. Using $\overline{M}$, $\overline{u}$, and $\overline{v}$ to indicate the means of these random variables, it is convenient that with no further assumptions,[11] Eq. 2 implies:

$$\overline{M}_{AB}(F_j, G_k) = \overline{u}(F_j) + \overline{v}(G_k). \qquad (3)$$

In what follows, I treat the levels of factors as ordered, which permits describing changes in level as increases or decreases. From Eq. 2 it is easy to show that F and G are *additive factors*: the combined effect on M_{AB} of increasing the levels of both F and G is the sum of the effect of increasing only F and the effect of increasing only G:

effect(F, G)
$$\equiv M_{AB}(F_2, G_2) - M_{AB}(F_1, G_1)$$
$$= [u(F_2) + v(G_2)] - [u(F_1) + v(G_1)]$$
$$= [u(F_2) - u(F_1)] + [v(G_2) - v(G_1)]$$
$$\equiv \textit{effect}(F) + \textit{effect}(G). \qquad (4)$$

Eq. 2 also implies that the effect of each factor will be invariant over levels of the other. Thus,

effect$(F|G = G_k)$
$$\equiv M_{AB}(F_2, G_k) - M_{AB}(F_1, G_k)$$
$$= [u(F_2) + v(G_k)] - [u(F_1) + v(G_k)]$$
$$= [u(F_2) - u(F_1)], \qquad (5)$$

regardless of G_k. A given measure may be pure or composite, depending on the factors being varied and the hypothesized modules of interest. This attribute of a measure is part of the joint hypothesis that is tested as part of the process-decomposition approach.[12,13]

2.3. Overview of examples and issues

Much of what follows consists of descriptions of successful examples of the process-decomposition approach. Examples will be referred to by the section numbers in which they are first discussed. With two exceptions, the successful examples involve factorial experiments with two factors. The exceptions are Ex. 3.1, in which the effects of the two factors are studied in separate experiments, and Ex. 4.3, in which the effects of three factors are considered. In all cases, the factors have been selected because it is hoped that they will be "process-specific": that they will selectively influence only one of the two or more processes that are hypothesized to underlie performance of the task. Three examples (10.2, 10.3, and 10.4) are intriguing and tantalizing cases where the approach could have been used but was not, because of incompleteness of design or analysis.

In Section 3 I discuss two applications based on electrophysiological measurements at the scalp from which pure measures are derived. In both cases, two neural modules are identified: In Ex. 3.1, in which the modules are associated with encoding two different aspects of the stimulus, they are found to operate in parallel. In Ex. 3.2, in which the modules are associated with preparation of two different aspects of the response, they are found to operate successively, as processing "stages". The RT data from Ex. 3.2 are discussed in Section 4.1, where the RT is treated as a composite measure and shown to lead to the identification of two mental modules that correspond to the neural modules inferred from the electrophysiological data discussed earlier. (By "correspond to" I mean that their durations are influenced selectively by the same factors and to the same extent.) The inference from the RT data of Ex. 3.2 exemplifies the method of additive factors (AFM), discussed more generally in Section 4.2, and applied

---

[11] Matters may not be so simple for other combination rules, such as multiplication; see Section 8.2.

[12] The reasoning described in Table 2 is sometimes erroneously expressed as "If we assume $H3$ then additivity confers support on $H1$." This ignores the support that additivity also confers on $H3$.

[13] It is important to note that whereas factors that selectively influence serially arranged processes will have additive effects on mean RT, this is not the only possible basis for additive effects on an interesting measure, despite beliefs to the contrary (e.g., Poldrack, 2010, p. 148; Jennings, McIntosh, Kapur, Tulving, & Houle, 1997, p. 237). The critical requirement for additivity is combination by summation, whatever its basis.

in Section 4.3 to the problem of locating the effect of a manipulation of interest (sleep deprivation) within a pair of already established mental modules, one for encoding the stimulus, the other for selecting the response.

As discussed in Section 5, signal detection theory has provided a widely applied method for measuring sensory processes in tasks that also involve decision processes, but has in general failed to isolate those decision processes from sensory factors. Ex. 5 illustrates a variant of the method that succeeds, and thereby demonstrates the modularity of the sensory and decision processes, in an experiment with pigeons in which the decision factor is not the traditional payoff matrix.

To the extent that there is localization of function in the brain, so that two or more modular processes are implemented in disjoint regions, and to the extent that the level of activation in a region varies with changes in the process it implements, the level of such activation can function as a pure measure of the process. In Sections 6.3 and 6.4 I discuss two examples in which fMRI (BOLD) signals in different brain regions were measured for this purpose; in both cases, RTs were measured as well. In Ex. 6.3 (number comparison), in which RT measurements in a similar experiment had already indicated separate stages for encoding the test number and comparing it to the target, both the new RT data and the fMRI data support this analysis, suggesting mental and neural modules that correspond. However, the fact that the direction of the effect of the encoding factor on the fMRI response differs in different brain regions is important. In Ex. 6.4 (manual choice-reaction with four stimulus-response pairs) the fMRI data support the hypothesis of modular neural processes for stimulus encoding and response selection, but unlike earlier observations of effects on $\overline{RT}$ from several similar paradigms, the effects of the two factors on $\overline{RT}$ interact rather than being additive, raising questions of interpretation. One important finding in this example is the additivity of effects of the encoding and response-selection factors on the fMRI measure in the two brain regions where both factors were found to have effects. In these regions, the fMRI signal appears to be a composite measure.

Examples 6.5 and 8.1 use the fMRI adaptation method; in both cases the measure, whose magnitude increases with the dissimilarity of the current stimulus to previous ones, is composite, raising the issue of the combination rule. Ex. 6.5, concerned with the perception and memory of scenes, shows that different modular processes are responsible for immediate and delayed adaptation effects in the parahippocampal place area, which seems to require different short-term and long-term memory representations.

Perhaps because factorial experiments are relatively rare in studies of brain activation, we have had little experience in considering the implications of the additivity of effects on fMRI measures. It is tempting to infer that modular brain processes are responsible. In Section 7 I consider for both RT (7.1) and fMRI (7.2) the conditions under which inferences from additivity to modularity are justified, and describe inferential requirements and limitations that are sometimes overlooked.

In Section 8 I provide brief summaries of four additional examples of the process-decomposition approach, using different composite measures, to show the diversity of applications. Ex. 8.1 uses the fMRI adaptation method to test the idea that perceptually separable dimensions are encoded by different neural processes, whereas perceptually integral dimensions are not. One reason for including Ex. 8.2, a classic study that provides evidence for modular spatial-frequency analyzers in visual pattern detection, is that unlike the other examples that use composite measures, the combination rule here is multiplication rather than summation, and the measure is the proportion of errors. An outline of the inferential logic is included. In Ex. 8.3, the composite measure with a multiplicative combination rule is the proportion of correct responses; the application is to speeded lexical decisions. Ex. 8.4 uses the amplitude of the event-related potential at multiple scalp locations as a set of related composite measures, powerful because of its fine temporal resolution and multiple locations.

In Section 9 I contrast the process-decomposition approach with the *task-comparison* method. Here, inferences are drawn from the effects on different tasks of various factors, together with theories about the processes used to accomplish those tasks. Examples of factors that have been used are the presence or absence of sleep deprivation and the presence or absence of a lesion in a particular brain region. To illustrate limitations of the method, I describe a comparison of the effects of repetitive transcranial magnetic stimulation (rTMS) on two tasks of tactile perception (Section 9.1). One variety of task comparison is Donders' subtraction method, originally developed for RT experiments, but, in recent years, applied to brain-activation measures (Section 9.2). Unlike task comparison, which is often used in a way that requires various assumptions (including modularity) to be made without test (Shallice, 1988, Ch. 11), the process-decomposition approach incorporates such tests. In Section 9.3, I describe the conflict between the conclusion from Ex. 4.3 that the effect of sleep deprivation is selective, and claims, based on task comparison, that the effect is global.

In Section 10, I consider experiments in which the effects of transcranial magnetic stimulation (TMS) on RTs in visual search and number-comparison judgements were measured. In these experiments, TMS of a brain region R is found to increase $\overline{RT}$ without otherwise disrupting performance. The presence and absence of TMS in such a region can be regarded as two levels of a factor, TMS_R. If this factor influences $\overline{RT}$, region R is inferred to play a role in performance of the task. However, the potential of TMS to associate brain regions with modular subprocesses and to provide evidence about separate modifiability is realized only when TMS_R is used together with other, process-specific factors, to determine which of their effects are modulated by TMS, and which are not. While promising with respect to these goals, the studies discussed are incomplete.

The traditional task of cognitive neuropsychology is to learn about the cognitive functions of the normal brain by studying what happens to them when it is damaged, typically by comparing the effects of brain damage in different tasks. Can brain damage also be used in the process-decomposition approach? This question is considered in Section 11; several considerations lead to a negative answer. Instead, the two approaches can inform each other.

Several additional issues are considered briefly in Section 12.

In Sternberg (2001), referred to as "SM:<Section>", I discuss and defend the process-decomposition approach in more detail, further discuss its inferential logic, describe its antecedents, provide more detail about Exs. 3.1, 3.2, 4.3, 5, 8.2, and 8.4, describe other examples using different species and different behavioural and neural measures, discuss the treatment of data, and consider issues of experimental design.

3. DECOMPOSING NEURAL PROCESSES WITH THE LATERALIZED READINESS POTENTIAL

3.1. Parallel modules for discriminating two stimulus features

Consider a trial in a choice-reaction experiment where two alternative responses are made by the two hands. When enough information has been extracted from the stimulus to permit selection of the hand, but before any sign of muscle activity, the part of the motor cortex that controls that hand becomes more active than the part that controls the non-selected hand. This asymmetric activity can be detected as an increase in the averages over trials of the difference between electrical potentials (ERPs) at the two corresponding scalp locations.[14] Let $A_{mc}(t)$ (an index of *motor-cortex asymmetry*) express this difference as a function of time after stimulus onset (if "stimulus locked"), or as a function of time before the overt response (if "response locked"). $A_{mc}(t)$ is normally

---

[14] As in some other brain measurements (e.g., PET, fMRI), the poor S/N ratio often means that averaging over trials is required for the measures to be interpretable. Here, the "noise" is due partly to neural events unrelated to the task being performed, whose contributions are reduced by combining subtraction of the pre-stimulus baseline level with an averaging process that reveals only those events that are consistently time-locked to the stimulus or the response.

zero, but is defined so as to become positive when the (correct) response hand is selected; the increase of such asymmetry is called the *lateralized-readiness potential* (LRP). The onset time of the LRP is thus an estimate of the time at which the side of the response (left or right) has been selected.

Consider a situation in which two different features of the same stimulus must be discriminated to determine how to respond. Are modular neural processes involved in doing so? And, if so, how are they organized temporally? Osman, Bashore, Coles, Donchin, and Meyer (1992) devised a clever way to ask these questions, using the LRP. On each trial, the visual stimulus had two features. Its *position* (left versus right, which was rapidly discriminated) indicated which response to make should a response be required. Its *category* (letter versus digit, which was discriminated more slowly) indicated whether this was a "Go" trial (on which the selected response should be activated) or a "NoGo" trial (on which no response should be made). Under these conditions, the LRP occurs even on trials with no overt response, and with an onset that is indistinguishable from the LRP on "Go" trials.

I shall use "Event 1" to mean the onset of the LRP; the latency T_1 of Event 1 can thus be used to indicate when the stimulus location has been discriminated and the response selected. Let us denote this *response selection* process by α. Normally (on "Go" trials) A_{mc} continues to rise until the overt response is initiated. If a "NoGo" signal tells the subject not to respond, however, A_{mc} starts falling. The time at which $A_{mc}(t; NoGo)$ diverges from $A_{mc}(t; Go)$—the latency T_2 of "Event 2"—can thus be used to indicate when the stimulus category (the Go versus NoGo signal) is discriminated and response preparation ceases. Let us denote this *category discrimination* process by β.

Events 1 and 2 indicate the completion of processes α and β. Can response preparation start when the location but not the category of the stimulus has been discriminated? And, if so, can category

discrimination proceed in parallel with response preparation? To answer such questions, Osman et al. (1992) examined the effects of two factors: One (in Exp. 1) is *Go-NoGo Discriminability*, *GND*, which should influence β; it could be *easy* (letter and digit with dissimilar shapes, GND_1) or *hard* (similar shapes, GND_2). The other factor (in Exp. 2) is the spatial compatibility of the stimulus-response mapping, *MC* (*Mapping Compatibility*), which should influence α; it could be *compatible* (respond with the hand on the same side as the stimulus, MC_1) or *incompatible* (respond with the hand on the opposite side, MC_2).

Idealizations of the resulting $A_{mc}(t)$ functions are shown in Figure 1. Each of the four panels shows the pair $A_{mc}(t; Go)$ and $A_{mc}(t; NoGo)$ for one condition. The two latency measures for a condition were derived in different ways from this pair of $A_{mc}(t)$ functions: The latency T_1 of Event 1 (onset of the LRP) is the time at which the *sum* of the two $A_{mc}(t)$ functions reliably exceeds baseline. The latency T_2 of Event 2 (divergence of the Go and NoGo LRPs) is the time at which their *difference* reliably exceeds zero. In Exp. 1, *GND* influenced $\overline{T}_2$ (by 43 ms) but not $\overline{T}_1$ (compare Figures 1A1 and 1A2), showing that *GND* influenced β but not α. ($\overline{T}_1 \approx 170$ ms on both Go and NoGo trials.)[15] Because the stimulus influenced response preparation before both of its features were discriminated, these findings from Exp. 1 demonstrate the transmission of "partial information" from the perceptual process to the response process.

In one of the conditions of Exp. 2, the stimulus-response mapping was incompatible, which was expected to delay selection of the response. To ensure that stimulus location had an opportunity to influence response preparation on NoGo trials in both conditions, it was important to prolong the Go-NoGo discrimination.[16] Osman et al. therefore reduced letter-digit shape discriminability so as to increase $\overline{T}_2$ from about 240 ms to about 350 ms. In this experiment, *MC*

---

[15] The effect of *GND* on $\overline{T}_1$ was 2.5 $\pm$ 5.0 ms; its effect on $\overline{T}_2$ was 43 $\pm$ 14 ms; the difference between these effects is 41 $\pm$ 11 ms ($N = 6$; $p \approx .01$).

[16] It is this requirement that would have made it difficult to implement a suitable factorial experiment.

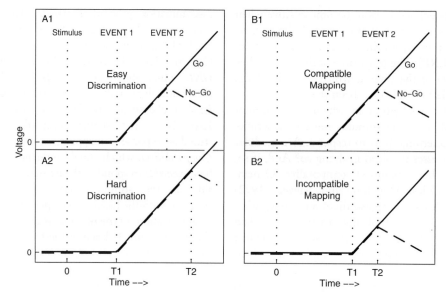

Figure 1. *Schematic idealized asymmetry functions* $A_{mc}(t)$ *from Osman, Bashore, Coles, Donchin, and Meyer (1992). Event 1 is the LRP onset; Event 2 is the onset of the divergence of* $A_{mc}(t; Go)$ *from* $A_{mc}(t; NoGo)$. *Panels A1 and A2: Asymmetry functions from Exp. 1, in which* Go-NoGo Discriminability *could be easy* $(GND = GND_1)$ *or hard* $(GND = GND_2)$. *Panels B1 and B2: Asymmetry functions from Exp. 2, in which* Mapping Compatibility *could be compatible* $(MC = MC_1)$ *or incompatible* $(MC = MC_2)$. *(Fig. 3 of Sternberg, 2001; adapted by permission.)*

influenced $\overline{T}_1$ (by 121 ms) but not $\overline{T}_2$ (compare Figures 1B1 and 1B2), showing that *MC* influenced $\boldsymbol{\alpha}$ but not $\boldsymbol{\beta}$. ($\overline{T}_2 \approx 350$ ms on both Go and NoGo trials.)[17] Increasing the level of mapping difficulty from MC_1 to MC_2 therefore *reduced* the interval between Event 1 and Event 2.

Taken together, the two experiments show that *MC* and *GND* influenced the two measures T_1 and T_2 selectively, supporting the hypothesis that they are pure measures of two different modular processes (Table 1). The results also show how $\boldsymbol{\alpha}$ and $\boldsymbol{\beta}$ are arranged in time. Suppose they were arranged sequentially, as stages. Prolonging the first of two stages by Δt ms should delay completion of the second by the same amount: the prolongation Δt should be *propagated* to the completion time of the next stage. If we assume equal delays between completion of each process and its effect on $A_{mc}(t)$, then the order of process completions would be the same as the order of

Events 1 and 2.[18] The finding (Exp. 2; Figure 1B) that the effect of *MC* on T_1 is not propagated to T_2 would then be sufficient to invalidate a stage model. If we relax the equal-delays assumption, permitting us to assume the opposite order of process completions, then the propagation property requires that any effects on T_2 propagate to T_1, contrary to what was found (Exp. 1; Figure 1A) for the effect of *GND*. An alternative to a stages arrangement is that $\boldsymbol{\alpha}$ and $\boldsymbol{\beta}$ operate in parallel, such that the $\overline{RT}$ (on Go trials) is determined by the completion time of the slower of the two. Such an arrangement is consistent with the further finding (from Exp. 2) that the effect of *MC* on $\overline{RT}$ (16 ms) is dramatically smaller than its effect on $\overline{T}_1$ (121 ms). This can happen because regardless of how much the duration of $\boldsymbol{\alpha}$ is shortened by changing the level of *MC*, response initiation on a Go trial must await completion of $\boldsymbol{\beta}$ as well.

---

[17] The effect of *MC* on $\overline{T}_1$ was 121 $\pm$ 17 ms; its effect on $\overline{T}_2$ was 3.3 $\pm$ 8.8 ms; the difference between these effects is 118 $\pm$ 21 ms ($N = 6$; $p \approx .01$).

[18] T_2 would then be a composite measure, influenced by both factors, with summation as the combination rule.

These findings about $\overline{RT}$ contrast to those of Ex. 3.2, below, in which pure measures based on the LRP provide evidence for a serial arrangement of two neural processes. In that case, unlike this one, a composite behavioural measure ($\overline{RT}$) leads to a similar analysis of corresponding mental processes, as we shall see in Section 4.1. In the present example, however, T_1 is a measure of a process (response selection, separated from response execution) for which there may be no behavioural measure, and whose contribution to $\overline{RT}$ may be large or small, depending on the level of *GND*.

3.2. Serial modules (stages) for preparing two response features

The LRP provides an estimate of the time when the side of the response is selected; this makes it possible to ask whether the neural process responsible for selecting the side of the response is separate from the neural process responsible for preparing other aspects of the response. This possibility was exploited in an experiment by Smulders, Kok, Kenemans, and Bashore (1995). It was a two-choice RT experiment with single-digit stimuli mapped on left-hand and right-hand responses. Two factors were varied orthogonally across blocks of trials: *Stimulus Quality* (SQ_j: digit intact versus degraded) and *Response Complexity* (RC_k: one keystroke—simple—versus a sequence of three keystrokes—complex—made by fingers of the responding hand). In addition to the composite measure RT_{jk}, Smulders et al.

measured the onset time of the LRP, based on both stimulus-locked (LRP$_s$) and response-locked (LRP$_r$) averaging of the $A_{mc}(t)$ functions. Let the LRP onset times be T_{sjk} (measured from the stimulus, and using LRP$_s$), and T^*_{rjk} (a negative quantity, measured from the response, and using LRP$_r$), and let $T_{rjk} = RT_{jk} + T^*_{rjk}$. T_{sjk} and T_{rjk} are then alternative estimates of the same time point between stimulus and response, measured from the stimulus; let $T_{.jk}$ be their mean.[19] Averaging over the four conditions, $RT_{..} = 416$ ms and $T_{...} = 264$ ms. If α is the neural process from stimulus to LRP onset, and β is the neural process from LRP onset to response, these values permit us to estimate their durations (pure measures of α and β) averaged over the four conditions: $D_{\alpha..} = T_{...} = 264$ ms and $D_{\beta..} = RT_{..} - T_{...} = 152$ ms.

Shown in the A and B panels of Figure 2 are the estimated durations of processes α and β separated by condition: $D_{\alpha jk} = T_{.jk}$, and $D_{\beta jk} = RT_{jk} - T_{.jk}$. Because T_{sjk} and T_{rjk} give similar estimates for effects of the two factors on D_α and D_β, the estimates are based on $T_{.jk}$. The results show that the two factors *SQ* and *RC* have selective effects on D_α and D_β. This supports the hypothesis that in this situation the LRP onset indeed defines a temporal boundary between two neural modules that function sequentially, as stages, consistent with the reasoning in Table 2.[20]

What are stages? They are functionally distinct operations that occur during nonoverlapping epochs.[21] In a process with two stages, the stream of operations between stimulus and

---

[19] When a mean is taken over values of a subscript, that subscript is replaced by a dot.

[20] The error variance values reported by Smulders et al. (1995) and the SE estimates provided here are likely to be overestimates (because balanced condition-order effects were treated as error variance); the data required to calculate better values are no longer available (F. T. Y. Smulders, personal communication, September, 1999).

[21] It is perhaps a confusion between time (process) and space (processor) that has led some commentators (e.g., Broadbent, 1984) to believe that a process whose modules are organized in stages cannot include feedback because it must be implemented by a "pipeline": an ordered set of processors through which information passes in a fixed direction from input to output. Broadbent's "pipelines" constrain the relation between process and representation: later processes must operate on representations that have been processed more highly—that are "further from the input". Stage models need not be constrained in this way; they merely partition processing operations into temporally successive components. There is no reason why a later stage cannot make use of new sensory information (such as feedback) in (re)processing earlier sensory information. For further discussion of Broadbent's (1984) critique of stage models, and the distinction among three kinds of stage (completion-controlled, outcome-contingent, and data-dependent), see Sternberg (1984).

response can be *cut*, separating Stage **A** (the processes before the cut) from Stage **B** (the processes after the cut). If **A** and **B** are influenced selectively by factors F and G, respectively, this means that F can have an effect only before the cut, and G only after the cut. In most analyses based on behavioural data, the cut is hypothetical, inferred from the additivity of factor effects. In the neural process analysis discussed above, the cut corresponds to a particular observable neural event, and divides the neural process into two subprocesses whose durations are selectively influenced by the two factors. This more direct observation of processing stages supports the inferences from the RT data. Note that by examining the effects of other factors, **A** (or **B**) might be further decomposed into stages or non-stage modules, only one of which needs to be influenced by F (or G).

In contrast to D_α and D_β, which are hypothesized (and confirmed) to be pure measures, RT_{jk}, shown in Panel C, is a composite measure: With two stages contributing to the time from stimulus to response, the RT reflects contributions from both. In Section 4.1, I consider the RT data from this experiment and how the inferred stages **A** and **B** relate to the neural processes α and β inferred from the LRP data.

4. MENTAL PROCESSING STAGES INFERRED FROM REACTION TIMES

4.1. Analysis of the reaction-time data in Ex. 3.2

The conclusion in Ex. 3.2 is that the time between the stimulus digit and the response (the RT) can be partitioned into two intervals, from stimulus to LRP (duration D_α, influenced by SQ but not RC), and from LRP to response (duration D_β, influenced by RC but not SQ). Consider just the mean reaction time, measured under the four factor-level combinations:

$$\overline{RT}_{jk} = \overline{D}_{\alpha j} + \overline{D}_{\beta k} = \overline{D}_\alpha(SQ_j) + \overline{D}_\beta(RC_k). \quad (6)$$

Suppose we had only those data and not the LRP data. It follows from the partitioning of $\overline{RT}$ shown in Eq. 6 that the combination rule for the contributions of neural processes α and β is summation. As discussed in Section 2.2, that and the selective influence of factors SQ and RC on α and β imply that the effects of SQ and RC on $\overline{RT}$ are additive. In general, factors that selectively influence the durations of distinct sequential components of the RT must have additive effects on the composite measure. Thus, if a hypothesis asserts that the RT in a particular task is the summed duration of two modular mental processes **A** and **B** arranged sequentially (as stages) with durations T_A and T_B, and selectively influenced by factors F and G, we should expect:

$$\overline{RT}(F_j, G_k) = \overline{T}_A(F_j) + \overline{T}_B(G_k). \quad (7)$$

The goodness of fit of the parallel unbroken lines in Figure 2C confirms the expectation of additivity for the RTs in the experiment by Smulders et al. and supports the joint hypothesis of Table 2. (The interaction contrast of SQ and RC was a negligible 2 ± 5 ms.) However, because in this case we also have measures of the durations of neural modules (from the analysis of the LRP data) we can go further: we can ask whether the mental modules derived from the purely behavioural analysis of the composite measure correspond to the neural modules inferred from the LRP-based pure measures.

Thus, suppose that the mental modules **A** and **B** responsible for the additive RT effects are implemented by the neural modules α and β, demarcated by the LRP. Then, not only should the same factors influence them selectively, but also the sizes of their effects should be the same. Agreement among the effect sizes can be examined by assuming that the two factors indeed have perfectly selective effects on α and β, and by using the appropriate subsets of the LRP data to "predict" the pattern of the $\{\overline{RT}_{jk}\}$. Thus, we should be able to use just the data in Figure 2A1 (averaging over RC levels) to obtain

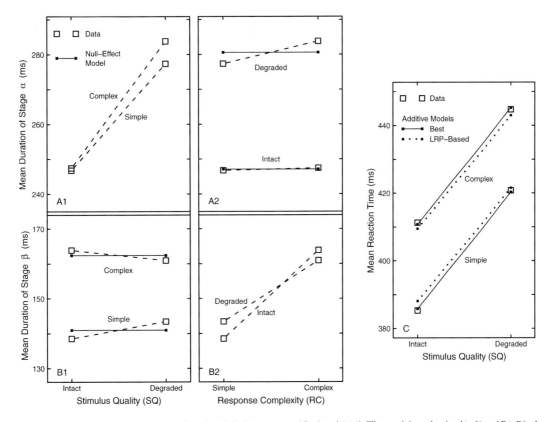

Figure 2. *Means over 14 subjects of data from Smulders, Kok, Kenemans, and Bashore (1995). The panels in each pair, A1–A2 and B1–B2, show the same values, plotted differently. Estimated duration $D_{\alpha jk}$ of Stage α, from stimulus presentation to LRP onset (Panels A1, A2); and duration $D_{\beta jk}$ of Stage β, from LRP onset to response (Panels B1, B2). These are shown as functions of Stimulus Quality (SQ$_j$, Panels A1, B1); and of Response Complexity (RC$_k$, Panels A2, B2). Data in Panels A1 and B1 are separated by level of RC; those in Panels A2 and B2 are separated by level of SQ. Also shown in Panels B1 and A2 are null-effect models. Main effects of SQ on D_α and D_β (with $\pm$ SE) are 33 $\pm$ 6 ms (Panel A1) and 1 $\pm$ 7 ms (Panel B1); main effects of RC on D_α and D_β are 4 $\pm$ 7 ms (Panel A2) and 21 $\pm$ 6 ms (Panel B2). The interaction contrasts are 6 $\pm$ 13 ms (stage α) and $-8 \pm$ 11 ms (stage β). The $\overline{RT}$ data (discussed in Section 4.1) are shown in Panel C, together with two fitted models. One (unbroken lines) is the best-fitting additive model (mean absolute deviation 0.5 ms); the other (dotted lines) is an additive model based on estimates of process durations from the LRP data (mean absolute deviation 1.8 ms). For the $\overline{RT}$s, the normalized interaction contrast is 7.0% [For a dimensionless normalized measure of the interaction in 2 × 2 data, I express the interaction contrast as a percentage of the geometric mean of the absolute values of the main effects. This facilitates comparison of the interaction magnitudes associated with different measures. See Roberts & Sternberg (1993), Table 26.1]. (Fig. 15 of Sternberg, 2001; adapted by permission.)*

the estimates $\hat{D}_\alpha(SQ_1)$ and $\hat{D}_\alpha(SQ_2)$. Similarly, we should be able to use just the data in Figure 2B2 (averaging over SQ levels) to obtain the estimates $\hat{D}_\beta(RC_1)$ and $\hat{D}_\beta(RC_2)$. If $\overline{RT} = D_\alpha + D_\beta$ we have the "predictions" $RT_{jk}^* = \hat{D}_\alpha(SQ_j) + \hat{D}_\beta(RC_k)$ for the four conditions.[22] The dotted lines in Figure 1C show that the agreement is

good: $\overline{RT}_{jk} \approx RT_{jk}^*$. Numerically, the effects of SQ and RC on the composite measure $\overline{RT}$ are 35 $\pm$ 3 ms and 25 $\pm$ 7 ms, close to their mean estimated effects (34 and 21 ms) on the pure measures D_α and D_β.

Another illustration of the independent use of two measures is provided by Ex. 6.3: again,

---

[22] This way of deriving the $\{RT_{jk}^*\}$ forces their means into agreement: $RT_{..}^* = \overline{RT}_{..}$; the question of interest is whether the differences among the four values agree.

pure measures to ask about the structure of a neural process, and a composite measure to ask about the structure of a corresponding mental process.

4.2. The method of additive factors

The approach to decomposing complex mental processes into subprocesses that is exemplified by the RT analysis described above depends on the observation that if a process can be partitioned into subprocesses arranged in stages, then the RT becomes an example of a composite measure with summation as the combination rule; in this case if two factors F and G change $\overline{RT}$ but influence no stages in common ("selective influence"), their effects on mean reaction time should be additive, as described in Table 2. Conversely, if the effects of factors F and G on $\overline{RT}$ in a process organized in stages interact, so that F modulates the effect of G rather than leaving it invariant, then F and G must influence at least one stage in common. Suppose that we have a process in which RT measurements have revealed two or more factors with additive effects. This supports the hypothesis that the process contains subprocesses arranged sequentially, in stages, with each of the factors selectively influencing a different subprocess.[23] Thus one approach to searching for the modular decomposition of a complex process is the method of additive factors (AFM), which involves determining whether two or more factors have additive or interacting effects on mean RT. See Section 7.1 for a discussion of the strength of such inferences. Example 4.3 illustrates how it is possible to reveal more complex processing structures by combining inferences from a pattern of additive and interacting factor effects.

4.3. Selectivity of the effect of sleep deprivation

One of the most provocative applications of the additive factor method is described by Sanders, Wijnen, and Van Arkel (1982, Exp. 1), and leads to the controversial conclusion that the effect of sleep deprivation is selective (process-specific) rather than global. What follows is a simplified description of their experiment and findings.

This example is especially powerful because it includes more than two factors. The stimuli were the single digits "2", "3", "4", and "5"; the responses were their spoken names, "two", "three", "four", and "five". Four factors were manipulated, each at two levels: The first was *Stimulus Quality* (*SQ*); the digits, presented as dot patterns, could be *intact*, or *degraded* by adding "noise" in the form of other dots. The second was the *Mapping Familiarity* (*MF*) from digits to names; it could either be *high* (respond to each digit with its name) or *low* (respond to "2", "3", "4", and "5" with "three", "four", "five", and "two", respectively). The third was *Sleep State* (*SLP*), which was either *normal* (data taken during the day after a normal night's sleep) or *deprived* (data taken during the day after a night awake in the lab). Test sessions occurred in both the morning and afternoon, creating a fourth two-level factor, *Time of Day* (*TD*). The $2^4 = 16$ conditions were run in separate blocks of trials. For simplicity the data shown in Figure 3 have been averaged over levels of *TD*. The measure was the RT for trials with correct responses. Other studies (see Section 6.4) had already suggested that *SQ* and *MF* were likely to influence two different stages of processing selectively, stages that might be described as stimulus encoding (**S**) and response selection (**R**).[24]

---

[23] Given a constraint on the durations of different stages that is stronger than zero correlation but weaker than stochastic independence, the assumption of stages plus selective influence implies numerous properties of aspects of the RT distributions in addition to their means (Sternberg, 1969; Roberts & Sternberg, 1993), such as additive effects on var(*RT*). However, without this constraint, stages plus selective influence don't require effects on var(*RT*) to be additive.

[24] The conclusion that *SQ* and *MF* influence separately-modifiable sequential processes, or stages, is further strengthened by analyses of complete RT-distributions (rather than just RT means) from similar experiments (Sternberg, 1969, Sec. V; Roberts & Sternberg, 1993, Exp. 2).

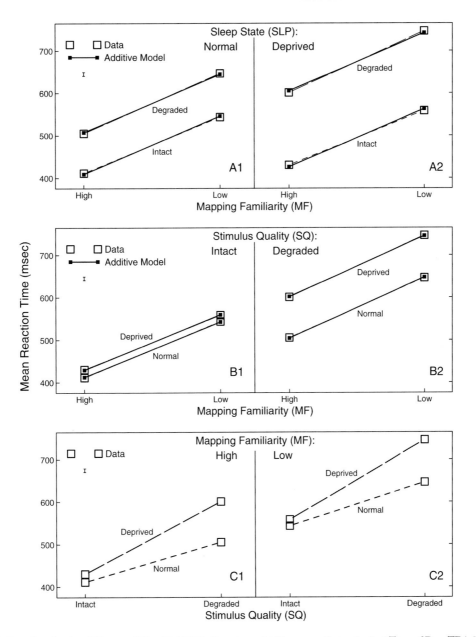

Figure 3. *Data from Sanders, Wijnen, and Van Arkel (1982, Experiment 1.) Means over the two levels of* Time of Day *(TD). The three pairs of panels show the same 2 × 2 × 2 = 8 data points (unfilled squares, broken lines), plotted differently. Each point is the mean of about 300 RTs from each of 16 subjects. A fitted additive model is also shown in each of the top four panels. Mean absolute deviations of data from model are 3.3 ms (Panels A1, A2) and 1.0 ms (Panels B1, B2). Because basic data are no longer available, values were obtained from Fig. 1 of Sanders et al. (1982). For the same reason, neither within-cell nor between-subject measures of variability are available. The ± SE bar was therefore determined by separating the data by TD, fitting a model that assumes the additivity of MF with SQ, SLP, and TD, and using the deviations (7 df) to estimate SE. The normalized interaction contrasts (see Figure 2 caption) for the six panels are A1: 8%, A2: 11%, B1: 9%; B2: 3%; C1: 88%; C2: 92%. (Fig. 14 of Sternberg, 2001; reprinted by permission.)*

The results in Figure 3 consist of the $\overline{RT}$s from the $2 \times 2 \times 2 = 8$ conditions. Panels A1 and A2 show that at each level of *SLP* there are additive effects of *SQ* and *MF* on $\overline{RT}$. This evidence supports:

(1) Performing the task involves at least two modules, arranged as stages, and
(2) Factors *SQ* and *MF* influence no stages in common.

Panels B1 and B2 show that at each level of *SQ* there are additive effects on $\overline{RT}$ of *MF* and *SLP*. That is, the extra time a subject takes to execute an unfamiliar S-R association rather than a well-learned one is invariant over sleep states, rather than being increased by sleep deprivation. This evidence lends further support to (1) and also supports:

(3) Factors *SLP* and *MF* influence no stages in common.

Panels C1 and C2 show that at each level of *MF* there are interactive effects of *SQ* and *SLP*: Increasing the level of *SLP* has a far greater effect on $\overline{RT}$ when the stimulus is degraded (98 ms) than when it is intact (17 ms). That is, sleep deprivation modulates the effect of the difficulty of stimulus encoding. This evidence supports

(4) Factors *SLP* and *SQ* influence at least one stage in common.

Taken together, the three pieces of evidence support a theory according to which the process used to perform the task contains at least two modules, **S** and **R**, these modules are arranged as stages, and among the factors *SQ*, *MF*, and *SLP*, *SQ* and *SLP* influence **S**, while *MF* alone influences **R**. It is reasonable to suppose that the stimulus is identified during **S**, and the response selected during **R**. (This is suggested by the nature of the factors *SQ* and *MF* that influence them.) The AFM has thus led us to the surprising conclusion that whereas *SLP* influences stimulus encoding, it does not influence response selection.

Unlike some other applications of composite measures, the findings from this experiment not only demonstrate separate modifiability and thereby permit us to divide the processes between stimulus and response into two modules

(here, stages) **S** and **R** (the former selectively influenced by *SQ*, the latter by *MF*); they also extend that analysis, providing an example of localizing the influence of a third factor *SLP* in one of the identified modules, **S**, thereby further characterizing **S** and **R**. And the additivity of the effects of *SLP* and *SQ* is of course further evidence for the separate modifiability of **S** and **R**.

5. SENSORY AND DECISION MODULES REVEALED BY SIGNAL-DETECTION THEORY

Probably the most influential approach to deriving pure measures of two processes underlying the performance of a task is the one associated with signal detection theory, SDT (Swets, Tanner, & Birdsall, 1961; Macmillan & Creelman, 2004). At the heart of this approach is the recognition that even simple psychophysical tasks involve decision processes as well as sensory processes. Consider a psychophysical experiment in which two types of trials are randomly intermixed, each with a slightly different light intensity. On one type of trial, the brighter light, S_T (the target stimulus) is presented; on the other type, the dimmer light, S_{NT} (the non-target stimulus) is presented. The observer's task is to respond with either R_T ("it was the target") or R_{NT} ("it was the non-target"). On each trial, according to SDT, the observer forms a unidimensional internal representation of the stimulus; let's call these representations X_T and X_{NT}, for S_T and S_{NT}. Because S_T is brighter than S_{NT}, X_T will tend to be larger than X_{NT}. It is also assumed, however, that because of external and internal noise, X_T and X_{NT} are random variables with distributions, rather than being fixed constants, and that because S_T and S_{NT} are similar, these distributions overlap. It is the overlap that creates the discrimination problem for the observer.

According to SDT the value of X on a trial results from the operation of a sensory process **S**; this value is then used by a decision process **D** to select one of the two responses, selecting R_T if X exceeds a criterion, and selecting R_{NT}

otherwise. The subject's choice of criterion determines the direction and magnitude of response bias.

The data from such an experiment can be described by four response proportions arranged in a 2 × 2 matrix, where the rows correspond to the two trial types S_T and S_{NT} and the columns correspond to the two responses R_T and R_{NT}. In the top row are the proportions of the target (S_T) trials that elicited each response, which estimate $Pr\{R_T|S_T\}$ (the true positive or "hit" probability), and $Pr\{R_{NT}|S_T\}$ (the false negative or "miss" probability). In the bottom row are the proportions of the non-target (S_{NT}) trials that elicited each response, which estimate $Pr\{R_T|S_{NT}\}$ (the false positive or "false alarm" probability) and $Pr\{R_{NT}|S_{NT}\}$ (the true negative or "correct rejection" probability). From such a matrix, two measures can be derived: One is d', presumed to be a pure measure of the sensory process **S**, and proportional to $\overline{X}_T - \overline{X}_{NT}$, which increases with discriminability. The other is an estimate of the criterion, presumed to be a pure measure of the decision process **D**.

Many factors have been used in attempts to influence **S** and **D**, some expected to influence just a sensory process (sensory-specific or *s-factors*), and some expected to influence just a decision process (decision-specific or *d-factors*). Stimulus features such as the luminance difference between S_T and S_{NT} are examples of s-factors used to influence the measure $M_S = d'$. In studies with human observers, 2 × 2 payoff matrices, containing positive or negative values associated with the four possible outcomes on a trial, have been used as a factor (*PM*) to influence the response bias associated with **D**. Unfortunately, selective influence by *PM* of **D** has not been shown; **D** also appears to be influenced by s-factors. However, a few animal studies, including the one described below, suggest that response bias is selectively influenced not by the conditional probabilities described by the payoff matrix, but by the distribution of rewards over the two

alternative responses (sometimes described as the "reinforcement ratio", *RR*). *RR* can be defined as $Pr\{R_{NT}|Reward\}$, the proportion of the total number of rewards (for both kinds of correct responses) that are given for R_{NT}.

In a luminance-discrimination experiment with six pigeons, McCarthy and Davison (1984) used a linked concurrent pair of variable-interval (VI) schedules to control *RR*. On each trial in a series, one of two light intensities appeared on the centre key of three keys; these two trial types were equally frequent. The correct response was to peck the left key (R_T) if the centre key was "bright," and to peck the right key (R_{NT}) if it was "dim". Correct responses were reinforced with food, with a mean probability of about 0.37, controlled by the VI schedules. Two factors were varied orthogonally: The *luminance ratio* (*LR*) of the two lights was varied by letting the dimmer luminance be one of five values, including, for the most difficult *LR* level, a value equal to the brighter luminance. The *reinforcement ratio* (*RR*), described by $Pr\{R_{NT}|Reward\}$, could be one of three values, 0.2, 0.5, or 0.8.[25] There were thus 5 × 3 = 15 conditions. For each bird, each condition was tested for a series of consecutive daily sessions until a stability requirement was satisfied; the data analyzed came from the last seven sessions in each condition (about 1060 trials per condition per bird).

For each condition and each bird, the data can be summarized by two proportions, $Pr\{R_T|S_T\}$ and $Pr\{R_T|S_{NT}\}$. If the distributions of X_T and X_{NT} are Gaussian with equal variances, and $z(\cdot)$ is the z-transform of a proportion (the inverse Gaussian distribution function), then the ("ROC") curve traced out when $z(Pr\{R_T|S_T\})$ is plotted against $z(Pr\{R_T|S_{NT}\})$ as *RR* is changed from 0.8 to 0.5 to 0.2, is expected to be linear with unit slope. Examination of the set of thirty such curves (6 birds × 5 levels of *LR*) supports this expectation, and hence the equal-variance Gaussian model. Given such support for the model, suitable estimators for the discriminability

---

[25] If $Pr\{R_{NT}|Reward\} = 0.2$, for example, for each rewarded R_{NT} response there are four rewarded R_T responses, encouraging a liberal (low) criterion for R_T.

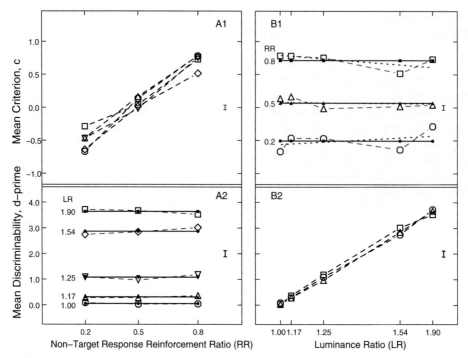

Figure 4. *Mean effects of* Reinforcement Ratio, RR = Pr{R$_{NT}$|Reward} *(Panels A1, A2) and* Luminance Ratio, LR *(Panels B1, B2) on criterion* ĉ *(Panels A1, B1) and on discriminability* d̂′ *(Panels A2, B2) are shown by unfilled points and broken lines. RR and LR levels have been scaled so as to linearize their mean effects on* ĉ*-value and* d̂′*-value (Panels A1 and B2). Filled points and unbroken lines in Panels A2 and B1 represent fitted models in which* c *and* d′ *are invariant with respect to factors RR and LR, respectively. The dotted lines in Panel B1 represent a fitted model with a multiplicative interaction of the two factors (see SM:7.2, SM:15.1), which is not statistically significant. The* ± SE *error bars reflect estimates of the variability of each plotted point after removing mean differences between birds. Plotting symbols correspond from top panels to bottom, but not from left to right; the plotted y-values are the same from left to right. From McCarthy and Davison (1984); basic data kindly provided by B. Alsop. (Fig. 5 of Sternberg, 2001; reprinted by permission.)*

and criterion measures for each condition are

$$\hat{d}' = z(Pr\{R_T|S_T\}) - z(Pr\{R_T|S_{NT}\}), \text{ and}$$

$$\hat{c} = -[z(Pr\{R_T|S_T\}) + z(Pr\{R_T|S_{NT}\})]/2.$$

The origin for the criterion measure is the midpoint between $\overline{X}_{NT}$ and $\overline{X}_T$; the sign of the criterion thus expresses the direction of the bias. Means over birds of these two measures are shown in Figure 4.

The left side of the figure shows that while the criterion responds strongly to factor *RR* (Panel A1), the often-demonstrated invariance of *d′*

with respect to d-factors is also persuasive here (Panel A2): there is neither a main effect of *RR* on *d′*, nor is there any modulation by *RR* of the effect of *LR*. The invariance model fits well. Thus we have evidence for the hypothesis that while *RR* is potent, as shown by its influence on the criterion *c* (hence on **D**), it leaves invariant our measure *d′* of discriminability (and hence of **S**). The complementary effects of *LR* are shown on the right side of the figure. Panel B2 shows the orderly effect of *LR* on *d′*; discriminability ranges widely, from *d′* ≈ 0 to *d′* ≈ 3.6. Panel B1 shows that to a good approximation the criterion is uninfluenced by *LR*.

6. NEURAL PROCESSING MODULES INFERRED FROM BRAIN ACTIVATION MAPS

6.1. fMRI signals as pure measures

Suppose there is localization of function (see, e.g., Op de Beeck et al., 2008, but also Haxby, 2004), such that two neural processes α and β are implemented by different processors P_α and P_β in non-overlapping brain regions R_α and R_β. The search for such processes has sometimes been stimulated by behavioural findings that support the existence of modular mental processes **A** and **B** that are influenced selectively by factors F and G. Because of their effectiveness in assessing the level of activity in localized brain regions, PET and fMRI are good techniques for such searches. Then, because process α should be influenced selectively by F, the activation level of region R_α, a pure measure, should vary with F, but not with G, and conversely for region R_β.[26] Thus, the existence of regions whose fMRI signals are influenced selectively by F and G provides evidence for modular *neural* processes that correspond to the modular *mental* processes inferred from the behavioural data. If such regions were found, it would support the modular decomposition inferred from the behavioural data, and would also support the conclusion that the processors that implement **A** and **B** are anatomically localized.

For examples 6.3 and 6.4, it was the modular decomposition into two processing stages inferred from RT data that suggested a new experiment that would incorporate fMRI measurements to search for corresponding neural processes. And in both experiments, concurrent RT data were taken, along with the fMRI data. While the RT data in Ex. 6.3 confirmed earlier findings, results in Ex. 6.4 did not, probably because of paradigm differences, which raises questions about the fMRI findings.

6.2. The fMRI signal as a composite measure

If α and β are implemented by different neural processors, P_α and P_β (or by the *same* processor $P_{\alpha\beta}$) in *one* region, $R_{\alpha\beta}$, then the activation level in $R_{\alpha\beta}$ is a composite measure that depends on both α and β. To test separate modifiability, we must know or show how their contributions to the activation measure are combined. For example, if the combination rule is *summation* (sometimes assumed without justification) and if factors F and G influence α and β selectively, then the effects of F and G will be additive. Finding such additivity in a factorial experiment would support the combination rule in that brain region, as well as selective influence. (If summation were assumed erroneously, selective influence might be obscured: the effect of each factor would appear to be modulated by the level of the other.) Additivity was found in examples 6.5 and 8.1, both of which used fMRI adaptation, as well as in the two brain regions in which it could be tested in Ex. 6.4. Some of the evidence that bears on the combination rule for fMRI signals is discussed in Section 7.2.

6.3. Modular processes in number comparison

In an experiment by Pinel, Dehaene, Rivière, and LeBihan (2001), subjects had to classify a sequence of visually displayed numbers, $\{k\}$, as being greater or less than 65. One factor was *notation* (N): the numbers k could be presented as Arabic numerals (e.g., "68") or number names (e.g., "SOIXANTE-HUIT"). The other was *Numerical Proximity* (P), defined as the absolute

---

[26] Such tests require no assumptions about whether a change in factor level causes an increase or decrease in activation. This contrasts with the assumption, sometimes used to infer modular neural processors (Kanwisher, Downing, Epstein, & Kourtzi, 2001), that stimuli more prototypical of those for which a processor is specialized will produce greater activation.

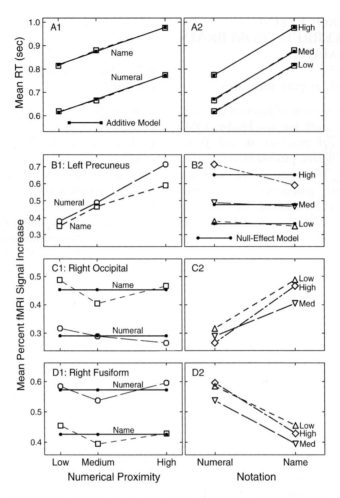

Figure 5. *Reaction-time and selected brain-activation data from Pinel, Dehaene, Rivière, and LeBihan (2001). The same data are plotted on the left as functions of* P *(Proximity, where "high" means closer), with* N *(Notation) the parameter, and on the right as functions of* N, *with* P *the parameter. Means over nine subjects of median RTs for correct responses are shown in Panels A, with a fitted additive model. The three levels of* P *have been scaled to linearize the main effect of* P *on* $\overline{RT}$; *this effect, from low to high* P, *is 159 ± 24 ms, while the main effect of* N *is 204 ± 34 ms. (SEs are based on variability over the nine subjects.) The difference across levels of* N *between the simple effects of* P *from low to high (a measure of interaction) is a negligible 4 ± 20 ms. (The SE may be inflated by unanalyzed condition-order effects.) The normalized interaction contrast (see Figure 2 caption), based on the four corners of the 3 × 2 design, is 4%. Mean activation measures from three sample brain regions, relative to an intertrial baseline, are shown in Panels B, C, and D, accompanied by fitted null-effect models in Panels B2, C1, and D1. Shown in Panels B1, C1, and D1, the main effects of* P *(from low to high, using fitted linear functions) are 0.29 ± 0.09% (p ≈ .01), −0.03 ± 0.03%, and 0.00 ± 0.04%. Shown in Panels B2, C2, and D2, the main effects of* N *are −0.06 ± 0.06%, −0.16 ± 0.05% (p ≈ .01), and −0.15 ± 0.05% (p ≈ .02). (Fig. 6.2 of Sternberg, 2004; reprinted by permission.)*

difference $|k - 65|$, and grouped into three levels. The interesting phenomenon here is the "symbolic distance effect" (Moyer & Landauer, 1967): the smaller the value of P (the closer the proximity), the slower the response. A similar

experiment (Dehaene, 1996) had shown additive effects of N and P on $\overline{RT}$; this was interpreted to indicate two modular subprocesses arranged as stages: encoding (**E**), influenced by N, which determines the identity of the stimulus and is slower for number names than numbers, and comparison (**C**), influenced by P, which uses the stimulus identity in performing the comparison and is slower for closer proximities. In the new experiment, in which fMRI as well as RT measurements were taken, most of the sixteen brain regions examined whose activation was influenced by N or by P were influenced significantly by only one of them, consistent with two separately modifiable neural processes ϵ and γ that are implemented by separately localized processors. When we average absolute effect sizes and SEs over the regions of each type, we find that for the nine N-sensitive regions the N effect was $0.17 \pm 0.05\%$ (median p-value $= .01$), while the P effect was $0.06 \pm 0.08\%$; for the seven P-sensitive regions the P effect was $0.32 \pm 0.10\%$ (median p-value $= .01$), while the N effect was $0.04 \pm 0.04\%$.

The fMRI data from three well-behaved regions are shown in Figure 5, Panels B, C, and D. The concurrently collected RT data (Figure 5, Panels A) replicated the earlier study, suggesting that we associate the neural modules ϵ and γ with the mental modules **E** and **C**; it is important that the mental and neural modules were selectively influenced by the same factors. However, while the direction of the effect of P was the same in all the brain regions it influenced, the direction of the effect of N was not: the change from numeric to verbal notation (which increased $\overline{RT}$) increased activation in some regions (e.g., Figure 5, Panels C) and decreased it in others (e.g., Figure 5, Panels D).[27,28]

6.4. Modular processes for stimulus encoding and response selection

A common finding has emerged from several studies of choice-reaction time (one of them discussed in Section 4.3), using various experimental arrangements and various realizations of the factors SQ (stimulus quality) and stimulus-response mapping difficulty (either MF, mapping familiarity, or MC, spatial mapping compatibility): these studies have shown that stimulus quality and mapping difficulty have additive effects on $\overline{RT}$, consistent with the idea that there are two processes, arranged in stages, that are selectively influenced by these factors. (These studies include Biederman & Kaplan, 1970, after a session of practice; Frowein & Sanders, 1978; Roberts & Sternberg, 1993, Exp. 2; Sanders, 1977, Exp. II; Sanders, 1980, Exp. 3; Sanders, Wijnen, & Van Arkel, 1982, Exp. I; and Shwartz, Pomerantz, & Egeth, 1977, Exp. 2.) The notion is that in initiating a response to a stimulus, the stimulus must first be identified (one stage, **S**) and then, starting with the identity, the response must be determined (a second stage, **R**).

Using a choice-reaction task with their versions of SQ and MC, Schumacher and D'Esposito (2002) measured RT and, concurrently, measured fMRI in six brain regions.[29] In their task, the stimulus was a row of four circular patches, one patch brighter than the others. The response was to press one of four keys, depending on which of the patches was the brighter one. The two factors, each at two levels, were the discriminability of the brighter

---

[27] Without requiring it, this finding invites us to consider that there are two qualitatively different encoding processes ε, one for each notation, rather than "one" process whose settings depend on N. This possibility is supported by the observation that "the notation factor affects the circuit where information is processed, not just the intensity of the activity within a fixed circuit" (S. Dehaene, personal communication, September 29, 2006). If so, we have a case where a change in the level of a factor (here, N) induces a task change (one operation replaced by another; see Section 12.1), but evidence for modularity emerges nonetheless: the proximity effect is invariant across the two tasks. Based on the idea that the processes implemented by different processors are probably different, the (multidimensional) activation data from such a simple (two-factor) experiment can support a claim of operations replacement. In contrast, an RT experiment that alone could support such a claim has yet to be devised.

[28] Using a dual-task experiment, Sigman and Dehaene (2005) have added to the evidence that distinguishes **E** from **C**: **E** could occur concurrently with all stages of the initial task, whereas **C** had to await completion of the "central" stage of the initial task.

[29] Extrastriate cortex was expected to respond to SQ; previous studies had implicated the remaining five regions (see Figure 6) in response selection.

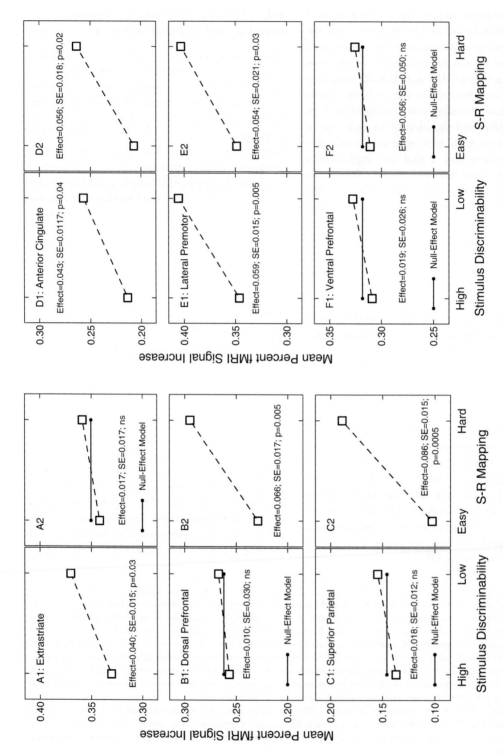

Figure 6. The six pairs of panels of Figure 6 provide brain activation data relative to a fixation baseline for the six regions measured by Schumacher and D'Esposito (2002). Mean main effects over nine subjects (eight for anterior cingulate) of Stimulus Discriminability and S-R Mapping in each region, with null effect models shown for each non-significant effect.

patch from the others (*SQ*), and the spatial compatibility of the patch-to-key mapping (*MC*). Each subject was tested under all four combinations of factor levels. Unlike Ex. 6.3, in every region where a factor had an effect on the fMRI signal, the "more difficult" level of that factor—the level that produced the longer $\overline{RT}$—also produced the larger fMRI signal. Figure 6 shows that in one of the regions, only *SQ* had a reliable effect (Panels A), in two of the regions only *MC* had reliable effects (Panels B and C), in two regions both factors had reliable effects (Panels D and E), and in one region neither factor had a reliable effect (Panels F). The selective effects found in three of the regions (where the fMRI signal was influenced by one of the factors but not the other) are consistent with **S** and **R** being implemented, at least in part, by anatomically distinct populations of neurons.[30]

The additivity found in earlier RT experiments suggests that there is no process influenced by both factors. But in two brain regions (Panels D and E), both factors were found to have effects. One possibility is that these regions each contain two specialized populations of neurons, each of which is influenced selectively by a different one of the two factors. If so, the total amount of neural activity in each of these regions would be influenced additively by the two factors. Alternatively, if **S** and **R** are sequential, as suggested by the RT data from the earlier experiments, the same neural processor in the same region could contribute to the implementation of both processes, and again it is plausible that

the summed neural activity would be influenced additively by the two factors. As shown in Figure 7, Panels A and B, the effects of *SQ* and *MC* on the fMRI signal were remarkably close to being perfectly additive.

Additive effects on the amount of neural activity by itself does not imply additive effects on the fMRI signal; assumptions required for this implication are discussed in Section 7.2. Given these assumptions, the additivity of the effects of *SQ* and *MC* on the fMRI signal supports additivity of their effects on the amount of neural activity, which in turn supports the idea that separate processes within the regions shown in Panels D and E contribute to the implementation of **S** and **R**.

In contrast to the earlier findings with various experimental arrangements mentioned above, the effects of the two factors on $\overline{RT}$ in the Schumacher-D'Esposito task were unfortunately not additive; as shown in Figure 7C there was a reliable interaction: the effect of raising the level of each factor was greater when the level of the other factor was higher (an "overadditive" interaction); such an interaction was found in the data for eight of the nine subjects. This finding seems inconsistent with the fMRI data, all of which support the idea that no neural process is influenced by both factors. One possibility is that there is such a process, but it happens not to be localized in any of the six regions that were examined, which suggests that stronger inferences require sampling more brain regions.[31,32]

---

[30] It is noteworthy and requires explanation that in each of the five cases where an effect is not statistically significant, it is nonetheless in the same direction as in those cases where the effect is significant. Is this because the neural populations that implement the **S** and **R** processes are incompletely localized, or because the measured regions don't correspond to the populations, or for some other reason?

[31] Schumacher and D'Esposito (2002) suggest that such a process might occur only under the stress of a subject's being in the scanner, and not under normal conditions. However, RT data from the practice session, outside the scanner, showed a non-significant interaction of about the same size and in the same direction. It is also of interest that a whole-brain analysis of the fMRI data did not reveal any additional task-sensitive regions (E. Schumacher, personal communication, November 27, 2006).

[32] There is an unresolved puzzle about these data that suggests that it would be valuable to replicate this experiment, using a procedure known to produce additive effects on $\overline{RT}$. The large SEs associated with the very small mean interaction contrasts for the data shown in panels 7A and 7B reflect the fact that the variability of the interaction contrast over subjects is quite large—so large relative to the mean that the reported *F*-statistics in both cases were 0.00. Indeed, relative to the variability, the reported mean interaction contrasts were significantly ($p < .05$) too small.

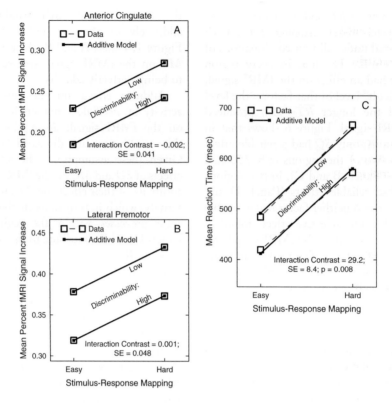

Figure 7. *Panels A, B show mean simple effects of the two factors on the brain activation measure, in the two regions where both main effects were significant in Schumacher and D'Esposito (2002). Also shown are fitted additive models, and the interaction contrasts that measure the badness of fit of these models. Panel C shows simple effects of the two factors on $\overline{RT}$, and the corresponding interaction contrast. The normalized interaction contrasts (see Figure 2 caption) are A: 4%; B: 1%; C: 25%. (The mean effect of Discriminability on $\overline{RT}$ when the Mapping was easy versus hard is 64 versus 94 ms, respectively.)*

6.5. Modular short-term and long-term memory processes in scene perception

Consider the process used to to recognize a scene and make a judgement about it. This process is influenced by the observer's previous experiences with the same scene and with other views of the same place. Epstein, Parker, and Feiler (2008) asked whether there are different subprocesses influenced selectively by such previous experiences, depending on whether the experiences are very recent ("short-interval"— within 2 sec) or less recent ("long-interval"—separated by about a half hour). Students at the University of Pennsylvania (Penn) saw two series of visual scenes, Series 1

before their brains were scanned, Series 2 while being scanned. During Series 1, all the scenes were from Penn, and subjects had to judge which half of the campus each scene was from.

In Series 2, two scenes were presented successively on each trial, with onsets separated by 1.2 sec. For two thirds of the trials, both scenes were from Penn; for the remaining third (whose data were discarded), one or both scenes were not from Penn. Subjects had to judge whether both scenes were from Penn, and make one speeded manual response to the second scene if so, the other response if not. Primary interest was in the RT and in the fMRI signal in the para-hippocampal place area (PPA) on each trial when both scenes were from Penn, and how these measures were influenced by two orthogonal factors: the *short-interval relation*: between the second scene and the first on trials in Series 2, and the *long-interval relation* between the second scene and scenes that had been displayed during Series 1.

fMRI Adaptation (also called "repetition suppression"; Grill-Spector & Malach, 2001) was expected both from Series 1 and from the first scene on each trial in Series 2: To the extent that a stimulus is similar to one shown earlier, the neural response to that stimulus is reduced. (One can also think of *recovery* from fMRI adaptation as a novelty effect: to the extent that aspects of a stimulus to which the measured neurons are sensitive are novel, their response is greater.[33]) Consistent with expectation, the fMRI signal in the PPA as well as the RT varied with both short-interval and long-interval relations. Answering the question whether short- and long-interval fMRI adaptation in the PPA are generated by a single process or by two separate processes therefore requires determining how their effects on the fMRI signal combine. Because the RT undoubtedly depends on other brain regions in addition to the PPA, analysis of the two measures might lead to different answers.[34]

There were three possible short-interval relations between the first and second scenes on a trial: they could be identical (second scene = old place, old view), similar (second scene = old place, new view), or different (second scene = new place).

Similarly, there were three possible long-interval relations: the Series 1 scenes could include one that was identical to the second scene, or one that was similar, or none that was either identical or similar. The ingenious design permitted these two kinds of relation to vary orthogonally. For the analysis presented here, the data were partitioned so as to separately examine (1) the *view effect*: the effect of increasing novelty by showing a different view of a previously seen place rather than the same view, and (2) the *place effect*: the effect of increasing novelty by showing a new place rather than repeating a previously seen place.[35] Thus there are two short-interval factors (*Sameness or Difference of View* and *Place*) and two long-interval factors (*Sameness or Difference of View* and *Place*), each with two levels. In asking how the effects of short-interval and long-interval factors combine, we can ask how each of the two short-interval factors combines with each of the two long-interval factors, giving us four separate tests.

Means of the PPA fMRI signal strengths over the sixteen subjects are shown in Figure 8.[36] All four of the main effects are significant, with $p < .01$. In each case the long- and short-interval effects are remarkably close to being additive. Whereas the long- and short-interval place effects are similar in magnitude (Panel B), with the former slightly greater, the long-interval view effect is substantially smaller than the short-interval view effect (Panel A). Indeed, the difference between the long- and short-interval main effects of the view factor is significantly greater than the difference between the main effects of the place factor, with $p < .01$. In addition

---

[33] The relation between fMRI adaptation and neuronal activity is controversial; see, e.g., Sawamura, Orban, and Vogels (2006), and Grill-Spector (2006).

[34] Suppose that the fMRI analysis leads to the conclusion that the two factors influence separate modules within the PPA. This would not preclude their having interactive effects on the mean RT. This could happen, e.g., if the processes that contribute to the RT include one or more processes, other than the one(s) implemented by the PPA, that are influenced by both factors. Or it could happen if the processes that contribute to the RT are selectively influenced by the two factors, but are arranged in parallel rather than as stages. On the other hand, suppose that the fMRI analysis leads to the conclusion that there is a single module influenced by the two factors. Then, unless the PPA does not play a role in generating the response, additivity of the RT effects of the two factors would be unexpected.

[35] In the present analysis of the effects of place change, the data for same place were collapsed over levels of the view factor. This analysis differs from that of Epstein et al. (2008).

[36] These are means of the BOLD signal strengths over the PPA regions in the two hemispheres.

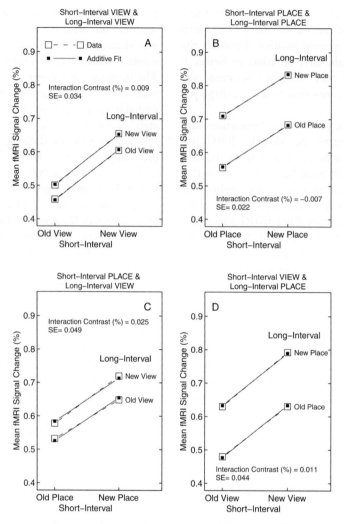

Figure 8. *Combined effects on the fMRI signal in the parahippocampal place area of two kinds of short-interval and long-interval novelty, from Epstein, Parker, and Feiler (2008). The normalized interaction contrasts (see Figure 2 caption) are A: 11%; B: 5%; C: 29%; D: 7%.*

to its significance level attesting to the remarkably high precision of these data, this three-way interaction supports the idea that the long-interval adapting effect is more "viewpoint invariant" than the short-interval effect.[37]

Means of the RT data are shown in Figure 9. There is one substantial interaction (in Panel D), but it is not statistically significant. The additivity in Panel A should probably not be taken seriously, because the long-interval view effect is small (just

---

[37] In a whole-brain analysis, reliable long- and short-interval effects were found in many other brain regions. There was no persuasive evidence that any region had just one of these effects. Furthermore, the number of regions in which the interaction of the two effects was significant (two among 21 tests) can be explained as the result of type I error. Thus, no regions were found that provided pure measures of either effect, and additional evidence was found of additivity of the two effects on the fMRI signal.

as in the fMRI data) and not statistically significant. As in the fMRI data, lengthening the interval reduces the view effect more than the place effect in the RT data; indeed, it reverses the effect in the RT data. It is interesting to consider whether the differences between short- and long-interval effects of view and place changes would alone argue that the short- and long-interval effects are generated by different processes. (See the discussion of *differential influence* in Section 12.4.)

To the extent that summation is a plausible combination rule for effects on fMRI (see Section 7.2), the additivity of the effects of short-interval and long-interval factors is consistent with their being generated by separate modular processes. However, the fMRI data alone don't tell us whether these processes are concurrent (resulting from the activity of different neural populations in the same region) or sequential. The fact that no brain regions were found in which just one process appears to be operating seems to argue against their being implemented by different neural populations. Both of the neurophysiological accounts suggested by Epstein et al. (2008) are consistent with the processes being sequential. If the additivity of the RT effects were more persuasive, we would have evidence for two processes being arranged as stages. However, as mentioned above, we don't know the relation between PPA activity and the processes that generate the response. Whatever their temporal arrangement, if two independent (modular) processes mediate the effects of the same experience, depending on how long ago it occurred, this seems to require separate short- and long-term memory representations.

7. MODULAR EXPLANATIONS OF ADDITIVE EFFECTS: HOW STRONG IS THE INFERENCE?

The inferences from composite measures to modular processes in Sections 4 and 6 based on RT and fMRI data have made use of the reasoning described in Table 2. How persuasive is such reasoning? Suppose that we make an observation—of the additivity of the effects of two factors on

a measure—that is consistent with a theory according to which the two factors influence a particular pair of processing modules selectively. Given the observation, how credible is the theory? This depends on the plausibility of the theory, the plausibility of alternative modular theories, and the plausibility of single-process (i.e., non-modular) theories that are also consistent with the observation (Howson & Urbach, 2006).

7.1. Inferences from reaction-time measurements

Let us first consider the case where the measure is $\overline{RT}$, and where the observation is of the additivity of the effects of two factors. When the additive-factor method was first proposed (Sternberg, 1969), there was a highly plausible and historically significant modular explanation: stages plus selective influence, with the combination rule (summation) inherent in the concept of stages. And there were no well-known plausible alternatives, either modular or non-modular. Since then, it has been discovered that under some conditions, other models, quite different in spirit from stage models, can also generate such additive effects. (Ashby, 1982; McClelland, 1979; Miller, van der Ham, & Sanders, 1995; Roberts & Sternberg, 1993). In all these cases, the prediction of means additivity derives from modularity plus selective influence; hence, from the viewpoint of discovering modular processes (but not of how these processes are arranged in time) the existence of these alternative possibilities does not weaken the argument outlined in Table 2. Their discovery, however, decidedly weakens the inference from the additivity of factor effects on $\overline{RT}$ to the organization in *stages* of the corresponding processes. To help distinguish among such modular alternatives one can sometimes use other aspects of the RT data (e.g., Roberts & Sternberg, 1993) or brain measurements. Examples of the use of brain measurements for this purpose include neurophysiological data (see Schall, 2003, and references therein, and Woodman, Kang, Thompson, & Schall, 2008) and the pure stage duration measures in the electrophysiological data of Ex. 3.2. As for non-modular theories, I know of no plausible way

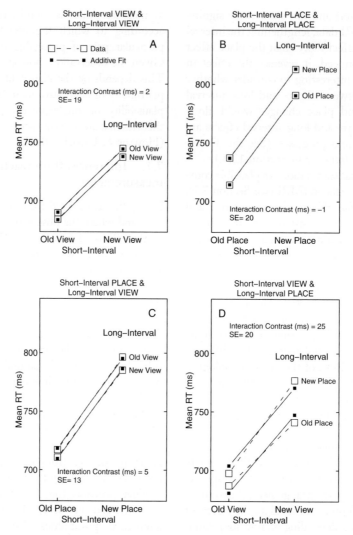

Figure 9. *Combined effects on* $\overline{\text{RT}}$ *of two kinds of short-interval and long-interval novelty, from Epstein, Parker, and Feiler (2008). The normalized interaction contrasts (see Figure 2 caption) are A: 11%; B: 3%; C: 18%; D: 64%.*

in which what is truly a single process can give rise to additive effects of two factors on mean $\overline{\text{RT}}$.[38] This could of course change, as we learn more about mental and neural processes.

7.2. Inferences from fMRI measurements

Suppose that we observe that the effects of two factors on the fMRI signal in a brain region are additive. It is tempting to conclude that they

---

[38] In the popular diffusion model (e.g., Ratcliff & Smith, 2010), the most natural way in which a factor has its effect is by changing the rate of evidence accumulation. Additive effects on this rate produce effects on $\overline{RT}$ that are overadditive.

influence different neural processes in that region. To do so, two propositions should be true:

Proposition 1: Summation is the combination rule for their contributions to the BOLD signal (*B*) of different processes in that region, either concurrent and implemented by different neural populations, or successive. (Only then can additivity of effects support the inference of selective influence.) This requires *B* to be linear in the total amount of neural activity in the region.

Proposition 2: Factors that influence the *same* neural process do *not* have additive effects on the amount of neural activity. (If they did, and *B* satisfied the linearity requirement, then additive effects could be produced by factors that influence the same neural process.) This leads to a requirement of *non*linearity for neural activity.

To see why these propositions are critical, consider what is required to correctly conclude in favour of modular processes in a region, and how we could be misled.

Different neural populations implement modular processes. Suppose first that α and β, modular processes selectively influenced by *F* and *G*, are implemented by two different populations of neurons in the measured region. Let us write $N_\alpha = N_\alpha(F_j)$ and $N_\beta = N_\beta(G_k)$ for the levels of neural activity in those two populations, and assume that the fMRI signal, *B* depends on both N_α and N_β, but possibly to different degrees. Assume further that *B* is a *linear* function of N_α and N_β: $B(N_\alpha, N_\beta) = B_0 + aN_\alpha + bN_\beta$, where B_0 is a baseline level, and *a* and *b* are nonnegative constants.[39] We can then write:

$$B_{jk} = B(F_j, G_k) = B_0 + aN_\alpha(F_j) + bN_\beta(G_k). \quad (8)$$

Because changes in *F* influence only the second term, and changes in *G* influence only the third term, the effects of F_j and G_k on B_{jk} must be additive, whatever the form of the functions $N_\alpha()$ and $N_\beta()$. The inferential logic for this case is described by Table 2, and, as described in that table, the

observation of additivity, as in Exs. 6.4, 6.5, and 8.1, supports the hypothesis that factors *F* and *G* influence different modules selectively, together with the hypothesis that the contributions to *B* of the two populations combine by summation, which in turn depends on *B* being linear in the level of neural activity.

One neural population implements successive modular processes. Because the fMRI signal reflects neural activity that occurs over a period of seconds, if processes α and β, selectively influenced by *F* and *G*, are implemented successively and sufficiently rapidly by the same population of neurons in the measured region, they would both contribute to the fMRI signal. With one proviso,[40] even if temporal summation were imperfect (e.g., Dale & Buckner, 1997), Eq. 8 would apply; the failure of perfect temporal summation would be reflected only in the parameters *a* and *b*.

Additive effects from a single process. As summarized in Table 2, the observation of additive effects of two factors *F* and *G* supports the joint hypothesis consisting of *H*1 and *H*3. An alternative explanation for such a finding is that there is a single process (α) influenced by both factors that operates in such a way that their effects on $M_\alpha(F, G)$ are additive. In evaluating the plausibility of this alternative we need to consider what would be required of the process for it to have this property, and how the requirement could be tested. For this purpose it is helpful to consider the idea of *factor-level strength*. Suppose two factors, *F* and *G*, each at two levels, in a 2×2 factorial design, and a measure $M = M(F, G)$. Associate a factor-level strength, s_f and s_g with each level of each factor; let the strengths for F_1, F_2, G_1, and G_2 be *q*, $q + r$, *u*,

---

[39] These constants would depend, for example, on the mean proximities of the two populations to the centre of the brain region in which the fMRI signal is measured, and on the time relation between the two activations.

[40] If the duration of either process is changed sufficiently by the change in factor level so that the temporal distribution of neural activation in the region is altered, additivity could fail. However, the findings in Ex. 6.4 are perhaps reassuring: Despite the fact that the $\overline{RT}$ data (Figure 7C) indicated substantial effects on the durations of both processes of interest, the additivity of the fMRI effects in both of the regions influenced by both factors was remarkably good. Apparently, even these duration changes are small relative to the sluggishness of *B*.

and $u + v$, respectively. To make it clear that s_f and s_g need to be specified only up to arbitrary multiplicative constants, we can write, for total factor-level strength, $tFLS = bs_f + cs_g$. Then for the four conditions in the experiment, (F_1, G_1), (F_1, G_2), (F_2, G_1), and (F_2, G_2), the total factor-level strengths are $bq + cu$, $bq + cu + cv$, $bq + br + cu$, and $bq + br + cu + cv$, respectively. Subtracting $bq + cu$, they become 0, cv, br, and $cv + br$, which makes it clear that the factor-level strengths in the four conditions are additive. Because the total strength is additive, a necessary and sufficient condition for the effects of the two factors on $M(F, G)$ to be additive is that M is a *linear* function of $tFLS$:

$$M(F, G) = M(tFLS) = M(bs_f + cs_g)$$
$$= a + b's_f + c's_g. \qquad (9)$$

To the extent that such linearity is plausible or valid, it prevents us from confidently inferring modular processes from additive effects on M. Applying this reasoning to fMRI, and assuming that B_α is linear in N_α, B_α is linear in $tFLS$ if (and only if) N_α is linear in $tFLS$: $N_\alpha(bs_f + cs_g) = a + b's_f + c's_g$. Thus, only to the extent that the linearity of N in $tFLS$ is implausible or invalid does the finding of additivity of factor effects on B support the hypothesis of modular processes.

In short, to justify the inferences in Exs. 6.5 and 8.1, and those based on the additive effects in two of the brain regions in Ex. 6.4, we have to believe that B is (approximately) linear in N, *and* that N is non-linear in $tFLS$. These requirements appear not to have been recognized by some investigators.

Evidence for linearity of B(N) (Proposition 1) and nonlinearity of N (Proposition 2). The neural basis of the BOLD response is controversial (e.g., Ekstrom, 2010; Logothetis & Wandell, 2004; Goense & Logothetis, 2008). That $B(N)$ is linear has been concluded from comparing the effects of motion coherence (Rees, Friston, & Koch, 2000) and contrast (Heeger, Huk, Geisler, & Albrecht, 2000) on B in humans with their effects on the single-cell spike rate in monkeys. Predictions from a linear transform model for the effects of certain visual stimulus variations on B were largely confirmed for area V1 in an influential study by Boynton, Engel, Glover, and Heeger (1996); see also Dale and Buckner (1997). The failures of linearity in such studies (such as failures of temporal summation) generally don't tell us whether it is $B(N)$, or the neural response N, or both, that are nonlinear (Boynton & Finney, 2003, Miller, Luh, Liu, Martinez, Obata, et al., 2001; Soltysik, Peck, White, Crosson, & Briggs, 2004). Generalization is problematic, because different brain regions may differ in linearity (Horner & Andrews, 2009; Soltysik et al., 2004). The authors of a study in which electrophysiological as well as fMRI measures were taken concluded that the source of nonlinearity in V1 is N, not $B(N)$ (Wan, Riera, Iwata, Takahashi, Wakabahyashi, & Kawashima, 2006). However, Miller et al.'s (2001) finding of a nonlinear relation between cerebral blood flow and B in primary visual and motor cortex is hard to explain unless $B(N)$ is nonlinear. And Boynton and Finney (2003) concluded that whereas some of the nonlinearity in higher visual areas is neural, some may be in $B(N)$.

Evidence, including that mentioned above, indicates that in response to contrast, duration, number of stimulus repetitions, and number of trials, the magnitude of the neural response N changes nonlinearly (Albrecht, Geisler, & Crane, 2003; Carandini & Heeger, 1994; Geisler & Albrecht, 1995; Heeger et al., 2000; Li, Miller, & Desimone, 1993; Meeter, Myers, & Gluck, 2005; Sawamura, Organ, & Vogels, 2006). This reduces the plausibility of a single neural process producing additive effects by responding linearly to $tFLS$. If we therefore assume that $N(tFLS)$ is nonlinear, we can conclude from additive effects of two factors on B in a brain region (as in Exs. 6.4, 6.5, and 8.1) that they influence different modules selectively.[41] Such instances of additive

---

[41] This argument is stronger for Ex. 6.4, where pure measures of each factor were found in three regions: This makes it more likely that the finding of effects of both factors in two other regions should be explained by those regions containing two populations of neurons, each responsive to one factor.

effects on B then provide evidence of the linearity of $B(N)$. However, taken together, the available evidence seems to permit us to treat the linearity of $B(N)$ only as a tentative working hypothesis.

8. BRIEF ACCOUNTS OF FOUR ADDITIONAL EXAMPLES WITH COMPOSITE MEASURES

8.1. Modular neural processes for perceptually separable dimensions

We considered an application of fMRI adaptation in Section 6.5; another example is a study by Drucker, Kerr, and Aguirre (2009). Suppose a set of visual stimuli that vary along two dimensions that are *neurally separable*, in the sense that they are evaluated by different modular neural processes (possibly implemented by different populations of neurons). Let S_1 and S_2 be successive stimuli, and let F_j and G_k be their proximities along the two dimensions. Then, given Eq. 8, the adapting effect of S_1 on the fMRI response to S_2 will be the sum of the adapting effects on the two processes, which in turn will depend additively on F_j and G_k. In an experiment to test this idea, Drucker et al. used two different sets of outline shapes, each varying over several levels of each of two dimensions. For one stimulus set the two dimensions were expected to be neurally separable because they are perceptually separable in the sense of Garner (1974);[42] for the other stimulus set they were expected to be *neurally integral*, that is, evaluated by a single process, because they are perceptually integral, and were therefore expected to have adapting effects on the two dimensions that would interact rather than being additive.[43]

Applying a single-df global measure of interaction to each subject's data for each stimulus set, they found results that supported their hypotheses. Unfortunately, they provided no breakdown of the multiple separate tests of additivity that their data permit, no comparison of measures of interaction with corresponding main effects, and no way to be sure that the global measure in the additive case was not the resultant of multiple interaction contrasts of opposite sign. (Their test is analogous to representing all the information about the combination of effects in Figure 8 as a single number.) One appeal of this study is that the same experimental and analytic methods and the same subjects revealed contrasting fMRI effects, additive and interactive, for the two sets of stimuli. Another appeal is that the results support an attractive neural theory of perceptual integrality and separability.

8.2. Evidence for modular spatial-frequency analyzers from the detectability of compound gratings

Consider a task in which a subject says "yes" when either or both of two detection processes respond, and says "no" if neither process responds. (For the present discussion we ignore the complication introduced by "guessed" yes responses that may occur when neither process responds.) If the behaviour of the two processes is uncorrelated, then the probability of neither process responding is the product of the individual nonresponse probabilities for the two processes. $Pr\{\text{"no"}\}$ is thus a composite measure of the two detection processes, with a multiplicative combination rule; this relationship is sometimes called "probability summation".

To describe the consequences of a multiplicative combination rule for a composite measure, it is helpful to introduce the idea of a proportional effect, or *p.effect*. We saw in Section 2.2 that the *effect* of a factor on a measure is defined as a *difference* (for a factor with two levels), as in Eq. 1, or can be defined as a vector of differences (for a factor with multiple levels). Similarly, the p.effect of a factor on a measure M_A is defined as a *ratio*

---

[42] For two perceptually separable (integral) dimensions, variation in one does not (does) interfere with making decisions based on the other, and perceptual distances obey a city-block (Euclidean) metric. See also, e.g., Ashby and Maddox (1994).

[43] While viewing each sequence of shapes, subjects reported on the position of a bisecting line.

Table 3. *Inferential logic for a composite measure with multiplication as the combination rule*

Joint Hypothesis
H1: Processes **A** and **B** are modules (separately modifiable).
H4: Contributions u_A, v_B of **A**, **B** to M_{AB}(**A**, **B**) combine by *multiplication*.
H5: Contributions of **A** and **B** to M_{AB} are uncorrelated.

Prediction
We may be able to find factors F and G that influence **A** and **B** selectively:
$p'_1{:}u_A \leftarrow F, \ \ p'_2{:}v_B \nleftarrow F, \ \ p'_3{:}v_B \leftarrow G, \ \ p'_4{:}u_A \nleftarrow G,$
and jointly influence no other process.
If so, their *proportional effects* on M_{AB} will be *multiplicative*.

Alternative Results	
We find factors F and G with *multiplicative p.effects* on M_{AB}.	We fail to find such factors.

Corresponding Inferences	
Support for joint hypothesis *H1 + H4 + H5*.	Refutes one/more of *H1, H4, H5,* *or* we didn't look enough for F, G.

(for a factor with two levels):

$$p.effect(F) = \frac{M_A(F_2)}{M_A(F_1)}, \qquad (10)$$

or a vector of ratios (for a factor with multiple levels). Suppose we have a composite measure with a multiplicative combination rule:

$$M_{AB}(F_j, G_k) = u(F_j) \times v(G_k). \qquad (11)$$

To derive the equivalent of Eq. 3 from Eq. 11 requires us to assume that the contributions u and v from processes **A** and **B** to M_{AB} are uncorrelated.[44] In that case, it follows from Eq. 11 that

$$\overline{M}_{AB}(F_j, G_k) = \bar{u}(F_j) \times \bar{v}(G_k), \qquad (12)$$

and, by analogy to Eq. 4, that

$$p.effect(F, G) = p.effect(F) \times p.effect(G). \qquad (13)$$

If the p.effects of the factors are multiplicative, as in Eq. 13, this supports the joint hypothesis that processes **A** and **B** are separately modifiable, that their contributions to M_{AB} combine by multiplication, and that their contributions are uncorrelated. The inferential logic in this case is outlined in Table 3.[45]

---

[44] This is a weaker requirement than stochastic independence, but may nonetheless be important.

[45] Adapted from Table 4 of Sternberg (2001) by permission.

This observation was exploited in a famous experiment in which the detectors were hypothesized spatial-frequency analyzers sensitive to different frequency bands. Sachs, Nachmias, and Robson (1971) independently varied the contrasts (F, G) of two widely separated frequencies that comprised a compound grating whose presence subjects had to detect. They found that reducing the contrast of one of the frequencies in the compound caused $Pr\{non\text{-}detect\}$ to increase by a constant factor, consistent with Eq. 13, thus supporting the joint hypothesis. This model failed badly when the component spatial frequencies in the compound were closer together. These findings provided important early evidence for modular analyzers for separated spatial frequencies and for the multiplicative combination rule.[46] One reason why this experiment was especially persuasive is that whereas one of the two gratings was either present or absent, the contrast of the other grating was varied over more than two levels.

More formally, let S_1 and S_2 represent the behaviour of the two modular subprocesses, here detection processes, with $S_j = 1$ indicating success (detection) and $S_j = 0$ otherwise, and assume that S_1 and S_2 are independent. In the present case, the combined process is successful (a "yes" response) if *either* of its subprocesses is successful. Under these conditions, it is the probability of *nonsuccess* ("nondetect") that is related to the subprocesses by a multiplicative combination rule:

$$Pr\{nonsuccess\} = Pr\{S_1 = 0 \ and \ S_2 = 0\}$$
$$= Pr\{S_1 = 0\} \times Pr\{S_2 = 0\}. \quad (14)$$

Shaw (1980) showed that Eq. 14 was a consequence of the attention-sharing version of an independent decisions model, and Mulligan and Shaw (1980) found that Eq. 13 (and neither of two alternative models) described the behaviour of three of their four observers detecting simultaneous auditory and visual signals in a 2×2

experiment in which each signal was either present or absent.

8.3. Modules inferred from multiplicative effects on the accuracy of lexical decisions

In contrast, suppose a situation in which the combined process is successful if and only if *both* of its independent subprocesses are successful. (This could occur if the output of the first is the input of the second.) It is then the probability of *success* that is related to the subprocesses by a multiplicative combination rule:

$$Pr\{success\} = Pr\{S_1 = 1 \ and \ S_2 = 1\}$$
$$= Pr\{S_1 = 1\} \times Pr\{S_2 = 1\}. \quad (15)$$

Equations 14 and 15 generalize, in the obvious way, to complex processes in which more than two (mutually independent) subprocesses are manipulated. One note of caution: If effects are *additive* within each of several subsets of the data (such as data from different subjects), they will also be additive in the mean data. (Additivity is preserved by the arithmetic mean.) However, if effects are *multiplicative* within data subsets, and are averaged using ordinary means (rather than geometric means, or arithmetic means after a logarithmic transformation), effects in the mean data may deviate from being multiplicative. (Multiplicative relationship may not be preserved by the arithmetic mean.) Pooling data from different subjects or from different levels of practice is also likely to induce correlation. Hence, when effects might be multiplicative, the units of analysis should be homogeneous subsets of the data, and experiments should be run so as to provide stability.[47]

In an important paper, Schweickert (1985) showed that effects of factors on $Pr\{correct\}$ in three diverse experiments satisfy a multiplicative combination rule. For example, one of the data sets (Schuberth, Spoehr, & Lane, 1981, Exp. 2) are the accuracies of the lexical decision process in a

---

[46] See SM:13 and SM:A.13 for more details.

[47] Numerical experiments show that under some plausible conditions, Eq. 12 is well approximated even when the contributions u and v to M_{AB} are highly correlated.

speeded task with orthogonal variation of three two-level factors: legibility of the test word, frequency of the word in English, and semantic congruity of the word with a sentence context. Schweickert found that a multiplicative combination rule is consistent with the effects of these factors on $Pr\{correct\}$, supporting theories in which the three factors influence three different mutually independent modular processes, all of which must succeed for a correct response. Because the error rate in these data never exceeded 8%, a multiplicative model for $Pr\{correct\}$ is virtually indistinguishable from an additive model for $Pr\{correct\}$, as Schweickert noted (which is equivalent to an additive model for $Pr\{error\}$); the mean absolute difference between fitted values of percent correct for multiplicative and additive models is a negligible 0.02%. This is a problem for inference only if a plausible additive model is available, which at this writing it appears not to be. For precise tests of models for $Pr\{correct\}$, more data are needed than in the Schuberth et al. experiment. For these data, with 672 observations per condition, the SEs of the mean $Pr\{correct\}$ for the eight conditions are large (0.3% to 1.0%), given the small main effects of 1.6%, 2.3%, and 2.9%.

8.4. Evidence from ERP amplitude for modular processes in semantic classification

At any particular time, the ERP at any point on the scalp is a composite measure of all the neural processors ("sources") in the brain that are active at that time. Furthermore, the physics of volume conduction tells us that the combination rule is summation.[48] Hence, unlike most other cases, the combination rule is not a part of the hypothesis that must be tested. Suppose there are two modular neural processes α and β, implemented by processors P_α and P_β, and influenced selectively by factors F and G. It follows that the effects of F and G on the ERP amplitude will be additive at all scalp locations. Furthermore, if P_α and P_β are at different locations in the brain, the topographies of the effects of F

and G (the way the effect sizes vary with location on the scalp) will differ. Because of the simplicity of the hypothesis and the richness of the possible tests, as well as the fine temporal resolution of the ERP, this approach is especially powerful.

Kounios (2007) exploited these properties in a study of the effects of priming on the semantic classification of a sequence of spoken nouns. Most of the words required no response, while 5% were targets (names of body parts) that called for a manual response. The words consisted of *primes* and *probes*. The factors (two levels each) were the *Semantic Relatedness* (*REL*) of the probe to the preceding prime, and the *Semantic Satiation* (*SAT*) of that prime (number of immediate repetitions of the prime before the probe). The data were the ERPs elicited by the non-target probes at several locations on the scalp. A composite measure $M_{\alpha\beta}$ is defined for each location as the mean ERP amplitude at that location during the epoch from 600 to 800 ms after probe onset. Consider the following theory, with three components:

*H*1 (Subprocesses): The complex process of recognizing the probe as a non-target contains (at least) two subprocesses, α and β, carried out by different neural processors, P_α and P_β.

*H*2 (Selective Influence): α and β are selectively influenced by *SAT* and *REL*, respectively.

*H*3 (Combination Rule): Each process is an ERP *source*; physics tells us that at any location the combination rule for sources is *summation*.

This theory implies that the effects of *SAT* and *REL* on $M_{\alpha\beta}$ will be additive at all scalp locations. Kounios found such additivity: The mean main effects of *REL* and *SAT* were $1.3 \pm 0.2\mu V$ and $2.1 \pm 0.4\mu V$, respectively, while the mean interaction contrast was $0.01 \pm 0.3\mu V$, making the normalized interaction contrast (see Figure 2 caption) 0.6% ($n = 36$). This finding supports the above theory and hence the modularity of α and β during the 600 to 800 ms epoch.[49] Also, the topographies of the two effects (their relative sizes across locations) differ markedly, indicating different locations in the brain for P_α and P_β,

---

[48] This follows from the electrical linearity of brain tissue (Nunez & Srinivasan, 2006, Ch. 1.5).

[49] Support for the theory is support for all of its three components. However, because the combination rule is given by physics in this application, there is no need to test component *H*3.

which adds to the evidence against a single-process explanation.[50]

9. PROCESS DECOMPOSITION VERSUS TASK COMPARISON

The applications above exemplify a process-decomposition approach whose goal is to divide the complex process by which a particular task is accomplished into modular subprocesses. The factor manipulations are not intended to produce "qualitative" changes in the complex process (such as adding new operations, or replacing one operation by another), which may be associated with a change in the task, just "quantitative" ones. The task-comparison method is a more popular approach to understanding the structure of complex processes. Here one determines the influence of factors on performance in different tasks, rather than on different parts of the complex process used to carry out one task. The data pattern of interest is the selective influence of factors on tasks, i.e., the single and double dissociation (Schmidt & Vorberg, 2006) of tasks. (A classical factor used in brain studies is the amount, usually presence versus absence, of damage in a particular region, which may affect performance in some tasks and not others; see Section 11.) Although it may achieve other goals, task comparison is inferior to process decomposition for discovering the modular subprocesses of a complex process or for investigating their properties: The interpretation usually requires assuming a theory of the complex process in each task, and the method includes no test of such theories. In contrast, process decomposition requires a theory of only one task, and, as illustrated by the examples above, incorporates a test of that theory.[51]

9.1. Comparison of two tactile perception tasks

An elegant example of task comparison, but one that is subject to its usual limitations, is provided by Merabet, Thut, Murray, Andrews, Hsiao, and Pascual-Leone (2004) in their experiment on the effects of repetitive transcranial magnetic stimulation (rTMS) of different brain regions on subjective numerical scaling of two tactile perceptual dimensions. Both tasks involved palpation by the fingers of one hand of a set of tactile dot arrays with varying dot spacings. The judged dimensions were roughness (r) in one task, and distance between dots (d) in the other. Where rTMS had an effect, it reduced the sensitivity of the obtained scale values to the differences among dot arrays. One measure of relative sensitivity is the slope, b, of the linear regression of post-rTMS scale values on non-rTMS scale values. If there were no effect we would have $b = 1.0$; if there is an effect, the value of b is reduced, so the effect of rTMS can be measured by $1 - b$. Means over the 11 subjects indicate that performance in the roughness-judgement task is influenced by rTMS$_s$ of the contralateral somatosensory cortex $(1 - \bar{b}_{rs} = 0.21 \pm 0.07; p = .02)$, but negligibly by rTMS$_o$ of the contralateral occipital cortex $(1 - \bar{b}_{ro} = 0.02 \pm 0.03)$, while performance in the distance-judgement task is influenced by rTMS$_o$ $(1 - \bar{b}_{do} = 0.16 \pm 0.07; p = .04)$, but negligibly by rTMS$_s$ $(1 - \bar{b}_{ds} = 0.05 \pm 0.04)$, a double dissociation of the two tasks.[52]

Plausible theories might include, for each task, processes for control of stimulus palpation (α), for generation of a complex percept (β), for extraction of the desired dimension (γ), and for conversion of its value into a numerical response (δ). Any or all of these processes might differ between tasks. The striking findings indicate

---

[50] In this application, modularity appears to change over time: During an earlier epoch (400 to 600 ms after probe onset) the two effects interacted substantially, while their topographies changed little from one epoch to the next. See SM:14 for more details.

[51] See SM:A.1.

[52] Subscripts d and r refer to the two tasks; subscripts s and o refer to the two stimulated brain regions. SEs are based on between-subject variability. Also supporting the claim of double dissociation, the differences $\bar{b}_{ro} - \bar{b}_{rs}$ and $\bar{b}_{ds} - \bar{b}_{do}$ are significantly greater than zero, with $p = .01$ and $p = .04$, respectively. However, because non-rTMS measurements were made only before rTMS, rather than being balanced over practice, straightforward interpretation of the slope values requires us to assume negligible effects of practice on those values.

that one or more of these processes in the two tasks depend on different regions of the cortex. In addition to specifying these four processes, a weak pair of task theories might also assert that γ_d and γ_r depend on occipital and somatosensory cortex, respectively. However, if nothing is said about the other processes, this would be insufficient to predict the results. A stronger pair of task theories might add the assumptions that $\alpha_d = \alpha_r = \alpha$ are identical, that $\beta_d = \beta_r = \beta$ are identical, and that $\delta_d = \delta_r = \delta$ are identical. This pair of theories would predict the results, which, together with the absence of effects in two of the conditions, would then also imply that none of processes α, β, or δ is sensitive to either rTMS_s or rTMS_o; this in turn would suggest that they are implemented by processors in neither of the stimulated regions. Unfortunately, the findings do not bear on the validity of such hypothesized task theories, weak or strong, or even on the question whether the operations in either task can be decomposed into modular subprocesses such as α, β, γ, and δ; inferential limitations such as these characterize the task-comparison method.

9.2. Donders' subtraction method: Task comparison with a composite measure

Perhaps the most venerable version of the task-comparison method is Donders' *subtraction method* (Donders, 1868/1969; Sternberg, 1998b, Appendix 2) for two tasks with measures $M_1 = \overline{RT}_1$ and $M_2 = \overline{RT}_2$. The joint hypothesis consists, first, of a pair of task theories that specify the constituent processes of each task, and second, a combination rule:

H1 (Task Theory 1): Task 1 is accomplished by process **A** (which may consist of more than one modular subprocess).

H2 (Task Theory 2): Task 2 is accomplished by processes **A** and **B**, where **A** is identical, at least in duration, to the corresponding process in Task 1. (That is, addition of **B** satisfies a "pure insertion" assumption.)

H3 (Combination Rule): Contributions $u = T_A$ of **A** and $v = T_B$ of **B** to $M_2 = \overline{RT}_2$ combine by *summation*, as in Table 2, and as implied by Donders' assumption that **A** and **B** occur sequentially, as stages.

Given these hypotheses, it follows that $M_1 = \overline{RT}_1$ is an estimate $\hat{T}_A$ of the mean duration of **A**, $M_2 = \overline{RT}_2$ is an estimate $\hat{T}_A + \hat{T}_B$ of the sum of the mean durations of **A** and **B**, and therefore, by subtraction, $\hat{T}_B = \overline{RT}_2 - \overline{RT}_1$ provides an estimate of the mean duration of **B**. It is a serious limitation of the subtraction method that it usually embodies a test neither of the combination rule nor of pure insertion. That is, *H2* and *H3* are assumed but not tested.[53,54] However, if these hypotheses are correct, then $\hat{T}_A$ and $\hat{T}_B$ are pure measures of processes **A** and **B**. One way to test the hypotheses is to find factors that influence the two measures selectively.[55] Another way to test them is to extend them by finding Tasks 3 and 4 that satisfy *H4* (Task 3 is accomplished by **A** and **C**)

---

[53] Tasks in which the number of iterations of the same process can be controlled, as in some search tasks, provide a special case of the subtraction method in which it is easier to validate the required assumptions. If the numbers of iterations in three variations of the same task are n_1, n_2, and n_3, the test is the linearity of $\overline{RT}(n_j)$; the slope of the function is an estimate of the duration of the iterated process.

[54] Tests of the invariance of the response process across tasks are provided by Ulrich, Mattes, and Miller (1999).

[55] The test would require finding factors F and G such that in a factorial experiment using Task 1 there would be an effect of F but not of G, and in a factorial experiment using Task 2 the effect of F would be equal to its effect in Task 1, and be additive with the effect of G. The inclusion of Task 1 in such a study could add to what was learned from Task 2: it would test the pure insertion assumption as well as permitting estimation of $\hat{T}_A$ and $\hat{T}_B$, rather than just of the effects on these quantities. For example, if we define the Smulders et al. (1995) experiment discussed in Section 3.2 and 4.1 as Task 2 (analogous to Donders "b"), with target stimuli for the left and right hand, one could add a Task 1 (analogous to Donders "c") in which the subject would respond with a single keystroke with the right hand if the right-hand target appeared, and make no response otherwise. One test of pure insertion would be to determine whether the effect of SQ on $\overline{RT}$ in Task 1 was equal to its effect on $\overline{RT}$ in Task 2.

and *H5* (Task 4 is accomplished by **A**, **B**, and **C**), and to include **C** in *H3*. The extended set of hypotheses can then be tested by confirming its prediction that $\overline{RT}_4 - \overline{RT}_3 = \overline{RT}_2 - \overline{RT}_1$.[56]

An analog of Donders' method, sometimes called "cognitive subtraction", has frequently been used with brain activation measures (e.g., Petersen, Fox, Posner, Minton, & Raichle, 1988; Cabeza & Nyberg, 1997; Lie, Specht, Marshall, & Fink, 2006; Poldrack, 2010). If localization of function were perfect, and if one could design pairs of tasks that were accomplished by processes such as those required by Task 1 and 2 above, differing by just the inclusion of one known subprocess, **B**, then brain mapping would benefit greatly from the resulting sets of pure measures. Unfortunately, neither of these requirements is typically satisfied. The method has been criticized (Friston, Price, Fletcher, Moore, Frackowiak, & Dolan, 1996; Sartori & Umiltà, 2000), and alternatives proposed (e.g., Friston et al., 1996; Price & Friston, 1997; Price, Moore, & Friston, 1997), but the alternatives usually also depend on task comparison with unverified task theories, as has been recognized (Caplan & Moo, 2004; Sartori & Umiltà, 2000). Even some critics of "cognitive subtraction" in brain imaging rely on task comparison with unverified task theories (Jennings, McIntosh, Kapur, Tulving, & Houle, 1997; Sidtis, Strother, Anderson, & Rottenberg, 1999).[57]

9.3. Finding the "mechanism of action" of a manipulation

It was in the context of the evidence for stages selectively influenced by *SQ* and *MF* that the interaction of *SLP* with *SQ* and its additivity with *MF* was interpreted in Ex. 4.3. The implication—that sleep deprivation has effects that are process-specific—contradicts the conclusions of others. For example, according to Dinges and Kribbs (1991, p. 117), there is "a generalized effect of sleepiness on all cognitive functioning", and according to Balkin, Rupp, Picchioni, and Wesensten (2008, p. 654), sleep loss "impairs some essential capacity that is basic to cognitive performance in general". (See also Lim and Dinges, 2010.) They based their conclusion not on the process-decomposition approach (which would lead to asking how sleep deprivation modulates the effects of process-specific factors), but on the finding, from dozens of studies using task comparison, that sleep deprivation impairs performance in a wide range of tasks. If they were correct, *SLP* should influence both **S** and **R**. Increasing the level of *SLP* should therefore exacerbate both kinds of difficulty: *SLP* should interact with both *SQ* and *MF* by amplifying the effects of both, contrary to what Sanders et al. found.[58] The problem for the task-comparison method in this application is perhaps the high likelihood that all tasks in which performance can be measured involve some perceptual operations, i.e., processes akin to **S**.

Process decomposition might be more fruitful than task-comparison also in investigating the mechanism of action of different drugs, for similar reasons: Even if a drug influences processes in class **A** and not in class **B** for many classes **A** and **B**, it may be difficult to find any task that does not involve processes in both classes. This may be why, for example, in a study that used task comparison to determine which processes are affected by clonidine versus temazepam (known to have different pharmacological

---

[56] This use of two related pairs of tasks is similar to the "cognitive conjunction" method for brain activation experiments introduced by Price and Friston (1997), except that they appear to have proposed no analogous test.

[57] An alternative approach (sometimes called "parametric design") is exemplified by variation of attentional load over six levels by Culham, Cavanagh, and Kanwisher (2001), the use of the same working-memory task with five retention intervals by Haxby, Ungerleider, Horwitz, Rapoport, and Grady (1995), and the use of a different working memory task with four sizes of memory load by Braver, Cohen, Nystrom, Jonides, Smith, and Noll (1997).

[58] Electrophysiological evidence that confirms the selectivity of the effect of *SLP* has been found by Humphrey, Kramer, and Stanny (1994).

mechanisms) in which 11 tasks were used, each drug produced statistically significant effects on all except one of the tasks (Tiplady, Bowness, Stien, & Drummond, 2005). The process-decomposition approach might be more helpful. Suppose, for example, that processes **A** and **B** in a task are known to be selectively influenced by factors F and G, respectively. Now suppose that processes **A** and **B** were also selectively influenced by Drugs 1 and 2, respectively. Then, whereas both drugs would affect task performance, the effect of F on that performance would be modulated only by Drug 1 and the effect of G only by Drug 2.

10. TRANSCRANIAL MAGNETIC STIMULATION (TMS) AND THE SEARCH FOR MODULES

10.1. An ideal experiment

It was recently discovered that even a single pulse of TMS at certain times and in some brain regions can prolong the RT in some tasks without reducing accuracy very much (Walsh & Pascual-Leone, 2003). Repetitive TMS (rTMS) either before or during performance of a task has produced similar results. This opens the intriguing possibility of employing TMS within the method of additive factors, just as sleep deprivation was used in Ex. 4.3.[59] By using TMS of a region R (TMS_R) in a factorial experiment, while varying the levels of other factors that are believed to influence different processing stages selectively, and determining which effects of the other factors on $\overline{RT}$ are modulated by TMS_R, it may be possible to learn whether R is involved in the implementation of any of those processing stages. For example, suppose there is a task in which we find that factors F and G have additive effects on $\overline{RT}$, from which we infer separate stages, **A** (influenced by F) and **B** (influenced by G). Now we add TMS_R as a third factor, and ask whether it interacts with F or G or neither. In the ideal results of such an experiment, TMS_R would (1) have an effect on RT, (2) interact with (modulate the effect of) one of the other factors, say, G, and (3) not interact with (have an effect that was additive with) the effect of the other factor, say, F. We would then have evidence that region R is involved in the implementation of **B**, but not of **A**. The selectivity of the effect would strengthen the inferences made without TMS about the existence of modular processes **A** and **B**, and would also associate region R with one process (**B**) and not the other.[60]

At this writing there appear to have been no satisfactory experiments of this kind. The primary outcome of many TMS experiments has been to associate a brain region with a task rather than with a subprocess; the goals have not included using TMS as a tool for process decomposition, even when doing so would not require a larger experiment. Although the examples below include ones where TMS is

---

[59] An important advantage of TMS over measures of brain activation (Section 6) in determining which brain regions are involved in implementing a process is that whereas activation of a region in conjunction with process occurrence does not mean that such activation is *necessary* for that process, interference with a process by stimulation of a region is better evidence for that region being necessary for the process to occur normally, just as does interference by a lesion in that region (Chatterjee, 2005). However, it needs to be kept in mind that the mechanism of TMS action is controversial (Harris, Clifford, & Miniussi, 2008; Johnson, Hamidi, & Postle, 2010; Miniussi, Ruzzoli, & Walsh, 2010; Siebner, Hartwigsen, Kassuba, & Rothwell, 2009).

[60] If the effect of TMS_R is time specific, as is likely with single-pulse TMS or a burst of rTMS after the trial starts ("on-line" TMS), the interpretation of its interactions with other factors may not be straightforward. Thus, in the present example, suppose that it is region R that implements process **B**, and that **B** follows **A**. Because effects on the duration of **A** influence the starting time of **B**, and hence the time of TMS relative to **B**, a change in the level of F might modulate the effect of TMS_R on **B**, and hence its effect on $\overline{RT}$. The resulting interaction of TMS_R with F would lead to the erroneous conclusion that region R is involved in the implementation of **A**. This argues for using rTMS before the task is performed ("off-line" TMS) in such studies, rather than using one or more TMS pulses during the task. When doing so, note that the cognitive aftereffects of TMS are short-lived and plausibly decline over time, which suggests that tests should be balanced in small blocks and that, to reduce error variance, trends over trials should be estimated and corrected.

shown to modulate effects generated by interesting processes, and hence to influence those processes, its influence has not been shown to be selective.

10.2. Visual search and parietal TMS

In visual search for a conjunction of features, it is usually observed that the $\overline{RT}$ for both present and absent responses increases approximately linearly with the number of elements to be searched (the *Display Size*, *DS*), suggesting a process of serial (or capacity-limited parallel) comparison of the search target with the displayed elements. If a linear function is fitted to such data, the slope of the function is sometimes interpreted to reflect the time per comparison, while the intercept reflects the summed durations of residual processes whose durations are not influenced by *DS*.[61] In search for a single feature, unlike search for a feature conjunction, $\overline{RT}$ may increase very little or not at all with *DS*, and the intercepts may also differ from those for conjunction search. Thus, feature and conjunction search appear to differ in residual processes as well as in the comparison process. The subprocess of most interest is the comparison process, whose measure is the slope of the function $\overline{RT}(DS)$ that relates $\overline{RT}$ to *DS*. To determine whether TMS influences the comparison process in conjunction search we need to discover whether it modulates the effect of *DS*—i.e., changes the slope of $\overline{RT}(DS)$. If TMS interferes with the comparison process, what effect would we expect? If the process is one of serial comparison, the time per comparison and hence the slope of $\overline{RT}(DS)$ function should increase. If the process is limited-capacity parallel, the capacity should decrease, which would also increase the slope.

In one of the first studies using TMS to investigate visual search, Ashbridge, Walsh, and Cowey (1997) examined the effect of single-pulse TMS of the right parietal cortex during feature and conjunction search. In a preliminary experiment in which TMS was not used but *DS* was varied, along with *Search Type* (feature versus conjunction), their observations conformed to the description above. However, in the experiment in which they applied TMS, they studied only one level of *DS*.[62] They found TMS to interact with search type, having an effect on conjunction search but not on feature search. However, they missed an opportunity: If they had varied *DS*, thus obtaining a measure of its effect (the slope of $\overline{RT}(DS)$) with and without TMS, their findings could tell us whether TMS produces its effect on conjunction search by influencing the comparison process, the residual processes, or both. Without varying *DS*, we do not know which subprocess is responsible for the effect of parietal TMS on conjunction search.

There may be several differences between the complex processes that underlie conjunction search and feature search. Thus, while finding that TMS influences one type of search but not the other is probably telling us something important, it is not clear which difference between processes is responsible. Because theories for the two tasks are not detailed enough to specify exactly how the associated complex processes differ, interpretation of the differential effects of parietal TMS on performance of the two tasks (and the inference, from this, of the role of parietal cortex in the comparison process in conjunction search) requires speculation.

Unfortunately, among 15 later attempts to determine the effects of TMS on RTs in visual search published during the past dozen years, *DS* was varied in only two, those by Ellison, Rushworth, and Walsh

---

[61] Which intercept is appropriate depends on details of the search process, and may differ for target-absent and target-present trials.

[62] O'Shea, Muggleton, Cowey, and Walsh (2006, p. 948) say that "a single set size was used because adding a set size doubles the number of trials ...". This reason is valid if a specified level of precision is desired for the effect of TMS_R for each level of *DS*, but not if the goal is to achieve a specified level of precision for the main effect of TMS_R, unless variability accelerates with *DS*. (But in their data, both *SD* and SD^2 decelerate with *DS*.) Thus, if one runs 50 TMS trials each with $DS = 4$ and $DS = 12$, instead of 100 trials with $DS = 8$ (and likewise for the non-TMS control condition), the precision of the estimated main effect of TMS_R (which depends on the means over *DS* levels) would be about the same, and, at minimal added cost one would also have an estimate of the effect of *DS*, and therefore an estimate of the extent to which TMS modulates that effect.

(2003, Exp. 3) and Rosenthal, Walsh, Mannan, Anderson, Hawken, and Kennard (2006). In both studies, rTMS of the right posterior parietal cortex starting with presentation of the search array was found to increase the slope of $\overline{RT}(DS)$.[63] More studies in this promising direction are needed.

10.3. Number comparison and rTMS of the angular gyrus

In Ex. 6.3 subjects had to classify numbers as being greater or less than 65. RT measurements, supported by fMRI data, indicated that performance in this task depends on (at least) two processing stages, one (encoding, **E**, influenced by *Notation, N*) to derive the identity of the comparison stimulus, and the other (comparison, **C**, influenced by numerical *Proximity, P*) to compare the derived identity to the criterion. The processing stage of particular interest, **C**, is that which produces the effect of *P*: slower responding for stimulus numbers that are closer to the criterion. In a pioneering study, Goebel, Walsh, and Rushworth (2001) found that brief rTMS applied to the left or right angular gyrus influences the RTs in such a task. Do these effects mean that the angular gyrus is involved in implementing **C**? Alternatively, it might be involved in some other process that contributes to the RT, such as **E**. They varied two other factors in addition to TMS_R: the magnitude and the sign of the difference between the stimulus number and the criterion. Measures to assess the effect of *P* could be the slopes of the (approximately linear) functions for positive and negative differences ($k > 65$ and $k < 65$) that relate $\overline{RT}$ to the difference, $|k - 65|$. To determine whether TMS_R influences **C**, we need to know whether it changes either or both of these slopes. Effects of TMS_R on the *heights* of these functions might reflect its influence on **E** or on other processes.

In principle, the data to answer this question were collected in this study. But focused tests of the effects of TMS_R on the relevant slopes were not conducted. We thus have a case where the design of the experiment seems ideal for examining whether and how rTMS modulates the proximity effect, which might indicate an effect on **C**, but the appropriate analysis was not reported.

10.4. Number comparison and rTMS of the intraparietal sulcus

Cappelletti, Barth, Fregni, Spelke, and Pascual-Leone (2007, Exp. 1) recognized the importance, for evaluating the relevance of a brain region to **C**, of determining whether TMS_R modulates the effect of numerical proximity. Using the same task as in Ex. 6.3, but with Arabic numerals only, they found that relative to sham TMS, after 1 Hz rTMS of the left intraparietal sulcus (IPS), but not of either angular gyrus, the effect of *P* increased, showing that this region is involved in the implementation of **C**. Figure 10 shows some of their results, based on an analysis different from theirs.

In this study, a different opportunity was missed. For findings such as these to contribute to process decomposition, we need to know not only which subprocesses a brain region implements, but also which subprocesses it does not implement. And the issue of functional specificity is also important in interpreting the association of brain regions with subprocesses, one of the primary goals of such studies. In addition to **C**, the left IPS might be important for other processes used to perform the task. And for this task there is a wealth of evidence for **E**, separate from **C**, and a factor (*N*) known to influence it selectively (Ex. 6.3). It would be helpful to use TMS to confirm that **E** and **C** are implemented in different brain regions, as suggested by fMRI. Without enlarging the experiment, the stimuli on half of the trials could have been number names ("SIXTY-EIGHT") rather than Arabic numerals, thus

---

[63] The first study used neither sham TMS nor TMS of a different brain region as the control condition. The authors, who reported only data from the target-present trials, in which the mean slope increased from 18.5 to 22.4 ms/item, claimed that they had found no effect of TMS on the slope, but they report neither a test of the slope difference nor a confidence interval. In the second study, in which the control condition was TMS of a different brain region, $\overline{RT}$s were shorter, slopes were smaller, and the effect of TMS on the slope was greater.

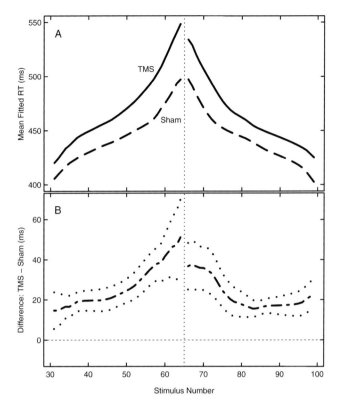

Figure 10. *Four functions fitted* [64] *to the RT data for correct responses in the left-IPS TMS and Sham TMS conditions from Cappelletti, Barth, Fregni, Spelke, and Pascual-Leone (2007, Exp. 1), in which subjects decided whether stimulus numbers were greater or smaller than 65. Panel A gives means of the four functions averaged over 10 subjects. Panel B gives means of the differences between the TMS and Sham functions (the* TMS_R *effect) together with their standard errors. Note the difference in scale. If the effects of* P *and* TMS_R *were additive, the two difference functions would be flat. Their increase with proximity shows the augmentation by rTMS of the* P*-effect, i.e., the interaction of the effects of the* P *and* TMS_R *factors.* [65]

including two levels of N. Given suitable balancing, data from the two subsets of trials could have been averaged to estimate the effect of P under TMS and control conditions. But in addition, by telling us whether the effect of N is modulated by rTMS of the left IPS, such an experiment would also permit asking whether that region is also important for E. Ideally, it would answer negatively, demonstrating the functional specificity of the left IPS by

showing invariance of the effect of N across levels of TMS_R.

11. PROCESS DECOMPOSITION AND THE EFFECTS OF BRAIN DAMAGE

Can localized brain damage (i.e., presence vs absence of lesions in particular locations) permit

---

[64] Data were retrieved for 11 of the 12 subjects; one of these, a clear outlier, was omitted. For each of the two conditions there were only about 50 RTs per subject for trials with each of the two responses. Starting with robust locally fitted polynomial regression (loess), a monotonic function was fitted to each of the four sets of observations for each subject. No adjustment was made for any decline over time in the aftereffect of rTMS.

[65] Future studies should concentrate observations on the closer proximities, where the P-effect is greater. Also, because there is considerable variation across individuals in the magnitude of the P-effect, subjects should perhaps be selected for large P-effects.

the demonstration of separate modifiability of two or more subprocesses that underlie performance of a task? Consider the hypothesis that a particular task is accomplished by a complex process consisting of modular subprocesses **A** and **B**. Suppose there is localization of function, such that a lesion in region R_A influences process **A**, while leaving process **B** invariant, and suppose that it does not replace **A** with a qualitatively different process. Define a *LesionR_A* factor that has two levels, no lesion and lesion. And suppose there is a factor, *G*, that influences process **B** but not **A**.[66] Given pure measures M_A and M_B we would need to show that *LesionR_A* influences M_A while leaving M_B (and hence the effect of *G*) invariant. Given a composite measure M_{AB} with summation as the combination rule, we would need to show that the effects of *LesionR_A* and *G* on that measure are additive. In a more complex scenario, our hypothesis might include the idea that **A** is also selectively influenced by non-lesion factor *F*. We would then also expect *LesionR_A* to modulate the effect of *F* on M_A or M_{AB}.

If the required selective influence could be shown, it would support the hypothesis. However, showing this faces two impediments.

(1) *Inadequate precision to demonstrate invariance.* Suppose first that we have pure measures and that the data are sufficiently precise so that the effect of *LesionR_A* on process **A** could be persuasively shown, by comparing M_A in a group of one or more patients with the lesion to a control group without the lesion. Unfortunately, it is unlikely that the invariance of M_B across levels of *LesionR_A* could be persuasively demonstrated. The difficulty in showing the absence of an effect is that there is virtually never any pre-lesion measurement,[67,68] which precludes within-subject comparison; given the ubiquity of individual differences among "normals", the sample size necessary for persuasive demonstration of equality of M_B between groups of patient and control subjects is likely to be impractically large.[69] Next consider the case where we have a composite measure M_{AB}. For example, **A** and **B** might be processing stages, and the measure might be mean reaction time, $\overline{RT}$. Assuming that *LesionR_A* influences $\overline{RT}$, additivity requires that the effect of *G* on $\overline{RT}$ is invariant across levels of *LesionR_A*. Again, the required precision would almost always require a comparison of large groups.[70]

(2) *Likelihood of qualitative change of the process under study.* The process-decomposition approach depends on measuring a complex process that is qualitatively the same (i.e., that consists of the same set of subprocesses) under different conditions (i.e., with different levels of factors that influence how much those subprocesses must accomplish). The effect of changing the level of a factor cannot be so great as to prevent the process that it influences from working; this would require that if the task is to be accomplished at all, it would require a qualitatively different complex process. Nor can the effect of changing the level of a factor be sufficiently great so as to induce the patient to learn over time to adopt a different "strategy"—a different complex process—from the normal one. But brain damage can sometimes have such effects.

---

[66] This factor could, but need not, be the presence or absence of a lesion in a region R_B within which process **B** was carried out.

[67] This problem need not arise when the lesion is produced surgically, as in Farah, Soso, and Dashieff (1992). However, because such lesions are produced to ameliorate some other pathology, such as epilepsy, they may be associated with more than one effect.

[68] Crawford and Garthwaite's (2006) methods are concerned with showing the presence of an effect in a single patient, not its absence.

[69] There is a sharp distinction between persuasive evidence of invariance and the failure to find a significant effect. In some papers it is concluded that brain damage has no effect merely from the fact that the test of the effect proves not to be statistically significant. Often no confidence intervals or other measures of the effect are provided that would permit one to decide how large the required effect would have to be, for significance. One such example can be found in the interesting study of lateral prefrontal damage by Gehring and Knight (2002).

[70] Furthermore, if the second factor was a lesion in region R_B, and only a composite measure was available, then a test of the hypothesized combination rule would require some patients who had lesions in both regions.

These impediments perhaps suggest the use within cognitive neuropsychology of task-comparison with its more limited goals, rather than process decomposition.[71]

It is possible that TMS may overcome the difficulties described above. First, TMS sometimes appears to be equivalent to a reversible lesion, which enables within-subject comparisons, hence greater precision. Second, the fact that the magnitude of TMS can be adjusted may mean that it can be arranged to modulate the process that it influences, rather than preventing it from functioning altogether. And third, because the functional lesion produced by TMS is presumably short-lived (rather than chronic) as well as being reversible, it may be less likely to lead to a change in the "strategy" by which a task is accomplished.

What should be the relation between traditional cognitive neuropsychology (i.e., making inferences about normal cognitive processes from the effects of brain damage) and the process-decomposition approach with normals? One goal they share is the identification of separately modifiable processes of the normal brain. I suggest that each can inform the other. The task theories, modular processes, and processor locations inferred or hypothesized on the basis of effects of brain damage can be tested by using the process-decomposition approach, the modules and task theories tested by using factors that vary the task, the processor locations by using fMRI or TMS. This seems to be close to the view expressed by Gurd and Marshall (2003, p. 194): "Double dissociations help us to make plausible conjectures about the functional architecture of mind, conjectures that can then be further explored with . . . 'process-

decomposition' methods . . ." It also appears to be close to the view expressed by Shallice (2003, p. S148): "Consider cognitive domains in which the functional architecture is poorly understood. Even today this includes nearly all the underpinnings of thought . . . For such poorly understood domains, the use of dissociations was essentially viewed as a discovery procedure, which needs converging evidence other than the dissociation per se in order to support the existence of an isolable system specifically impaired in the relevant patients." And the task theories and modular processes inferred from the process-decomposition approach in normals (along with the inferred processor locations, if process decomposition is augmented with fMRI or TMS) can be used to inform the interpretation of the effects of brain damage.

12. ADDITIONAL ISSUES

12.1. Quantitative versus qualitative task changes

As shown by Ex. 6.3, the distinction between process decomposition (with its avoidance of task changes) and task comparison can be subtle. In that example, the fMRI data suggest that the effect of the notation factor is probably better thought of as qualitative rather than quantitative—as replacing one encoding process by another, rather than influencing the settings or parameters of the "same" encoding process. Nonetheless, because of the invariance of the effects of proximity on both RT and brain activation, the findings in that example provide evidence for modular processes. In general, qualitative task changes should be

---

[71] Other impediments to using brain damage as a factor in process decomposition are:

(3) The victims of strokes often have widespread cerebrovascular disease. Traumatic head injuries tend to produce widespread minor damage, as well as localized major damage. This may be why damage that appears to be localized seems often to produce at least small effects on many functions.

(4) Even where functionally distinct brain regions are spatially distinct there is no reason to expect that the region of damage due to a stroke (which is determined by the brain's vascular organization) corresponds, so as to be functionally specific. Indeed, the localized effects of a stroke may be to damage nerve tracts that project to many brain regions.

(5) It may be difficult to find undamaged control subjects with overall levels of performance that are poor enough to be comparable. One approach is to increase the difficulty of the task for these subjects, but such increases may themselves have differential effects on different aspects of performance. Another approach is to select the better performing among the brain damaged subjects, but such selection is also a potential source of bias.

avoided because they reduce the likelihood of such invariance, and hence the likelihood of identifying modules. However, evidence is required to assert qualitative task invariance. One kind of evidence is the pattern of factor effects: for each factor, each change in level should influence the same operations and leave the same other operations invariant. The usefulness of such evidence is one of several reasons for using factors with more than two levels (see SM:A.2, SM:A.9).

12.2. Specialized processors and modular processes

Does the existence of localized neural processors that implement functionally distinct processes imply the modularity of those process? To address this question, consider one kind of evidence used to establish the existence of two processors: Suppose that T_1, T_2, and T_3 are three tasks, such that distinct brain regions R_α and R_β are activated during T_1, R_α but not R_β is activated during T_2, and neither region is activated during T_3. Many would conclude that processes α and β (carried out in R_α and R_β respectively) are functionally distinct, and that tasks T_1, and T_2 use α, task T_1 uses β, and task T_3 uses neither. While it may seem plausible, such task-specificity of R_α and R_β does not require the processes they implement in T_1 to be modular, in the sense of being separately modifiable. For example, suppose, that α provides a motivational or attentional resource required by β, or controls which of several variants of β is being used. A change in α would then induce a change in β, and the effect of a change in β would depend on the status of α.

12.3. Relation between mental and neural processing modules

Consider modular mental processes in a task, supported by behavioural evidence, and modular neural processes in that task, supported by brain measurements. Does either of these imply the other? On which psychophysical-physiological "linking propositions" (Teller, 1984) does the answer to this question depend? It would be helpful to have more studies (such as Exs. 3.2, 6.3, 6.4, and 6.5), in which both brain and behavioural measures are taken, both directed at process decomposition. One starting point would be to take cases where behavioural data already exist that persuasively favour a modular decomposition, as was done in Exs. 6.3 and 6.4, and ask whether there is a corresponding decomposition based on brain data into modular neural processes that are influenced by the same factors and invariant with respect to the same other factors. In this respect Ex. 6.4 backfired: although the fMRI data supported the expected modularity of stimulus encoding and response selection, the RT data did not. In general, fMRI measures in some subsets of regions might show modularity (selective effects on pure measures, additive effects on composite measures), but because other regions are involved, the mental processes might not be decomposable.

12.4. Differential influence as a criterion for modularity

Is separate modifiability too strong or too weak to be a useful criterion for partitioning a process? What are the relative merits of alternative criteria for modularity, and alternative approaches to module identification? Is the weaker *differential influence* more useful than selective influence?[72] It is helpful to be precise about the meaning of differential influence in a way that clarifies its relation to selective influence. Assume that factor levels are assigned so that an increase in level produces an increase in the measure of the corresponding process, consider the case where both measures of interest change in the same direction, and let F_j and G_k be numerical factor-level strengths of factors with two levels. Let $M_A(\Delta F) = M_A(F_2) - M_A(F_1)$ represent the effect of a change in factor F on a measure of process $\mathbf{A}$,

---

[72] If one variety of differential influence obtains, one can find factors F and G such that both factors influence both processes $\mathbf{A}$ and $\mathbf{B}$, but for $\mathbf{A}$ ($\mathbf{B}$) the effect of F (G) is the larger (Kanwisher et al., 2001). Whether differential or selective influence characterizes processors is controversial (Haxby, 2004; Reddy & Kanwisher, 2006).

etc. Then selective influence can be described as the combination of four properties: $M_A(\Delta F) > 0$, $M_B(\Delta G) > 0$, $M_A(\Delta G) = 0$, and $M_B(\Delta F) = 0$. The first two properties show that factors F and G are both potent and that measures M_A and M_B are both sensitive. If measures M_A and M_B were measures of the *same* process, the second pair of properties would therefore be impossible. In this terminology, differential influence is satisfied if either $M_A(\Delta F) > M_A(\Delta G)$ and $M_B(\Delta F) < M_B(\Delta G)$, or if $M_A(\Delta F) > M_B(\Delta F)$ and $M_A(\Delta G) < M_B(\Delta G)$.[73] Suppose we are willing to assume that the functions relating M_A and M_B to factor levels differ by at most additive and multiplicative constants:

$$M_B(x) = gM_A(x) + h. \tag{16}$$

Then differences in sensitivity or potency can explain neither of these pairs of properties; M_A and M_B must be measures of different processes. However, without that assumption, such pairs of properties could result from differences between measures of the same process.[74] Whether constraint (16) is plausible or valid depends on the nature of M_A and M_B.

12.5. Factorial experiments: Verification plus discovery

Despite R. A. Fisher's (1935) explanation of the advantages of factorial experiments, they are used too seldom with behavioural or brain measurements, and are then usually limited to two factors. Factorial experiments are efficient: there is virtually no loss of precision from adding a second orthogonal factor to a one-factor experiment, or a third orthogonal factor to a two-factor experiment, for example, without adding trials. In the case of composite measures we have seen that factorial experiments are essential for determining how effects

combine, which is theoretically critical. By including subsidiary factors with those of primary interest (as in "fishing expedition") it is possible to combine discovery with verification, as well as testing the generality of the effect of primary interest. In blocked designs the resulting increase in the number of conditions adds to the difficulty of balancing conditions across levels of practice, but even this issue doesn't arise in random designs, such as "event-related" fMRI experiments and many TMS experiments. For examples of missed opportunities to learn more by including additional factors in TMS experiments without increasing their size, see Sections 10.2 and 10.4.

When it is possible to define more than two levels of a factor, this should be considered. As well as having other advantages (Section 12.1; SM:A.9), multiple levels permit more powerful tests of interaction,[75] and permit focused tests of monotone interaction, the interaction of most interest. (SM:7, SM:15)

12.6. Implications of brain metabolism constraints

The metabolic requirements of brain activity are large relative to the available energy supply, with the implication that, given the spike rates of active neurons, no more than about 1% of the neurons in the brain can be concurrently active (Lennie, 2003). Implications of these severe metabolic limitations for the plausibility and possibility of alternative processing architectures, and for the modularity of processors, have to be considered.

13. CONCLUSION

Considerable evidence has accumulated, some of it documented here, for the existence within complex mental and neural processes of modular

---

[73] With suitable normalization, these pairs of inequalities are equivalent.

[74] For example, suppose that $M_A(x) = x^2$ and $M_B(x) = x$, where x is the level ("strength") of a factor. Let $F_1 = 1.4$, $F_2 = 1.6$, $G_1 = 0.3$, and $G_2 = 0.6$. Then both of the above pairs of properties are satisfied.

[75] For example, a 2×2 design, with four conditions, provides only one df for interaction, whereas a 3×3 design, with nine conditions, provides four df.

subprocesses that are separately modifiable and that carry out distinct functions. Of course, the identification of such subprocesses is only a first step in the understanding of the complex processes to which they belong; it needs to be followed by detailed understanding of how each of the modules works, sometimes in the form of quantitative models, and about the relationship of the neural and mental modules. The success thus far across a range of cognitive domains encourages further searching, and raises questions about how best to do so.

RELATED DISCUSSIONS

For Hadley's defense of the existence and plausibility of mental modules against attacks by Fodor (2000), Kosslyn (2001), and Uttal (2001), see Hadley (2003). For other discussion of the properties that Fodor (1983) ascribed to modular processes, see Coltheart (1999) and Jacobs (1997). For discussions of double dissociation of tasks, as in the task-comparison method, a good place to start is with Schmidt and Vorberg (2006). For more on the process-decomposition approach see Sternberg (2001) (described in Section 2.3) and references therein. For the method of additive factors and numerous examples of its application, see SM:16, SM:A.16, Roberts and Sternberg (1993), Sternberg (1998a), Sanders (1998), and references therein.

AUTHOR NOTE

Supplementary data (a table of features of the nineteen examples in Sternberg, 2001, and this article) is published online alongside this article at: www.psypress.com/cogneuropsychology.

ABBREVIATIONS GLOSSARY

Listed here are the main abbreviations used, the numbers of the sections where they are introduced, and brief definitions.

A,B	1	processes: mental
$A_{mc}(t)$	3.1	motor cortex asymmetry as a function of time
B	7.2	level of the BOLD fMRI signal
$B(N)$	7.2	function relating B to amount of neural activity, N
BOLD	2.3	blood-oxygen-level dependence (fMRI signal)
C	6.3	process: comparison
c	5	criterion
D	5	process: decision
d	9.1	distance dimension to be judged
d', d-prime	5	discriminability measure
d-factors	5	factors that are likely to influence the decision process
DS	10.2	factor: display size
D_α, D_β	3.2	durations of processes α, β
$D_{\alpha jk}$	3.2	duration of α when $SQ = SQ_j$ and $RC = RC_k$
$D_{\alpha\cdot\cdot}$	3.2	mean duration of α, over levels of SQ and RC
E	6.3	process: encoding
ERP	2.2	event-related potential
F,G	2.1	factors
fMRI	1	functional magnetic resonance imaging
F_j	2.2	Factor F at level j
GND	3.1	factor: go-nogo discriminability
H1	2.2	hypothesis 1
$LesionR_A$	11	factor: presence or absence of a lesion in region R_A
LRP	3.1	lateralized-readiness potential
LRP_s, LRP_r	3.2	stimulus-locked LRP, response-locked LRP
MC	3.1	factor: mapping compatibility
MF	4.3	factor: mapping familiarity
M_A	2.2	(pure) measure of process A
M_{AB}	2.2	composite measure to which A and B contribute
N	6.3	factor: notation

N_α, N_β	7.2	amount of neural activity in populations that implement α and β
P	6.3	factor: numerical proximity |k - 65|
p.effect	8.2	proportional effect
PET	6.1	positron emission tomography
PM	5	factor: payoff matrix
PPA	6.5	parahippocampal place area
Pr{nonsuccess}	8.2	probability of nonsuccess
P_α, P_β	6.1	neural processors that implement α, β
$P_{\alpha\beta}$	6.2	neural processor that implements both α and β
R	4.3	process: response selection
r	9.1	roughness dimension to be judged
RC	3.2	factor: response complexity
REL	8.4	factor: semantic relatedness
RR	5	factor: reinforcement ratio: $Pr\{R_{NT}\|Reward\}$
R_α, R_β	6.1	brain regions that contain P_α, P_β
$R_{\alpha\beta}$	6.2	brain region that contains $P_{\alpha\beta}$
R_T, R_{NT}	5	target and nontarget responses
rTMS	2.3	repetitive transcranial magnetic stimulation
RT, $\overline{RT}$	2.2	reaction time, mean reaction time
S	4.3	process: stimulus encoding, or process: sensory
SAT	8.4	factor: semantic satiation
s-factors	5	factors that are likely to influence the sensory process
SLP	4.3	factor: sleep state
SM	2.3	reference to Sternberg (2001)
SQ	3.2	factor: stimulus quality
S_T, S_{NT}	5	target and nontarget stimuli
TD	4.3	factor: time of day
TMS	2.3	transcranial magnetic stimulation
TMS_R	2.3	factor: presence or absence of TMS of brain region R
u, v	2.2	contributions of A and B to M_{AB}
X_T, X_{NT}	5	target and nontarget representations
α, β	1	processes: neural
ε	6.3	process: neural that implements E
γ	6.3	process: neural that implements C

REFERENCES

Albrecht, D. G., Geisler, W. S., & Crane, A. M. (2003). Nonlinear properties of visual cortex neurons: Temporal dynamics, stimulus selectivity, neural performance. In L. Chalupa & J. Werner (Eds.), *The visual neurosciences* (pp. 747–764). Cambridge, MA: MIT Press.

Ashbridge, E., Walsh, V., & Cowey, A. (1997). Temporal aspects of visual search studied by transcranial magnetic stimulation. *Neuropsychologia, 35,* 1121–1131.

Ashby, F. G. (1982). Deriving exact predictions from the cascade model. *Psychological Review, 89,* 599–607.

Ashby, F. G., & Maddox, W. T. (1994). A response time theory of separability and integrality in speeded classification. *Journal of Mathematical Psychology, 38,* 423–466.

Balkin, T. J., Rupp, T., Picchioni, D., & Wesensten, N. J. (2008). Sleep loss and sleepiness: Current issues. *Chest, 134,* 653–660.

Berger, R. L., & Hsu, J. C. (1996). Bioequivalence trials, intersection–union tests and equivalence confidence sets. *Statistical Science, 11,* 283–319.

Biederman, I., & Kaplan, R. (1970). Stimulus discriminability and stimulus response compatibility: Evidence for independent effects on choice reaction time. *Journal of Experimental Psychology, 86,* 434–439.

Boynton, G. M., Engel, S. A., Glover, G. H., & Heeger, D. J. (1996). Linear systems analysis of functional magnetic resonance imaging in human V1. *Journal of Neuroscience, 16,* 4207–21.

Boynton, G. M., & Finney, E. M. (2003). Orientation–specific adaptation in human visual cortex. *Journal of Neuroscience, 23,* 8781–7.

Braver, T. S., Cohen, J. D., Nystrom, L. E., Jonides, J., Smith, E. E., & Noll, D. C. (1997). A parametric study of prefrontal cortex involvement in human working memory. *Neuroimage, 5,* 49–62.

Broadbent, D. E. (1984). The Maltese cross: A new simplistic model for memory. *Behavioral and Brain Sciences, 7,* 55–68.

Cabeza, R., & Nyberg, L. (1997). Imaging cognition: An empirical review of PET studies with normal subjects. *Journal of Cognitive Neuroscience, 9,* 1–26.

Caplan, D., & Moo, L. (2004). Cognitive conjunction and cognitive functions. *Neuroimage, 21,* 751–756.

Cappelletti, M., Barth, H., Fregni, F., Spelke, E. S., & Pascual-Leone, A. (2007). rTMS over the intraparietal sulcus disrupts numerosity processing. *Experimental Brain Research, 179,* 631–642.

Carandini, M., & Heeger, D. J. (1994). Summation and division by neurons in primate visual cortex. *Science, 264,* 1333–1336.

Chatterjee, A. (2005). A madness to the methods in cognitive neuroscience? *Journal of Cognitive Neuroscience, 27,* 847–849.

Coltheart, M. (1999). Modularity and cognition. *Trends in Cognitive Sciences, 3,* 115–120.

Crawford, J. R., & Garthwaite, P. H. (2006). Methods of testing for a deficit in single-case studies: Evaluation of statistical power by Monte Carlo simulation. *Cognitive Neuropsychology, 23,* 877–904.

Culham, J. C., Cavanagh, P., & Kanwisher, N. G. (2001). Attention response functions: Characterizing brain areas using fMRI activation during parametric variations of attentional load. *Neuron, 32,* 737–745.

Dale, A. M., & Buckner, R. L. (1997). Selective averaging of rapidly presented individual trials using fMRI. *Human Brain Mapping, 5,* 329–340.

Dehaene, S. (1996). The organization of brain activations in number comparison: Event-related potentials and the additive-factors method. *Journal of Cognitive Neuroscience, 8,* 47–68.

Dinges, D. F., & Kribbs, N. B. (1991). Performing while sleepy: Effects of experimentally-induced sleepiness. In T. H. Monk (Ed.), *Sleep, sleepiness and performance* (pp. 97–128). London, UK: Wiley.

Donders, F. C. (1868/1969). Over de snelheid van psychische processen [On the speed of mental processes]. *Onderzoekingen gedaan in het Physiologisch Laboratorium der Utrechtsche Hoogeschool, 1868-1869, Tweede reeks, II,* 92-120. Transl. by Koster, W. G. (1969). In *Attention and performance II,* Koster, W. G., Ed., *Acta Psychologica, 30,* 412–431.

Drucker, D. M., Kerr, W. T., & Aguirre, G. K. (2009). Distinguishing conjoint and independent neural tuning for stimulus features with fMRI adaptation. *Journal of Neurophysiology, 101,* 3310–3324.

Ekstrom, A. (2010). How and when the fMRI BOLD signal relates to underlying neural activity: The danger in dissociation. *Brain Research Reviews, 62,* 233–244.

Ellison, A., Rushworth, M., & Walsh, V. (2003). The parietal cortex in visual search: A visuomotor hypothesis. *Clinical Neurophysiology Supplement, 56,* 321–330.

Epstein, R. A., Parker, W. E., & Feiler, A. M. (2008). Two kinds of fMRI repetition suppression? Evidence for dissociable neural mechanisms. *Journal of Neurophysiology, 99,* 2877–2886.

Erickson, R. P. (2001). The evolution and implications of population and modular neural coding ideas. *Progress in Brain Research, 130,* 9–29.

Farah, M. J., Soso, M. J., & Dashieff, R. M. (1992). Visual angle of the mind's eye before and after unilateral occipital lobectomy. *Journal of Experimental Psychology: Human Perception and Performance, 18,* 241–246.

Fisher, R. A. (1935). "VI. The factorial design in experimentation". In *The design of experiments.* Edinburgh, UK: Oliver & Boyd.

Fodor, J. (1983). *The modularity of mind: An essay on faculty psychology.* Cambridge, MA: MIT Press.

Fodor, J. (2000). *The mind doesn't work that way: The scope and limits of computational psychology.* Cambridge, MA: MIT Press.

Friston, K. J., Price, C. J., Fletcher, P., Moore, C., Frackowiak, R. S. J., & Dolan, R. J. (1996). The trouble with cognitive subtraction. *Neuroimage, 4,* 97–104.

Frowein, H. W., & Sanders, A. F. (1978). Effects of visual stimulus degradation, S-R compatibility and foreperiod duration on choice reaction time and movement time. *Bulletin of the Psychonomic Society, 12,* 106–108.

Gallistel, C. R. (2009). The importance of proving the null. *Psychological Review, 116,* 439–453.

Garner, W. R. (1974). *The processing of information and structure.* Potomac, MD: Lawrence Erlbaum Associates.

Gehring, W. J., & Knight, R. T. (2002). Lateral prefrontal damage affects processing selection but not attention switching. *Cognitive Brain Research, 13,* 267–279.

Geisler, W. S., & Albrecht, D. G. (1995). Bayesian analysis of identification performance in monkey visual cortex: Nonlinear mechanisms and stimulus certainty. *Vision Research, 35,* 2723–2730.

Ghorashi, S., Enns, J. T., Klein, R. M., & Di Lollo, V. (2010). Spatial selection and target identification are separable processes in visual search. *Journal of Vision, 10,* 1–12.

Goebel, S., Walsh, V., & Rushworth, M. F. S. (2001). The mental number line and the human angular gyrus. *NeuroImage, 14,* 1278–1289.

Goense, J. B. M., & Logothetis, N. K. (2008). Neurophysiology of the BOLD fMRI signal in awake monkeys. *Current Biology, 18,* 631–640.

Goodale, M. A. (1996). Visuomotor modules in the vertebrate brain. *Canadian Journal of Physiology and Pharmacology, 74,* 390–400.

Grill-Spector, K. (2006). Selectivity of adaptation in single units: Implications for fMRI experiments. *Neuron, 11,* 170–171.

Grill-Spector, K., & Malach, R. (2001). fMR-adaptation: A tool for studying the functional properties of human cortical neurons. *Acta Psychologica, 107,* 293–321.

Gurd, J. M., & Marshall, J. C. (2003). Dissociations: Double or quits? *Cortex, 39,* 192–195.

Hadley, R. F. (2003). A defense of functional modularity. *Connection Science, 15,* 95–116.

Harris, J. A., Clifford, C. W. G., & Miniussi, C. (2008). The functional effect of transcranial magnetic stimulation: Signal suppression or neural noise generation? *Journal of Cognitive Neuroscience, 20,* 734–740.

Haxby, J. V. (2004). Analysis of topographically organized patterns of response in fMRI data: Distributed representations of objects in ventral temporal cortex. In N. Kanwisher & J. Duncan (Eds.), *Attention and performance XX: Functional neuroimaging of visual cognition* (pp. 83–97). Oxford, UK: Oxford University Press.

Haxby, J. V., Ungerleider, L. G., Horwitz, B., Rapoport, S. I., & Grady, C. L. (1995). Hemispheric differences in neural systems for face working memory: A PET-rCBF study. *Human Brain Mapping, 3,* 68–82.

Heeger, D. J., Huk, A. C., Geisler, W. S., & Albrecht, D. G. (2000). Spikes versus BOLD: What does neuroimaging tell us about neuronal activity? *Nature Neuroscience, 3,* 631–633.

Horner, A. J., & Andrews, T. J. (2009). Linearity of the fMRI response in category-selective regions of human visual cortex. *Human Brain Mapping, 30,* 2628–2640.

Howson, C., & Urbach, P. (2006). *Scientific reasoning: The Bayesian approach* (3rd ed.). Chicago, IL: Open Court.

Humphrey, D. G., Kramer, A. F., & Stanny, R. R. (1994). Influence of extended wakefulness on automatic and nonautomatic processing. *Human Factors, 36,* 652–669.

Jacobs, R. A. (1997). Nature, nurture, and the development of functional specializations: A computational approach. *Psychonomic Bulletin & Review, 4,* 299–309.

Jacobs, R. A. (1999). Computational studies of the development of functionally specialized neural modules. *Trends in Cognitive Sciences, 3,* 31–38.

Jacobs, R. A., & Jordan, M. I. (1992). Computational consequences of a bias toward short connections. *Journal of Cognitive Neuroscience, 4,* 323–336.

Jennings, J. M., McIntosh, A. R., Kapur, S., Tulving, E., & Houle, S. (1997). Cognitive subtractions may not add up: The interaction between semantic processing and response mode. *Neuroimage*, *5*, 229–239.

Johnson, J. S., Hamidi, M., & Postle, B. R. (2010). Using EEG to explore how rTMS produces its effects on behavior. *Brain Topography*, *22*, 281–293.

Kanwisher, N., Downing, P., Epstein, R., & Kourtzi, Z. (2001). Functional neuroimaging of visual recognition. In R. Cabeza & A. Kingstone (Eds.), *Handbook of functional neuroimaging of cognition* (pp. 109–151). Cambridge MA: MIT Press.

Kosslyn, S. M. (2001). The strategic eye: Another look. *Minds and Machines*, *11*, 287–291.

Kounios, J. (2007). Functional modularity of semantic memory revealed by event-related brain potentials. In J. Hart, Jr. & M. A. Kraut (Eds.), *Neural basis of semantic memory* (pp. 65–104). Cambridge, UK: Cambridge University Press.

Lennie, P. (2003). The cost of cortical computation. *Current Biology*, *13*, 493–497.

Li, L., Miller, E. K., & Desimone, R. (1993). The representation of stimulus familiarity in anterior inferior temporal cortex. *Journal of Neurophysiology*, *69*, 1918–1929.

Lie, C.-H., Specht, K., Marshall, J. C., & Fink, G. R. (2006). Using fMRI to decompose the neural processes underlying the Wisconsin Card Sorting Test. *NeuroImage*, *30*, 1038–1049.

Lim, J., & Dinges, D. F. (2010). A meta-analysis of the impact of short-term sleep deprivation on cognitive variables. *Psychological Bulletin*, *136*, 375–389.

Logothetis, N. K., & Wandell, B. A. (2004). Interpreting the BOLD signal. *Annual Review of Physiology*, *66*, 735–769.

Machamer, P., Darden, L., & Craver, E. (2000). Thinking about mechanisms. *Philosophy of Science*, *67*, 1–25.

Macmillan, N. A., & Creelman, C. D. (2004). *Detection theory: A user's guide* (2nd ed.). Mahwah, NJ: Erlbaum.

Marr, D. (1976). Early processing of visual information. *Philosophical Transactions of the Royal Society, London B*, *275*, 483–524.

McCarthy, D., & Davison, M. (1984). Isobias and alloiobias functions in animal psychophysics. *Journal of Experimental Psychology: Animal Behavior Processes*, *10*, 390–409.

McClelland, J. L. (1979). On the time relations of mental processes: An examination of systems of processes in cascade. *Psychological Review*, *86*, 287–330.

Meeter, M., Myers, C. E., & Gluck, M. A. (2005). Integrating incremental learning and episodic memory models of the hippocampal region. *Psychological Review*, *112*, 560–585.

Merabet, L., Thut, G., Murray, B., Andrews, J., Hsiao, S., & Pascual-Leone, A. (2004). Feeling by sight or seeing by touch? *Neuron*, *42*, 173–179.

Miller, J., van der Ham, F., & Sanders, A. F. (1995). Overlapping stage models and reaction time additivity: Effects of the activation equation. *Acta Psychologica*, *90*, 11–28.

Miller, K. L., Luh, W-M., Liu, T. T., Martinez, A., Obata, T., Wong, E. C., Frank, L. R., & Buxton, R. B. (2001). Nonlinear temporal dynamics of the cerebral blood flow response. *Human Brain Mapping*, *13*, 1–12.

Miniussi, C., Ruzzoli, M., & Walsh, V. (2010). The mechanism of transcranial magentic stimulation in cognition. *Cortex*, *46*, 128–130.

Moyer, R. S., & Landauer, T. K. (1967). Time required for judgements of numerical inequality. *Nature*, *215*, 1519–1520.

Mulligan, R. M., & Shaw, M. L. (1980). Multimodal signal detection: Independent decisions vs. integration. *Perception & Psychophysics*, *28*, 471–478.

Nunez, P. L., & Srinivasan, R. (2006). *Electric fields of the brain: The neurophysics of EEG*. New York: Oxford University Press.

Op de Beeck, H. P., Haushofer, J., & Kanwisher, N. G. (2008). Interpreting fMRI data: Maps, modules and dimensions. *Nature Reviews Neuroscience*, *9*, 123–135.

O'Shea, J., Muggleton, N. G., Cowey, A., & Walsh, V. (2006). On the roles of the human frontal eye fields and parietal cortex in visual search. *Visual Cognition*, *14*, 934–957.

Osman, A., Bashore, T. R., Coles, M. G. H., Donchin, E., & Meyer, D. E. (1992). On the transmission of partial information: Inferences from movement-related brain potentials. *Journal of Experimental Psychology: Human Perception and Performance*, *18*, 217–232.

Petersen, S. E., Fox, P. T., Posner, M. I., Minton, M., & Raichle, M. E. (1988). Positron emission tomographic studies of the cortical anatomy of single-word processing. *Nature*, *331*, 585–589.

Pinel, P., Dehaene, S., Rivière, D., & LeBihan, D. (2001). Modulation of parietal activation by semantic distance in a number comparison task. *NeuroImage*, *14*, 1013–1026.

Poldrack, R. A. (2010). Subtraction and beyond: The logic of experimental designs for neuroimaging. In S. J. Hanson & M. Bunzl (Eds.), *Foundational issues in human brain mapping* (pp. 147–159). Cambridge, MA: MIT Press.

Price, C. J., & Friston, K. J. (1997). Cognitive conjunction: A new approach to brain activation experiments. *Neuroimage, 5,* 261–270.

Price, C. J., Moore, C. J., & Friston, K. J. (1997). Subtractions, conjunctions, and interactions in experimental design of activation studies. *Human Brain Mapping, 5,* 264–272.

Ratcliff, R., & Smith, P. L. (2010). Perceptual discrimination in static and dynamic noise: The temporal relation between perceptual encoding and decision making. *Journal of Experimental Psychology: General, 139,* 70–94.

Reddy, L., & Kanwisher, N. (2006). Coding of visual objects in the ventral stream. *Current Opinion in Neurobiology, 16,* 408–414.

Rees, G., Friston, K., & Koch, C. (2000). A direct quantitative relationship between the functional properties of human and macaque V5. *Nature Neuroscience, 3,* 716–723.

Roberts, S., & Sternberg, S. (1993). The meaning of additive reaction-time effects: Tests of three alternatives. In D. E. Meyer & S. Kornblum (Eds.), *Attention and performance XIV: Synergies in experimental psychology, artificial intelligence, and cognitive neuroscience – a silver jubilee* (pp. 611–653). Cambridge, MA: MIT Press.

Rogers, J. L., Howard, K. I., & Vessey, J. T. (1993). Using significance tests to evaluate equivalence between two experimental groups. *Psychological Bulletin, 113,* 553–565.

Rosenthal, C. R., Walsh, V., Mannan, S. K., Anderson, E. J., Hawken, M. B., & Kennard, C. (2006). Temporal dynamics of parietal cortex involvement in visual search. *Neuropsychologia, 44,* 731–743.

Rouder, J. N., Speckman, P. L., Sun, D., Morey, R. D., & Iverson, G. (2009). Bayesian *t* tests for accepting and rejecting the null hypothesis. *Psychonomic Bulletin & Review, 16,* 225–237.

Rumelhart, D. E., McClelland, J. L., & the PDP Research Group (1986). *Parallel Distributed Processing: Explorations in the microstructure of cognition, Volume 1: Foundations.* Cambridge, MA: MIT Press.

Sachs, M. B., Nachmias, J., & Robson, J. G. (1971). Spatial-frequency channels in human vision. *Journal of the Optical Society of America, 61,* 1176–1186.

Sanders, A. F. (1977). Structural and functional aspects of the reaction process. In S. Dornic (Ed.), *Attention and performance VI* (pp. 3–25). Hillsdale, NJ: Erlbaum.

Sanders, A. F. (1980). Some effects of instructed muscle tension on choice reaction time and movement time. In R. S. Nickerson (Ed.), *Attention and performance VIII* (pp. 59–74). Hillsdale, NJ: Erlbaum.

Sanders, A. F. (1998). *Elements of human performance: Reaction processes and attention in human skill.* Mahwah, NJ: Erlbaum.

Sanders, A. F., Wijnen, J. L. C., & Van Arkel, A. E. (1982). An additive factor analysis of the effects of sleep loss on reaction processes. *Acta Psychologica, 51,* 41–59.

Sartori, G., & Umiltà, C. (2000). How to avoid the fallacies of cognitive subtraction in brain imaging. *Brain and Language, 74,* 191–212.

Sawamura, H., Orban, G. A., & Vogels, R. (2006), Selectivity of neuronal adaptation does not match response selectivity: A single-cell study of the fMRI adaptation paradigm. *Neuron, 11,* 307–318.

Schall, J. D. (2003). Neural correlates of decision processes: Neural and mental chronometry. *Current Opinion in Neurobiology, 13,* 182–186.

Schmidt, T., & Vorberg, D. (2006). Criteria for unconscious cognition: Three types of dissociation. *Perception & Psychophysics, 68,* 489–504.

Schuberth, R. E., Spoehr, K. T., & Lane, D. M. (1981). Effects of stimulus and contextual information on the lexical decision process. *Memory & Cognition, 9,* 68–77.

Schumacher, E. H., & D'Esposito, M. (2002). Neural implementation of response selection in humans as revealed by localized effects of stimulus-response compatibility on brain activation. *Human Brain Mapping, 17,* 193–201.

Schweickert, R. (1985). Separable effects of factors on speed and accuracy: Memory scanning, lexical decision, and choice tasks. *Psychological Bulletin, 97,* 530–546.

Shallice, T. (1988). *From neuropsychology to mental structure.* Cambridge, UK: Cambridge University Press.

Shallice, T. (2003). Functional imaging and neuropsychology findings: How can they be linked? *Neuroimage, 20,* S146–S154.

Shaw, M. L. (1980). Identifying attentional and decision-making components in information processing. In R. S. Nickerson (Ed.), *Attention and performance VIII* (pp. 277–296). Hillsdale, NJ: Erlbaum.

Shwartz, S. P., Pomerantz, J. R., & Egeth, H. E. (1977). State and process limitations in information processing: An additive factors analysis. *Journal of Experimental Psychology: Human Perception and Performance, 3,* 402–410.

Sidtis, J. J., Strother, S. C., Anderson, J. R., & Rottenberg, D. A. (1999). Are brain functions really additive? *Neuroimage, 9,* 490–496.

Siebner, H. R., Hartwigsen, G., Kassuba, T., & Rothwell, J. C. (2009). How does transcranial magnetic stimulation modify neuronal activity in the brain? Implications for studies of cognition. *Cortex, 45,* 1035–1042.

Sigman, M., & Dehaene, S. (2005). Parsing a cognitive task: A characterization of the mind's bottleneck. *PLoS Biology, 3,* 334–349.

Simon, H. A. (1962). The architecture of complexity. *Proceedings of the American Philosophical Society, 106,* 467–482.

Simon, H. A. (2005). The structure of complexity in an evolving world: The role of near decomposability. In W. Callebaut & D. Rasskin-Gutman (Eds.), *Modularity: Understanding the development and evolution of natural complex systems* (pp. ix–xiii). Cambridge, MA: MIT Press.

Smulders, F. T. Y., Kok, A., Kenemans, J. L., & Bashore, T. R. (1995). The temporal selectivity of additive factor effects on the reaction process revealed in ERP component latencies. *Acta Psychologica, 90,* 97–109.

Soltysik, D. A., Peck, K. K., White, K. D., Crosson, B., & Briggs, R. W. (2004). Comparison of hemodynamic response nonlinearity across primary cortical areas. *Neuroimage, 22,* 1117–1127.

Sternberg, S. (1969). The discovery of processing stages: Extensions of Donders' method. In W. G. Koster (Ed.), *Attention and performance II, Acta Psychologica, 30,* 276–315.

Sternberg, S. (1984). Stage models of mental processing and the additive-factor method. *Behavioral and Brain Sciences, 7,* 82–84.

Sternberg, S. (1998a). Discovering mental processing stages: The method of additive factors. In D. Scarborough & S. Sternberg (Eds.), *An invitation to cognitive science, Volume 4: Methods, models, and conceptual issues* (pp. 703–863). Cambridge, MA: MIT Press.

Sternberg, S. (1998b). Inferring mental operations from reaction-time data: How we compare objects. In D. Scarborough & S. Sternberg (Eds.), *An invitation to cognitive science, Volume 4: Methods, models, and conceptual issues* (pp. 365–454). Cambridge, MA: MIT Press.

Sternberg, S. (2001). Separate modifiability, mental modules, and the use of pure and composite measures to reveal them. *Acta Psychologica, 106,* 147–246.

Sternberg, S. (2003). Process decomposition from double dissociation of subprocesses. *Cortex, 39,* 180–182.

Sternberg, S. (2004). Separate modifiability and the search for processing modules. In N. Kanwisher & J. Duncan (Eds.), *Attention and performance XX: Functional neuroimaging of visual cognition* (pp. 125–139). Oxford, UK: Oxford University Press.

Swets, J. A., Tanner, W. P., Jr., & Birdsall, T. G. (1961). Decision processes in perception. *Psychological Review, 68,* 301–340.

Teller, D. (1984). Linking propositions. *Vision Research, 24,* 1233–1246.

Tiplady, B., Bowness, E., Stien, L., & Drummond, G. (2005). Selective effects of clonidine and temazepam on attention and memory. *Journal of Psychopharmacology, 19,* 259–265.

Ulrich, R., Mattes, S., & Miller, J. (1999). Donders's assumption of pure insertion: An evaluation on the basis of response dynamics. *Acta Psychologica, 102,* 43–75.

Uttal, W. R. (2001). *The new phrenology: The limits of localizing cognitive processes in the brain.* Cambridge, MA: MIT Press.

Walsh, V., & Pascual-Leone, A. (2003). *Transcranial Magnetic Stimulation: A Neurochronometrics of Mind.* Cambridge, MA: MIT Press.

Wan, X., Riera, J., Iwata, K., Takahashi, M., Wakabayashi, T., & Kawashima, R. (2006). The neural basis of the hemodynamic response nonlinearity in human primary visual cortex: Implications for neurovascular coupling mechanism. *Neuroimage, 32,* 616–625.

Woodman, G. F., Kang, M.-S., Thompson, K., & Schall, J. D. (2008). The effect of visual search efficiency on response preparation: Neurophysiological evidence for discrete flow. *Psychological Science, 19,* 128–136.

COGNITIVE NEUROPSYCHOLOGY, 2011, 28 (3 & 4), 209–223

How to discover modules in mind and brain:
The curse of nonlinearity, and blessing of neuroimaging.
A comment on Sternberg (2011)

R. N. Henson

MRC Cognition & Brain Sciences Unit, Cambridge, UK

Sternberg (2011) elegantly formalizes how certain sets of hypotheses, specifically modularity and pure or composite measures, imply certain patterns of behavioural and neuroimaging data. Experimentalists are often interested in the converse, however: whether certain patterns of data distinguish certain hypotheses, specifically whether more than one module is involved. In this case, there is a striking reversal of the relative value of the data patterns that Sternberg considers. Foremost, the example of additive effects of two factors on one composite measure becomes noninformative for this converse question. Indeed, as soon as one allows for nonlinear measurement functions and nonlinear module processes, even a cross-over interaction between two factors is noninformative in this respect. Rather, one requires more than one measure, from which certain data patterns do provide strong evidence for multiple modules, assuming only that the measurement functions are monotonic. If two measures are not monotonically related to each other across the levels of one or more experimental factors, then one has evidence for more than one module (i.e., more than one nonmonotonic transform). Two special cases of this are illustrated here: a "reversed association" between two measures across three levels of a single factor, and Sternberg's example of selective effects of two factors on two measures. Fortunately, functional neuroimaging methods normally do provide multiple measures over space (e.g., functional magnetic resonance imaging, fMRI) and/or time (e.g., electroencephalography, EEG). Thus to the extent that brain modules imply mind modules (i.e., separate processors imply separate processes), the performance data offered by functional neuroimaging are likely to be more powerful in revealing modules than are the single behavioural measures (such as accuracy or reaction time, RT) traditionally considered in psychology.

Keywords: Cognitive neuroscience; Cognitive psychology; functional magnetic resonance imaging; Electroencephalography; Dissociations.

1. INTRODUCTION: INFERENTIAL LOGIC

Sternberg's target article in this issue (Sternberg, 2011) illustrates the importance of formal analyses of the methodological approaches adopted in experimental psychology: formalization of ideas often held implicitly by most researchers, but rarely examined explicitly for their assumptions and limitations.

Correspondence should be addressed to Dr. R. N. Henson, MRC Cognition & Brain Sciences Unit, 15 Chaucer Road, Cambridge, CB2 7EF, UK. (E-mail: rik.henson@mrc-cbu.cam.ac.uk).

This work is funded by the UK Medical Research Council (MC_US_A060_0046). The author thanks John Dunn, Niko Kriegeskorte, and the three reviewers for their helpful comments.

http://dx.doi.org/10.1080/02643294.2011.561305

Sternberg has continued this worthy enterprise ever since his pioneering work in the late 1960s (e.g., Sternberg, 1969, 2001), and his analyses are just as relevant, if not more relevant (as I argue below), to the more recent field of cognitive neuroscience, which tackles the mind–brain relationship "head-on". For this pioneering work, Sternberg is to be congratulated, and the wider research community would do well to consider his arguments carefully. In this reply, I suggest a related, but alternative, perspective, at least for the specific question of inferring the number of modules from behavioural and neuroimaging data.

More specifically, while Sternberg's recent analysis (Sternberg, 2011) has focused on the implications of modularity for patterns of behavioural or neuroimaging data, I consider the converse case of what patterns of behavioural or neuroimaging data support modularity. Interestingly, this "inverse" perspective actually diminishes the value of some of Sternberg's principles, such as "additive factors", and emphasizes the value of other principles, such as "selective effects" of factors, when applied to multiple measurements. This argument is formalized below, before three examples are given to illustrate what one might conclude about modules from certain patterns of behavioural and/or neuroimaging data, which are then discussed more generally in terms of modules in mind and brain.

1.1.   Form of present argument

The inferential logic in Section 2.2 of Sternberg's paper is of the form (where $\rightarrow$ should be read as "implies"):

$$H_1 \& H_2 \rightarrow p_1 \& p_2 \qquad (1)$$

where H_i are hypotheses (related to the number of modules and the nature of their measurement, M) and p_i are properties of the data (e.g., significant experimental effects). It follows logically that (where $\sim$ should be read as "not"):

$$\sim (p_1 \& p_2) \rightarrow \sim (H_1 \& H_2)$$

This is the classical "modus tollens", or "denying the consequent", argument: that failing

to find that both p_1 and p_2 are true (ignoring for the moment the issues of null results in classical statistics; see Sternberg's Footnote 8) implies that at least one of the original hypotheses H_i is incorrect. However, a possible danger here is inappropriate "affirmation of the consequent"—that is, it does not follow logically that:

$$p_1 \& p_2 \rightarrow H_1 \& H_2 \qquad (2)$$

I am not suggesting that Sternberg ever made this logical error (he refers to this situation of confirming p_1 and p_2 as providing "support for joint hypotheses H_i"). Nonetheless there is the danger that finding additive effects in the data of the type described by Sternberg is erroneously taken by others to imply modules. Thus in a nutshell, the gist of the present argument is that, while modules might imply additive factors, additive factors do not imply modules. I demonstrate this in the first example (Section 3.1) below.

Instead, I focus on the idea that, if there is only one module (H_1), and measurements are monotonic functions of a module's output (H_2), then certain properties of the data cannot be found—that is:

$$H_1 \& H_2 \rightarrow \sim (p_1 \& p_2),$$

and therefore if those patterns are found (and assuming H_2 is always true), then more than one module can be inferred—that is:

$$p_1 \& p_2 \rightarrow \sim (H_1 \& H_2)$$
$$\sim (H_1 \& H_2) \& H_2 \rightarrow \sim H_1 \qquad (3)$$

Before proceeding, it should be noted that the deductive "implications" in the above statements of propositional logic (Statements 1–3) are predicated on the terms (H_i, p_i) being either true or false. The truth value of a property of data, p_i, however, is difficult if not impossible to ascertain, given that there are sources of measurement noise and fundamental measurement limits that generally make statements about data properties probabilistic rather than absolute (even if those probabilities satisfy conventional scientific levels of "significance"). With this in mind, for typical behavioural or neuroimaging data, Statement 3 should be read as "assuming monotonic measurement functions, certain patterns of data provide evidence against a single module account" (for further elaboration of deductive vs. abductive inference in science, see Coltheart, 2011).

2.   TERMINOLOGY

I will adopt the same terminology as that of Sternberg (2011). In brief, let **A** and **B** be modules, F and G be experimental factors, and $M_i(F,G)$ be a measurement function that maps the response of Modules A and B to F and G to the ith behavioural or neural dependent variable. One important aspect of the present argument is that M_i may not be linear in the levels of experimental factors (e.g., F, G); indeed, in the general case, it would seem unwise to assume that our measures are linearly related to underlying psychological processes. For example, many perceptual judgements (e.g., of "pitch") are logarithmic functions of physical manipulations of a stimulus (e.g., frequency). Rather, the only assumption necessary in what follows is that M_i is monotonic.

Another important addition in the present argument is that Modules **A** and **B** perform nonlinear operations on their inputs, expressed by the functions $a(F,G)$ and $b(F,G)$ respectively—that is, $M_i(F,G) = M_i(a(F,G),b(F,G))$. The reason for this assumption becomes more apparent when considering interconnected neural processors later: However, in brief, there is little value in each processor within a system performing a linear operation, otherwise the same ultimate linear relationship between the system's inputs and outputs could be implemented in a single processor (since any linear combination of linear functions can be expressed as a single linear function; an argument also used to justify nonlinear activation functions within layers of an artificial neural network; e.g., Grossberg, 1988). If the mapping between the inputs to a module and its output (e.g., a), and between its output and the experimental measurement (M_i), are both nonlinear and unknown, it may seem difficult to draw conclusions about modules from M_i alone; fortunately, the assumption that M_i is monotonic provides some leverage, as illustrated in the examples below.

3.   THREE EXAMPLES

To illustrate the different perspective arising from making statements about modules from data, rather than testing predictions of modules with data, I consider three examples below. The first example (Section 3.1) is based on applying "additive factors" logic to two factors and a single behavioural measure, as formalized in Section 2.2 of Sternberg's (2011) article (when assuming a "summation" rule for the composite measure M_{AB}). The purpose of this first example is to demonstrate the invalidity of Statement 2 above (i.e., to show how finding additive effects does not constitute strong evidence for multiple modules). This example also goes on to illustrate that the same problem applies to interactions, even cross-over interactions, between two factors on a single measurement.

The purpose of the second example (Section 3.2) is to illustrate the utility of Statement 3 above— namely, to argue that certain other, nonadditive patterns of data (with only a single factor but at least two different measurements) do provide strong evidence for multiple modules. This example also extends the argument to functional neuroimaging, which normally automatically provides multiple measurements (across different brain regions and/or different time points).

The third and final example (Section 3.3) reconsiders the case of two factors, but which now show selective effects on two independent measurements, a pattern that (providing one accepts the null hypothesis of no interaction) again provides strong evidence for multiple modules. This example also raises the difficult problem of applying the present argument to a network of modules, where the output of one module becomes the input of another (and where neural measurements may only be available on a subset of modules).

3.1. Two factors, one measurement: Insufficiency of additive factors

If we start with Sternberg's example of a single, composite measure, then my slightly modified version of his argument is as follows:

- H_1: There are two modules, **A** and **B**, selectively affected by factors F and G respectively—that is, with processes $a(F)$ and $b(G)$.
- H_2: The measurement M_{AB} is a linear function of a and b—that is, $M_{AB}(F,G) = u \cdot a(F) + v \cdot b(G)$, where u and v are constants (and ignoring an overall intercept term).

These hypotheses are illustrated schematically in Figure 1-A1. Now consider the case of a 3×2 design, where Factor F has three levels, and Factor G has two levels. An elegant example of such as design is the study of Pinel, Dehaene, Riviere, and LeBihan (2001) that Sternberg considers in his Section 6.3. In this first example, we consider just the behavioural data from that study—namely, the mean response times (M_{AB}) to classify a probe number as greater or smaller than a target number, as a function of whether (a) the probe number is presented as a numeral or by its name (G), and (b) the absolute numerical difference between the probe and target, which was low, medium, or high (F). The results are shown schematically in Figure 1-B1, where F and G had additive effects on M_{AB}.

Using Sternberg's notation, the properties of the data associated with "additive factors" in this example are (where F_1 and F_2 refer to first and second level of F, etc.):

$$p_1 : M_{AB}(F_1, G_1) - M_{AB}(F_2, G_1) = $$
$$M_{AB}(F_1, G_2) - M_{AB}(F_2, G_2)$$
$$p_2 : M_{AB}(F_2, G_1) - M_{AB}(F_3, G_1) = $$
$$M_{AB}(F_2, G_2) - M_{AB}(F_3, G_2)$$
$$p_3 : M_{AB}(F_1, G_1) - M_{AB}(F_1, G_2) = $$
$$M_{AB}(F_2, G_1) - M_{AB}(F_2, G_2)$$
$$p_4 : M_{AB}(F_2, G_1) - M_{AB}(F_2, G_2) = $$
$$M_{AB}(F_3, G_1) - M_{AB}(F_3, G_2)$$

In a factorial analysis, this pattern entails (at a minimum) significant main effects of F and G, with no evidence for an interaction. In other words, the pattern reflects no differences among the simple main effects of the first factor over the different levels of the second.

Now simple algebra (in terms of u and v) shows that, provided the operations of the modules, $a(F)$ and $b(G)$, are linear, the assumption of linear measurement (H_2) means that:

$$H_1 \& H_2 \to p_1 \& p_2 \& p_3 \& p_4$$

In other words, finding additive effects would be consistent with Sternberg's "separately modifiable" modules, **A** and **B**. However, finding additive effects can also be consistent with a single module. To appreciate this, consider a single module, **C**, whose operation depends on both F and G, as in Figure 1-A2. In the general case, the module's output, $c(F,G)$, can be nonlinear, and the measurement of that output, $M_{AB} = w(c(F,G))$, is assumed only to be monotonic. But to make the present point, we can assume that both of these functions are linear—that is, that $c(F,G) = u \cdot F + v \cdot G$, and $M_{AB} = w \cdot c(F,G)$ (ignoring intercepts, and where u,v,w are now constants)—and still reproduce the pattern of additive factors. To see this, define a new, unidimensional (latent) variable, $E = u \cdot F + v \cdot G$, onto which the factors F and G map, and on which the functionality of **C** solely depends, and assume that the output $c(E)$ is measured proportionally by M_{AB}. This is shown in Figure 1-B2, which is simply a replotting of the data in Figure 1-B1.[1] In other words, the fact that we do not know how experimental factors F and G map onto the psychological dimension over which **C** operates means that additive factors on a single dependent variable do not constitute evidence for more than one module.

3.1.1. *Insufficiency of other interaction patterns*
Though the insufficiency of finding additive effects on a single composite measure is the main

---

[1]Note that this still holds, even if the data points for different levels of F and G (i.e., red and blue points in Figure 1-B1) overlap; in other words, the fact that $M_{AB}(F_1,G_3) < M_{AB}(F_2,G_1)$ in these examples is just to aid visualization.

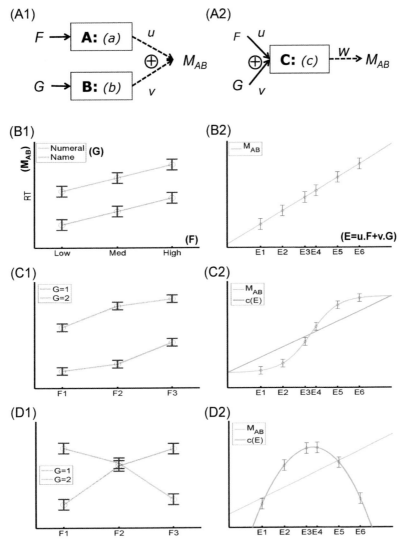

Figure 1. *Two factors, one measurement: insufficiency of additive factors. Possible manner in which two experimental factors, F and G, could affect single measurement (M$_{AB}$) of two modules, A and B (Panel A1), or of a single module, C (Panel A2). The functions a, b, and c describe processes performed by modules; u, v, and w are measurement functions (or constants that control linear measurement functions in the discussion of Sternberg's, 2011, additive factors in the text). Example data when F (with three levels) and G (with two levels) have additive effects (Panel B1), and how these data are explained by linear measurement of the single module C, whose output, c(E), is a linear function of E, itself a linear combination of F and G (Panel B2; see text). Example data when F and G interact (Panel C1), and how these data are explained by nonlinear (but monotonic) measurement of a single module whose output is a linear function of F and G (Panel C2). Example data when F and G show a cross-over interaction (Panel D1), and how these data are explained by linear measurement of a single module, whose output is a nonlinear function of F and G (Panel D2). None of these data patterns therefore constitute evidence against a single module account (according to present framework).*

message of this example, it is instructive to consider other patterns of data. For example, what if there is an interaction between *F* and *G*, of the form shown in Figure 1-C1: Does this provide strong support for two modules? The answer is no, because even if the operation of module C,

$c(E)$, in Figure 1–A2 is linear (green line in Figure 1–C2), a nonlinear but monotonic (e.g., sigmoidal) measurement function, $w(c(E))$, for M_{AB} (cyan line in Figure 1–C2) can still explain the data (as could the converse case of a sigmoidal module process, c, and a linear measurement function, w).

Or what if there is a cross-over interaction between F and G, of the form shown in Figure 1-D1: Does this provide strong support for two modules? The answer is again no. Unlike Figure 1-C, these data cannot be explained by a linear module and a nonlinear but monotonic measurement function. However, assuming that modules should perform nonlinear operations on their input (as argued in Section 2 above), a cross-over interaction can be explained by a nonlinear function $c(E)$ (green line in Figure 1-D2), even if the measurement function, w, is linear (cyan line in Figure 1-D2). Thus, while I have argued that non-linearity is an important property of modules, the reason that I refer to it as a "curse" in the title of this article is that it makes the task of inferring modules even more challenging.

Fortunately, there are more compelling ways to question a single module account within the present framework, provided one takes more than one measurement of each experimental condition. The reason for this is expanded below, but in short, because the form of c is invariant over any measurement, then assuming that each measurement is monotonic in the output of c, certain patterns of data across multiple measurements cannot be explained even if c is nonlinear and unknown.

3.2. One factor, two measurements: Reversed associations

Now consider the case of one experimental factor, F, with three levels, and two measurements, M_A and M_B (note that the labels M_A and M_B are not meant to imply pure measures of **A** and **B**, as will be seen below, but are used for consistency with Sternberg's article). The question then concerns what pattern of data would constitute

evidence for two modules (Figure 2-A1) rather than one single module (Figure 2-A2).

Let us start by considering the cross-over interaction in Section 3.1.1 above (Figure 1-D1), but where the two lines in Figure 2-B1 now refer to two measurements, rather than two levels of an orthogonal experimental factor. This pattern is not evidence against a single module explanation, because M_A and M_B could both be monotonic functions: one monotonic increasing (w, for M_A) and one monotonic decreasing (x, for M_B), as shown in Figure 2-B2.

Consider, however, the pattern shown in Figure 2–C1. This pattern is called a "reversed association" (Dunn & Kirsner, 1988), because it involves an association (positive correlation between effects of F_2 versus F_1 on both M_A and M_B) that is reversed at other levels of F (a cross-over interaction between F_3 versus F_2 on M_A and M_B). More precisely, it consists of:

$$p_1 : [M_A(F_2) > M_A(F_1) \,\&\, M_B(F_2) > M_B(F_1)]$$
$$\text{or } [M_A(F_2) < M_A(F_1) \,\&\, M_B(F_2) < M_B(F_1)]$$
$$p_2 : [M_A(F_3) > M_A(F_2) \,\&\, M_B(F_3) < M_B(F_2)]$$
$$\text{or } [M_A(F_3) < M_A(F_2) \,\&\, M_B(F_3) > M_B(F_2)]$$

As Dunn and Kirsner originally observed, this pattern questions a single underlying psychological process (module). Given that the mapping from F to the outputs $c(F)$ of a single module **C** must be invariant across all measurements, there is no single way to remap the relative values of $c(F_1)$, $c(F_2)$, and $c(F_3)$ (even if c is nonlinear) and simultaneously fit the reversed association when assuming monotonic measurement functions (e.g., function x for M_B in Figure 2-C2 would need to be nonmonotonic in this case, violating our hypothesis H_2, as indicated by the cross by its legend). In other words, a reversed association suggests that the modules respond in a *qualitatively* different manner to the levels of a factor, in that the relative order of effect sizes across levels produced by one module, $a(F)$, does not match the relative order across levels produced by another module, $b(F)$.

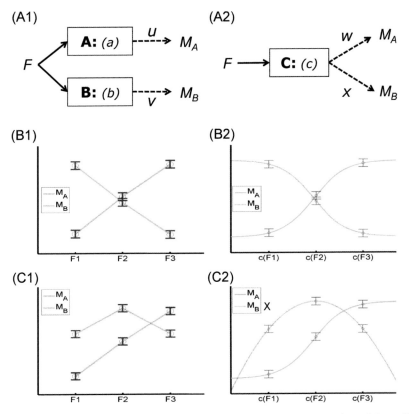

Figure 2. *One factor, two measurements: reversed associations. Possible manner in which one experimental factor, F, could affect two independent measurements (M_A and M_B) of two modules A and B (Panel A1), or a single module C (Panel A2). Example data when F (with three levels) has opposite effects of M_A and M_B (Panel B1), which can be explained by two modules (even with linear measurement functions u and v), but can also be explained by different, (non)linear but monotonic measurement functions, w and x, of the single module C (Panel B2). Example data that comprise a reversed association (Panel C1), which monotonic functions M_A and M_B cannot explain, given only a single module, even if that module implements a nonlinear function of F, c(F) (Panel C2; the cross by the label for M_B indicates that this measurement function has to be nonmonotonic in order to fit the data, violating the present assumptions). This data pattern therefore does constitute evidence against a single module account (see text).*

3.2.1. *Processors and neuroimaging data*

This is a suitable juncture to extend the present argument to brain modules and functional neuroimaging data. As Sternberg (2011) observes, it is important to distinguish psychological processes from the neural implementation of those processes (the "processors"). This is illustrated in Figure 3: Two modules **A** and **B** might be implemented by two separate processors, α and β (Figure 3-A1), or two modules **A** and **B** might be implemented within the same processor χ (Figure 3-B1), or the same module **C** might be implemented by two separate processors, χ_1 and χ_2 (Figure 3-A2).

Furthermore, as Sternberg also notes: "The existence of functionally specialized processors (either localized or distributed) is a sufficient condition but not necessary one for functionally distinct processes ... " (Sternberg, 2011, Section 1). In other words, there is an asymmetry in the relationship between processors and processes: Modular processes need not imply modular processors, but there would seem little point in evolving modular processors unless they implemented modular processes (see also Shallice, 1988, for a similar argument about the relationship between double dissociations and isolable subsystems, and present

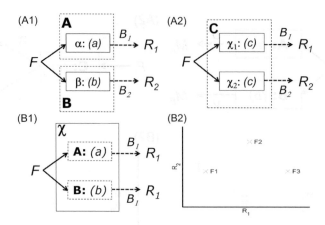

Figure 3. *Possible neural implementations of Modules A, B, and C. Greek letters α, β, χ₁, and χ₂ refer to distinct neural components (processors). Two modules implemented by two separate processors (Panel A1); the same module implemented by two separate processors (Panel A2); two modules implemented within the same processor (Panel B1). In the example of functional magnetic resonance imaging (fMRI) data in the text, B₁ and B₂ refer to the neural-to-BOLD (BOLD = blood-oxygen-level-dependent) mappings (monotonic measurement functions) for spatially resolvable brain regions R₁ and R₂. Panel B2 is a replotting of the reversed association data in Figure 2–C1, but now as BOLD signal in one region against that in another; the fact that these data points do not fall on a monotonic function again suggests that a single module (Panel A2)—that is, the same process that happens to be implemented across multiple processors—is unlikely.*

Discussion for further consideration of modules in mind and brain).

For existing, noninvasive human neuroimaging techniques, the measurements (*M*) are now some signal integrated over many neurons within a brain region. This neural activity is also either integrated over time, as in haemodynamic techniques like functional magnetic resonance imaging (fMRI), or integrated over multiple brain regions, as in extracranial electrophysiological techniques like electro- and magnetoencephalography (E/MEG). For the present argument, we stick with fMRI, where the measurements are now labelled R_1 and R_2 to represent the fMRI signal from two brain regions (corresponding to processors α and β, or χ₁ and χ₂).

However, the same basic argument can be extended to E/MEG measurements at different time points (or even electrophysiological signals occurring at the same time but believed to derive from different brain regions following source reconstruction of E/MEG data; Baillet, Mosher, & Leahy, 2001). Given the complex biophysical processes that govern, for example, the blood-oxygenation-level-dependent (BOLD) signal that is normally measured by fMRI, it would seem even more judicious to make minimal assumptions about how neuroimaging measurements relate to hypothetical psychological processes—that is, assume only that the measurement functions B_1 and B_2 in Figure 3 are monotonic.[2] Nonetheless, the reason that I

[2]The measurement function *B* in Figure 3 subsumes both of Sternberg's (2011) mappings from an experimental factor *F* to the neural activity within a processor (akin to *N* in Section 7.2 of Sternberg's article) and from neural activity within a processor to the BOLD signal measured by fMRI (Sternberg's *B*). The distinction between these mappings is not important for the present argument, but would become important if relating fMRI data to more direct neurophysiological measures. In other words, a 10% change in a parametric factor *F*—that is, $(F_2 - F_1)/F_1 = 0.1$ (e.g., visual contrast) may or may not result in a 10% increase in neuronal firing rate (or local field potentials), which in turn may or may not result in a 10% increase in BOLD. Though Sternberg notes that the latter linearity has been observed under some conditions (e.g., Rees, Friston, & Koch, 2000), other (monotonic) nonlinearities, particularly in the mapping from blood flow to BOLD, have also been demonstrated (Friston, Mechelli, Turner, & Price, 2000). More generally, however (e.g., in the example of networks of processors in Figure 5), it might be prudent to introduce additional mappings from experimental factors (or psychological variables) to neural activity (e.g., that form the input to the "sensory" processors in a network) and possibly from the neural activity output from one processor to the input to another (reflecting effective connectivity between processors).

refer to neuroimaging as a "blessing" in the title of this article is that it normally automatically provides multiple, simultaneous measurements of brain activity.

Thus, according to the argument in Section 3.1 above, the finding of additive effects of two factors on the BOLD signal within a single region (such as the "parahippocampal place area" of the Epstein, Parker, & Feiler, 2008, study considered in Section 6.5 of Sternberg's, 2011, article) would not constitute evidence for multiple modules. Rather, one must find certain patterns, such as the reversed association described in Section 3.2, in the BOLD signal across *two or more* regions. This application of "reversed association logic" to neuroimaging data was originally outlined in Henson (2005), together with further examples of how one might use neuroimaging data from two or more brain regions to distinguish between competing psychological theories (and for a concrete example in the context of testing single- versus dual-process theories of recognition memory, see Henson, 2006a).

Note that another way of depicting the reversed association in Figure 2-C1 is to plot the two measurements directly against each other: If the data points fall on a monotonic function, then they can be explained by a single psychological process (dimension). This is the basis of "state-trace" analysis, of which the reversed association is a special case (Newell & Dunn, 2008). The analogous proposal here is that if neural measurements for two brain regions, R_1 and R_2, do not fall on a monotonic function (as in Figure 3-B2), then those two regions are unlikely to be implementing the same module. In other words, the pattern of neuroimaging data in Figure 3-B2

questions the scenario depicted in Figure 3-A2 and supports the scenario depicted in Figure 3-A1.[3]

3.3. Two factors, two measures: Selective effects on neuroimaging data

Despite their potential inferential power, few neuroimaging studies have produced a clear reversed association across three or more conditions and two or more brain regions, at least when those brain regions are defined independently (Henson, 2006a; though see Weber & Huettel, 2008, for one example). This is a shame, because reversed associations can be defined simply by four significant pairwise effects in the data (corresponding to data patterns p_1 and p_2 in Section 3.2 above), unlike the general case of "state-trace" analysis, for which statistical methods for quantifying deviations from monotonicity are yet to be fully established (Newell & Dunn, 2008). On the other hand, if one is prepared to accept the null hypothesis of no effect in the data, there are other patterns of data that also question a single module account.[4] Here the combination of two or more factors that show selective effects on two or more independent measurements (related to Sternberg's Section 6.4) become informative, as illustrated below.

Consider an fMRI study with two experimental factors, F with three levels and G with two levels, and data from two regions of interest, R_1 and R_2. The desire is to distinguish the multiple modules (and multiple processors) from the single module (implemented by multiple processors) depicted in Figures 4-A1 and 4-A2, respectively. Now if one finds a main effect of Factor G but no effect of Factor F in region R_1 (Figure 4-B1), plus a main

---

[3]The scenario depicted in Figure 3-B1 is not relevant because it only entails one brain measurement (R_1), but serves to remind us that this measurement may itself be the product of multiple modules. This may be either because the spatial resolution of the neuroimaging technique is not sufficient to distinguish activity of different processors, or even because the same processor might implement different processes, dependent, for example, on control signals from other processors (i.e., networks of connected brain regions; see Section 3.3.1).

[4]The issue of null effects in classical statistics is discussed by Sternberg in his Footnote 8. While not in total agreement, I am happy to confer them with the same evidential value for the purpose of the present argument. More generally, Bayesian approaches would seem more suitable, in which one can assign a probability to an effect being within a certain range of zero (particularly "empirical Bayesian" approaches, in which the prior can be defined by the data themselves, provided there is an implicit hierarchical model; see Friston et al., 2002, for an example application in fMRI analysis).

effect of Factor *F* but no effect of Factor *G* in region R_2 (Figure 4-B2), then one can question the single module in Figure 4-A2. (This was actually the general pattern and claim made from the fMRI data of the Pinel et al., 2001, study described in Section 3.1 above.) This is because again, there is no way that a single nonlinear function within Module C can simultaneously fit the data from two monotonic measurement functions, even if that same function $c(F,G)$ happens to be implemented in two different brain regions, χ_1 and χ_2, on which the two independent measurement

functions operate (to produce R_1 and R_2). This is illustrated in Figures 4-C1 and 4-C2. In Figure 4-C1, a linear mapping of *F* and *G* to E_1–E_6, over which $c(E)$ operates, in conjunction with a sharp, sigmoidal measurement function R_1 (cyan line), can fit the main effect of Factor *G* on R_1, but cannot simultaneously fit the main effect of Factor *F* on R_2, whatever the measurement function (i.e., the magenta dotted line requires a different relative ordering of E_1–E_6 in order to fit the data and remain monotonic, as indicated by the cross by its legend). In Figure 4-C2, this is

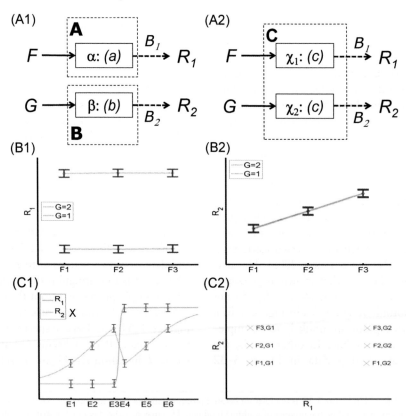

Figure 4. *Two factors, two measurements: selective effects on two brain regions. Two modules implemented by two separate processors (Panel A1); the same module implemented by two separate processors (Panel A2). Example neuroimaging data where measurement R_1 of one region shows a main effect of Factor G but not Factor F (Panel B1), and measurement R_2 of a different region shows a main effect of F but not G (Panel B2). These data (accepting null hypotheses of no effects) are evidence against a single module C—that is, a single nonlinear function $c(F,G) = c(E)$, where E is a linear function of F and G—even with different neural-to-BOLD (BOLD = blood-oxygen-level-dependent) mappings (measurements) in the two regions (Panel C1; the cross by the label for R_2 indicates that this measurement function has to be nonmonotonic in order to fit the data, violating the present assumptions). This is again illustrated by fact that a plot of BOLD signal in two regions against one another (Panel C2) cannot be fitted by a monotonic function (see text).*

demonstrated by the fact that the six data points from plotting R_1 against R_2 do not fall on a monotonically increasing or decreasing function (Newell & Dunn, 2008). Thus, while I agree with Sternberg that the combination of factorial experimental designs and neuroimaging techniques offers a powerful way to find evidence of "separately modifiable" processors, which in turn provides evidence for multiple modules, I would emphasize different aspects of the data, particularly the value of having multiple measurements across brain regions.

3.3.1. *Networks of processors*

Once one begins to consider seriously the operation of a complex system like the brain, in which a number of modules are assumed to interact with one another, the inferences one can make from neuroimaging (or behavioural) data become less specific, however. To see this, consider the toy network shown in Figure 5. Here there are three modules, implemented across four processors, where Module **C** is implemented in two separate processors, χ_1 and χ_2, and where the inputs to **C** are the outputs of **A** and **B**. According to the argument in Section 3.2 above, a reversed association across three levels of a factor F and the two measurements R_1 and R_2 of χ_1 and χ_2 would question the existence of a single module **C**. However, the perturbations to the system induced by manipulating the levels of F may not impinge directly on module **C** (as was assumed in the examples above), but only indirectly via two earlier modules, **A** and **B**. For example, the levels of F could correspond to different levels of visual contrast, and the processors α and β could correspond to brain regions early in the visual processing pathway, while processors χ_1 and χ_2 could correspond to "higher order" brain regions further along that pathway, related, for example, to perceptual decisions (e.g., in prefrontal cortex).

In this case, because **A** and **B** are able to implement different, nonlinear operations on their input (the levels of F), and because their resulting outputs form separate inputs to χ_1 and χ_2, respectively, a reversed association on

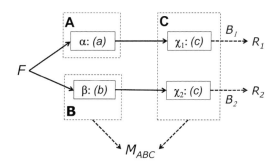

Figure 5. *Example network of modules, where different inputs to Module C, by virtue of different "upstream" modules A and B, mean that a reversed association between Factor F and measurements of two regions R_1 and R_2 (or any other discriminative data pattern considered in Figures 3–4) does not constitute evidence that regions χ_1 and χ_2 implement distinct modules, only that at least two different modules exist somewhere within the network including, or upstream of, χ_1 and χ_2 (see text). Note that the arrows between α and χ_1, and between β and χ_2, refer to the direction of causal influence (but not to a specific form of temporal interaction, e.g., staged or cascaded)— that is, a feedforward architecture here. In the alternative case of bidirectional arrows—that is, a fully interactive architecture where the outputs of Process c could also affect the outputs of Processes a and b—the same reversed association across measurements R_1 and R_2 would only constitute evidence of more than one module somewhere in the network (i.e., could arise from any two processors whose influence could be traced directly or indirectly to χ_1 and χ_2; see text).*

measurements R_1 and R_2 of χ_1 and χ_2 is no longer evidence against a single module **C**—that is, χ_1 and χ_2 may implement the same function, c, but the relative values of the input to χ_1 and χ_2 may differ by virtue of different prior nonlinear operations $a(F)$ and $b(F)$, respectively, causing a reversed association. For example, $a(F)$ may be a linear function that maintains the relative order of $F_1 < F_2 < F_3$, while $b(F)$ may be a nonlinear function, like that in Figure 1-D2, which reorders the relative levels of F to $F_1 < F_2 > F_3$, thereby jointly allowing **C** to produce a reversed association of the type shown in Figure 3-B2. This ambiguity can be resolved by simultaneous consideration of neuroimaging data from processors α and β (e.g., R_3 and R_4, not shown in Figure 5), but it is possible that such data might simply not be available for these processors for some reason (e.g., because of types of neural activity that are undetectable by fMRI). In this case, the specificity of the inference drawn from the reversed association on measurements R_1 and R_2, given the network depicted in Figure 5, is reduced to the claim that there are at least two different modules either within χ_1 and χ_2, *or upstream of those processors*. The same limitations would seem to apply to neuroimaging dissociations over time, as in the EEG examples considered in Sternberg's Section 3.1: Selective effects of factors on different poststimulus time windows would allow one to claim only that "separately modifiable" processes occur at some time prior to, or including, the measured time windows. Relating such neuroimaging data to simultaneous behavioural data also becomes a challenge, given that a behavioural measurement, M_{ABC} (e.g., accuracy), will be influenced by more than one module (e.g., a motor region driving that behavioural response, not shown in Figure 5, might "read out" the activity of both β and χ_2, i.e., depend directly on both **B** and **C**, and indirectly on **A**).

However, even the above restriction of inferring modules to "within or upstream of χ_1 and χ_2" is predicated on unidirectional communication from α to χ_1, and from β to χ_2—that is, a "feedforward" architecture. In the alternative case of a fully interactive architecture (i.e., bidirectional arrows between modules in Figure 5), where the outputs of Process c could also affect the outputs of Processes a and b, the same reversed association between the levels of F and measurements R_1 and R_2 would only constitute evidence of more than one module *somewhere* in the network as a whole (i.e., the reversed association could arise from any two processors whose influence could be traced directly or indirectly to χ_1 and χ_2). Indeed, in this highly interactive case, even knowing the BOLD signal in all the relevant processors will not help localize the multiple modules. While one might think that evidence for more than one module (nonlinear process) somewhere in the brain is not particularly informative, it should be remembered that one still has evidence for more than one module that is sensitive specifically to the experimental manipulation (F), which can still be theoretically important. More generally, this challenge of localizing modules within

highly interactive systems probably requires testing multiple explicit, network models (e.g., structural equation modelling; see below).

4. DISCUSSION: MODULES IN BRAIN AND MIND

The present methodological argument continues a line of thinking introduced by Henson (2005), where it was called "function-to-structure deduction", as one of two types of inference about psychological processes that one might make from neuroimaging data. The critical pattern of a reversed association across three experimental conditions and two brain regions was later spelled out in more detail by Henson (2006a), where it was called an example of "forward inference" (in contrast to the "reverse inference" coined by Poldrack, 2006). Here, the same basic argument is formalized more explicitly, using the terminology introduced by Sternberg (2011), and extended to data patterns beyond a reversed association (e.g., the selective effects of two factors described in Section 3.3 above). It has been explained how this perspective questions what Sternberg would conclude from additive effects on a single behavioural measure (e.g., the RT data of Pinel et al., 2001, considered in Sternberg's Section 6.3), or from additive effects on a single neural measure (e.g., the fMRI data from the parahippocampal place area of Epstein et al., 2008, considered in Sternberg's Section 6.5), but concurs with what Sternberg would conclude from selective effects on multiple neural measures (e.g., the fMRI data of Pinel et al., 2001, considered in Sternberg's Section 6.3).

More theoretical issues—for example, of what defines a module—have deliberately been avoided (though see Henson, 2006b, for some thoughts along these more philosophical lines, e.g., in terms of "locality" and "directionality"). Indeed, in many of these issues, I am in agreement with Sternberg. Thus I also accept the computational/evolutionary argument for the existence of modules (exemplified by the elegant quote of Marr's given in Footnote 2 of Sternberg's article in this issue) and do not use the word "module" in the strict Fodorian sense (Fodor, 1983).[5] Rather, I use it in the same, simpler sense of Sternberg—that is, of being "separately modifiable", analogous to Shallice's definition of "isolable subsystems" (Shallice, 1988). In this sense, modularity really describes a methodological approach, rather than purely theoretical enterprise—that is, the proposal that a complex system may be "decomposed" into its constituent parts (before those parts can be reassembled in a model of the system), an approach that has dominated biology (Bechtel, 2003).

Do dissociable processors imply separate processes (modules)? Page (2006) gives an example that questions the inference of multiple psychological processes from a reversed association in neuroimaging data: Imagine that one measured neural activity at distinct locations along a topologically organized part of cortex, where neurons show nonlinear (e.g., Gaussian) tuning curves as a function of a factor F (e.g., tone frequency). Comparison of three levels of F (e.g., three frequencies) might then produce a reversed association across two locations within that topographic map (see Henson, 2005, and Page, 2006, for further explanation). Does this imply two modules operating at those two locations? Well the answer depends on the level of theoretical description. At the level of those two processors (implementing nonlinear functions of their input), one would have to argue that they implement different processes—that is, are tuned to detect different frequencies. At the level of part of cortex as a whole, one could describe it as one module, whose function is to code the frequency of auditory input. This issue of multiple levels of description is discussed at greater length by Henson (2005).

Inferring the existence of more than one module is of course not the end goal of cognitive (neuro)scientists. The present criteria for inferring multiple modules do not proscribe the precise

processes performed by each. The same scientists normally want to go further and describe the precise operation of those modules (e.g., the nature of processes a,b,c in examples above). This is generally achieved by hypothesizing further factors that affect those modules and testing these hypotheses in new experiments (see Henson, 2006a, for an example in the context of theories of recognition memory). Indeed, these hypothesize–test–hypothesize iterations appear a good description of most empirical sciences. This is the counterargument to the claim that one can always find dissociable data patterns (whatever the precise definition of "dissociable"), in the sense that if a participant can tell you the difference between two stimuli/tasks/contexts, then there must be a difference somewhere in their brain: It is the nature of that difference that is vital. So, for example, I was once asked whether, if one found different patterns of fMRI activity for pictures of Chinese versus Japanese food, would one infer separate modules for these two types of cuisine? Well, one might infer that (assuming that the fMRI data met the criteria for multiple modules in Section 3), but one would not stop there, but rather propose further experiments (experimental manipulations) that attempt to distinguish the "national cuisine" hypothesis from alternative hypotheses related to, for example, differences in the form or colour of the pictures of the foodstuffs (e.g., by using verbal labels instead), or gustatory differences normally experienced in the sugar/salt content of those foodstuffs, and so on.

A practical point that emerges from the above considerations is the importance of multifactorial, parametric designs for neuroimaging experiments: multiple factors in order to find selective effects of the type described in Section 3.3 above, and parametric in order to provide at least some insight into the nature of the psychological–neural (or "neurometric") mapping (e.g., possibility of a linear mapping). This is, of course, advice that Sternberg has long given for behavioural

---

[5]Nonetheless, a potentially important additional criterion I have proposed here for a module is that it implement a nonlinear function of its input (for the reasons given in Section 2). Whether this criterion is strictly necessary might be a topic for future discussion.

experiments, though he states that "factorial experiments are relatively rare in studies of brain activation" (Sternberg, 2011, Section 2.3). While it is true that in practice most early neuroimaging studies focused on categorical, subtraction designs—where a handful of conditions are compared that are assumed to differ qualitatively in their component processes (often entailing different tasks), rather than conforming to parametrically related factors—the theoretical importance of factorial, parametric designs for neuroimaging has, in fact, been appreciated for many years (e.g., Friston et al., 1996; see also Friston & Price, 2011).

I should also note that much of Sternberg's article in this issue (Sternberg, 2011) concerns the use of additive factors on time-resolved measurements like reaction times (RTs) and event-related potentials (ERPs), in order to infer serial or parallel processing "stages" (e.g., Sternberg's Sections 3 and 4). This has perhaps been the most influential application of Sternberg's work since his seminal 1969 paper (Sternberg, 1969). I have not considered such temporal issues here. Rather, my focus has been on the basic process decomposition approach (outlined in Sternberg's Section 2) and its application to "stationary" data like behavioural accuracy or fMRI data (as in Sternberg's Section 6). Nonetheless, I do believe that an important future goal for neuroscientific methodological consideration will be to establish the types of inference one can make, if any, about staged versus cascaded, and/or independent versus interactive, processing of modules (Coltheart, 2011). Given what we know about the highly connected and complex dynamics of the brain's physiology, I suspect such direct inferences will be limited, and instead we will need to rely on indirect inferences based on formal model comparison of a range of explicit, dynamic, network models, which differ in the sets of connections, "forward" and/or "backward", that are affected by an experimental manipulation (e.g., Stephan et al., 2007).

Finally, while I have argued for certain patterns of data being necessary to provide evidence for modules, I accept that scientists in practice normally consider a continuum of evidence, with some data patterns simply being more compelling

than others (Henson, 2005). Nonetheless, the formalization of the assumptions and limitations associated with each type of evidence, as exemplified by Sternberg's continued endeavours, are vital for determining the relative value of that evidence for the precise inference intended.

REFERENCES

Baillet, S., Mosher, J. C., & Leahy, R. M. (2001). Electromagnetic brain mapping. *IEEE Signal Processing Magazine, 18*(6), 14–30.

Bechtel, W. (2003). Decomposing the mind-brain: A long-term pursuit. *Brain and Mind, 3*, 229–242.

Coltheart, M. (2011). Methods for modular modelling: Additive factors and cognitive neuropsychology. *Cognitive Neuropsychology, 28*, 224–240.

Dunn, J. C., & Kirsner, K. (1988). Discovering functionally independent mental processes: The principle of reversed association. *Psychological Review, 95*, 91–101.

Epstein, R. A., Parker, W. E., & Feiler, A. M. (2008). Two kinds of fMRI repetition suppression? Evidence for dissociable neural mechanisms. *Journal of Neurophysiology, 99*, 2877–2886.

Fodor, J. (1983). *The modularity of mind: An essay on faculty psychology.* Cambridge, MA: MIT Press.

Friston, K. J., Glaser, D. E., Henson, R. N., Kiebel, S., Phillips, C., & Ashburner, J. (2002). Classical and Bayesian inference in neuroimaging: Applications. *NeuroImage, 16*, 484–512.

Friston, K. J., Mechelli, A., Turner, R., & Price, C. J. (2000). Nonlinear responses in fMRI: The balloon model, Volterra kernels and other hemodynamics. *NeuroImage, 12*, 466–477.

Friston, K. J., & Price, C. J. (2011). Modules and brain mapping. *Cognitive Neuropsychology, 28*, 241–250.

Friston, K. J., Price, C. J., Fletcher, P., Moore, C., Frackowiak, C. J., & Dolan, R. (1996). The trouble with cognitive subtraction. *NeuroImage, 4*, 97–104.

Grossberg, S. (1988). Nonlinear neural networks: Principles, mechanisms, and architectures. *Neural Networks, 1*, 17–61.

Henson, R. N. (2005). What can functional imaging tell the experimental psychologist? *Quarterly Journal of Experimental Psychology, 58A*, 193–233.

Henson, R. N. (2006a). Forward inference in functional neuroimaging: Dissociations vs associations. *Trends in Cognitive Science, 10*, 64–69.

Henson, R. N. (2006b). What has (neuro)psychology told us about the mind (so far)? A reply to Coltheart (2006). *Cortex, 42,* 387–392.

Newell, B. R., & Dunn, J. C. (2008). Dimensions in data: Testing psychological models using state-trace analysis. *Trends in Cognitive Science, 12,* 285–290.

Page, M. P. A. (2006). What can't functional neuroimaging tell the cognitive psychologist? *Cortex, 42,* 428–443.

Pinel, P., Dehaene, S., Riviere, D., & LeBihan, D. (2001). Modulation of parietal activation by semantic distance in a number comparison task. *NeuroImage, 14,* 1013–1026.

Poldrack, R. A. (2006). Can cognitive processes be inferred from neuroimaging data? *Trends in Cognitive Science, 10,* 59–63.

Rees, G., Friston, K., & Koch, C. (2000). A direct quantitative relationship between the functional properties of human and macaque V5. *Nature Neuroscience, 3,* 716–723.

Shallice, T. (1988). *From neuropsychology to mental structure.* Cambridge, UK: Cambridge University Press.

Stephan, K. E., Harrison, L., Kiebel, S. J., David, O., Penny, W. K., & Friston, K. J. (2007). Dynamic causal models of neural system dynamics: Current state and future extensions. *Journal of Biosciences, 32,* 129–144.

Sternberg, S. (1969). The discovery of processing stages: Extensions of Donders method. *Acta Psychologica, 30,* 276–315.

Sternberg, S. (2001). Separate modifiability, mental modules, and the use of pure and composite measures to reveal them. *Acta Psychologica, 106,* 147–246.

Sternberg, S. (2011). Modular processes in mind and brain. *Cognitive Neuropsychology, 28,* 156–208.

Weber, B. J., & Huettel, S. A. (2008). The neural substrates of probabilistic decision making. *Brain Research, 1234,* 104–115.

COGNITIVE NEUROPSYCHOLOGY, 2011, 28 (3 & 4), 224–240

Methods for modular modelling: Additive factors and cognitive neuropsychology

Max Coltheart

Macquarie Centre for Cognitive Science, Macquarie University, Sydney, NSW, Australia

Theorizing about how people perform any cognitive information-processing task typically takes the form of proposing a modular model of the cognitive system that people use to accomplish that task. Some of these models are stage models; many are not. In particular, models in which the passage of information from one module to another is cascaded rather than discrete are currently very popular, but these by definition are not stage models. The additive factor method as described by Sternberg (2011) is designed specifically for working with stage models. How useful is it for theorists whose models are not stage models? The goal of the additive factor method is the verification or discovery of the parts (modules) of cognitive systems. That is also the goal of the method of cognitive neuropsychology. I concur with Sternberg's view that these are complementary methods that can inform each other.

Keywords: Modularity; Additive factors; Computational modelling.

Let me begin with a quotation. "It can be argued within the sciences that the most important approach to the understanding of complex systems, such as mental processes, is to analyse them into parts or *modules*—to decompose them—and then discover what each part does, what other parts influence it, and what influence it has on other parts. Thus one of the goals of cognitive science in understanding the mental process that underlies the performance of even a simple task, such as naming a digit, is to determine what the parts of that process are" (Sternberg, 1998, p. 705). This paper is about that goal.

Two methods that have been widely used by cognitive scientists to learn more about what parts some particular mental process is composed of are the additive-factors (AF) method as described by Sternberg (2011 this issue) and the method of cognitive neuropsychology (CN) as documented in this journal over the past quarter of a century.

These two methods have a great deal in common, most importantly the attitude they take with regard to the relationship between data and theory. Both methods take this to be a two-way relationship.

First, one can begin with some theory and then use the AF method or the CN method to derive predictions about what the data of a particular investigation must be like if the theory is correct. The form of inference used to derive predictions

Correspondence should be addressed to Max Coltheart, Macquarie Centre for Cognitive Science, Macquarie University, Sydney, NSW 2109, Australia. (E-mail: max.coltheart@mq.edu.au).

I thank Saul Sternberg, Derek Besner, Claudio Mulatti, and Veronica Cembrani for much useful discussion.

http://www.psypress.com/cogneuropsychology

http://dx.doi.org/10.1080/02643294.2011.587794

here is deductive inference: The premises are stated in the theory, and the predictions are deduced from these premises. Work using the AF method can show, for example, that, if the theory is correct, a particular pair of experimental variables should show additive effects in the data whilst some other pair of experimental variables should interact. Work using the CN approach can show that, if the theory is correct, one should see patients with a particular pattern of cognitive impairment but should never see patients with some other particular pattern of cognitive impairment. Sternberg (2011 this issue) refers to this way of using the AF method as "module verification" because if the prediction generated from a modular theory is supported by the data, that strengthens one's belief in the theory and hence in the specific proposals that theory makes about what the modules of the relevant cognitive processing system are. I prefer the term "theory evaluation" here because this kind of work, whether it uses the AF or CN method, can result in the strengthening of one's belief in the theory (when the predictions are met by the data) or the weakening of one's belief in the theory (when the predications are violated by the data).

Alternatively, one can begin with the data and work backwards to a new theory: Sternberg (2011 this issue) calls this "module discovery", and so will I. In the case of the AF method, one might include in one's experiments some factor about whose additive or interactive effects no theory makes any predictions.[1] Having discovered what the effects of this factor actually are, one can then seek to infer some theory that can explain why this factor has the effects it has: Such a theory will hypothesize the existence of some new module or modules.

The same thing happens with the CN method. For example, in working with a patient A.C. with impaired spoken-word comprehension after brain damage, Coltheart et al. (1998) noticed that A.C. could provide correct semantic information about spoken concrete nouns provided that what was requested was information about nonperceptual properties of the object denoted by the noun; and if auditory or olfactory properties of the objects named were probed, the patient also succeeded. But if the requested information about an object was visual (such as colour, shape, or number of legs possessed), the patient was at chance in providing such information. This led the authors to suggest that the semantic system is not a single module, but consists of different modules representing different sensory modalities of perceptual information about concrete objects, with A.C. having lost the module that represents visual perceptual information.

The form of inference used when inferring a theory from the data is not deductive inference: Data can never serve as premises from which a theory must follow as a conclusion, since in all sciences there can be many theories that are consistent with the same set of data. Nor is the inference used when going from data to theory inductive inference: it is not of the form "I have seen 12 swans, and they have all been white; I therefore infer that all swans are white". Instead, it is a third kind of inference, known as abductive inference (Pierce, 1903/1997) or "inference to the best explanation" (Lipton, 1991). Abductive inferences are of the form "Here is a theory, which, if true, would predict (i.e., deductively imply) the data that have been observed". Such inferences may be supplemented by statements of the form "Here are some other theories, which, if true, would also deductively imply these data, and here is my reason for preferring the theory that I am advocating to these other theories". Or they may be supplemented by challenges of the form "Show me another theory that, if true, would also deductively imply these data, and then I will consider whether I have reason for preferring the theory that I am advocating to that other theory".

---

[1] Sternberg refers to this kind of practice—I think with approval—as a "fishing expedition". I share his approval of scientific fishing expeditions. Not all journal-article reviewers do.

WHAT IS A MODULE?

When the functional architecture of a proposed cognitive information-processing system consists of a set of distinct information-processing subsystems, each responsible for carrying out a particular defined and restricted information-processing job, I will refer to these subsystems as modules and will say that the system as a whole possesses the property of modularity. Sternberg (2011 this issue) does the same.

It is worth comparing this conception of modularity with that of Fodor (1983).

Fodor's conception of modularity is very widely misunderstood. Consider the title of the paper by Bowers and Davis (2004), which was "Is speech perception modular or interactive?" The authors take these two properties as mutually exclusive and, indeed, explicitly state this in the first sentence of their paper: Their view is that if a system is interactive, then it cannot be termed modular. But why should one take such a view? The authors cite Fodor (1983) as an advocate of the view that a system with feedback cannot be described as modular. But Fodor never proposed such a view. Indeed, the view of context effects in speech perception that Bowers and Davis offer as a nonmodular account of the phoneme restoration effect is precisely the view that Fodor offers too, but Fodor was offering this as, in his terms, a modular account! Bowers and Davis (2004, p. 3) say:

> The question arises as to whether phonemic processing is influenced by feedback from higher levels of processing. It is well-established that phoneme identification is often influenced by lexical context. For example, listeners who hear an input like ?ape, where the ? denotes an ambiguous phoneme that is somewhere between /t/ and /d/, are biased towards interpreting the ambiguous phoneme as a /t/, so that the input is consistent with a word (tape).

That is also how Fodor explains the phoneme restoration effect, and the reason why this counts as a modular explanation is explained by Fodor (1983, p. 76) as follows:

> The claim that input systems are informationally encapsulated must be very carefully distinguished from the claim that there is top-down information flow within these systems . . . phoneme

restoration provides considerable prima-facie evidence that phoneme identification has access to what the subject knows about the lexical inventory of his language. If this interpretation is correct, then phoneme restoration illustrates top-down information flow in speech perception. It does not, however, illustrate the cognitive penetrability of the language input system. To show that that system is penetrable [hence informationally unencapsulated], you would have to show that its processes have access to information that is not specified at any of the levels of representation that the language input system computes. . . . If . . . the "background information" deployed in phoneme restoration is simply the hearer's knowledge of the words in his language, then that counts as top-down flow within the language module.

So there is nothing contradictory about claiming that a system is modular in the Fodorian sense and simultaneously claiming that it includes feedback: These are not mutually exclusive alternatives.

This point exemplifies a wider problem. Fodor (1983) listed a number of properties that modules can possess: domain-specificity, innateness, informational encapsulation, fast operation, hardwiredness (neural specificity), autonomy, and the property "not assembled". It has frequently been claimed that here Fodor was offering a *definition* of modularity—that is, was proposing these as defining characteristics of modularity, so that a system cannot be called a module unless it possesses all of these properties. But in his book Fodor explicitly disavowed such an aim: "I am not, in any strict sense, in the business of defining my terms. . . . So what I propose to do instead of defining "modular" is to associate the notion of modularity with a pattern of answers to such questions as 1–5" (Fodor, 1983, p. 37; the five questions were about possible features of modularity). He continued: "the notion of modularity ought to admit of degrees. . . . The notion of modularity that I have in mind certainly does. When I speak of a cognitive system as modular, I shall therefore always mean "to some interesting extent" (Fodor, 1983, p. 37). So, contrary to many claims about Fodor's views, there is no property X such that one can say "The system lacks property X, so it is not modular". Hence even if noninteractivity were one of the Fodorian characteristic features of modules, a system that possesses interactivity could still be called modular.

Let's turn now from the Fodorian conception of modularity to the Sternbergian. As Sternberg (2011 this issue, Footnote 3) observes, his criterion for modularity is far weaker than the set of properties suggested by Fodor. For Sternberg, two cognitive (sub)systems **A** and **B** are modular with respect to each other if and only if each (sub)system can be changed independently of the other. That is, there needs to be at least one variable F that when manipulated affects the operation of **A** but not of **B** and at least one variable G that affects the operation of **B** but not of A. Such results demonstrate *selective influence* and satisfy the criterion of *separate modifiability*. It is the satisfaction of that criterion that justifies the claim that **A** and **B** are modules. This criterion for modularity is weaker than Fodor's in one sense: It offers only one characteristic feature rather then the seven offered by Fodor and listed above. But it is much stronger than Fodor's in another sense. For Fodor, there is no property X such that one can say: The system does not have property X, and therefore it is not modular. But for Sternberg there *is* such a critical property. If two cognitive components do not exhibit the property of selective influence, than they are not distinct modules in Sternberg's sense.

With the AF approach, there are two ways in which one can investigate whether a system putatively containing two modules **A** and **B** shows the property of separate modifiability. If it is possible to directly measure changes in **A** and also directly measure changes in **B**—that is, if pure measures of the activity of **A** and of **B** are available—then one can directly investigate whether variable F affects **A** but not **B**, and variable G affects **B** but not **A**. If it is not possible to measure the activities of module **A** and module **B** separately—that is, if only a composite measure of the operation of the **A**–**B** system as a whole is available (reaction time to perform some task requiring that system, for example)—then one needs to carry out a factorial experiment varying factors F and G orthogonally. If F affects only **A**, and G affects only **B**, then in such an experiment, F and G will have additive effects on the composite measure—for example, on RT. In this paper I consider only

the composite-measure case as occurs, for example, in typical RT studies of the performance of cognitive tasks.

Interestingly, Sternberg (2011 this issue, Footnote 3) observes that the Fodorian property of domain specificity appears to imply separate modifiability, since it is hard to imagine, if one hypothesized a system of, say, two modules each with a different processing domain, that one could not identify experimental variables that affected processing in one domain but not in the other. Coltheart (1999) also singled out domain specificity as an especially significant element in the Fodorian list of module properties and even suggested that modularity be *defined* with respect to this property, proposing that "A cognitive system is modular when and only when it is domain-specific" (Coltheart, 1999, p. 115). So if one adopted Coltheart's definition of modularity, then Sternberg's criterion of separate modifiability would be implied. Hence both authors, unlike Fodor (1983), are advocating a property that must be satisfied if a system is to be referred to as modular—and they are advocating the same property. So for both authors, a cognitive subsystem can be referred to as a module even if it is assembled (from more basic modules) is not innate, is not fast, is not informationally encapsulated, is not autonomous, and is not neurally hardwired. But most (sub)systems referred to by these authors as modules would, as a matter of fact though not of definition, possess most of these Fodorian properties.

For Sternberg (2011 this issue), the concept of modularity applies both at the neural level and at the cognitive, information-processing level. Thus there can be *neural modules*, and there can be *mental modules*. This needs to be true if the CN method is to succeed. The criterion of separate modifiability is central to both the AF and CN methods, and the CN approach depends upon modules being represented in the brain in such a way that a certain form of brain damage can modify the operation of module **A** but not module **B**, whereas some other form of brain damage can modify the operation of **B** but not **A**. Here the region of brain subserving **A** and the region of brain subserving **B** are separately modifiable (here, separately damageable). That is why the CN method for investigating mental modules requires that there be neural modularity as well as mental modularity.

MODULAR MODELLING OF COGNITION

Suppose we hypothesize a cognitive model consisting of two mental information-processing subsystems **A** and **B**, each charged with the performance of some specific information-processing job. **A** is a subsystem that receives input directly from the stimulus (or perhaps from low-level perceptual processing subsystems that lie outside the scope of our cognitive model). **B** is a subsystem whose output generates a response directly (or perhaps goes to low-level response-construction subsystems that lie outside the scope of our cognitive model). If **B** receives information about the stimulus via **A** (rather than directly from the stimulus or from low-level perceptual processing systems that feed **A**), then we depict this cognitive model as shown in Figure 1.

The arrows in such diagrams are intended to depict the direction in which information flows. They are *not* intended to depict the direction in which time flows as the system does its work in real time (though they often correspond to direction of time flow as well as direction of information flow); this point is considered again below.

Communication between A and B in this model

There are three theoretical possibilities concerning the communication between **A** and **B** here.

Staged processing
"In the stage model, processes *a* and *b* operate in sequence . . . one process begins when its predecessor is complete" (Roberts & Sternberg, 1993,

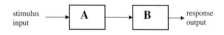

Figure 1. *A modular model without feedback.*

p. 613). So in our example, if communication from **A** to **B** is staged, Subsystem **A** must complete its job (whatever that is) before Subsystem **B** can begin its job (whatever that is). Here an experimental variable that specifically affects processing in Subsystem **A** will affect how long processing in **A** takes for its completion (it will affect "the duration of A"), but will have no effect on the nature or quality of the information **A** sends to **B**. That information will be the same whether Module **A** completed its job easily and quickly or slowly and with difficulty.

Cascaded processing
An alternative to staged processing is cascaded processing (McClelland, 1979). If there is cascaded processing between **A** and **B**, this means that as soon as there is any activity at all in Module **A**, information is passed on to Module **B**, which begins immediately to do its job on this information, whatever that job is. Here the quality and/or nature of the information that **A** sends to **B** may well change over time as processing in the whole system unfolds. And here the concept "the duration of A", which is critical in stage models, is not important and sometimes does not even apply to a model (for example, a modular model with cascaded processing may posit that strength of activation in a module may over time approach some asymptotic value that is never actually reached).

Sternberg (1998) discusses the idea of cascaded processing, referring to it as "overlapping processes: complete overlap". His characterization of this as "activation begins to rise at the output of the final unit as soon as the stimulus is applied to the input of the first . . . thus . . . the units . . . are not ordered temporally and can be regarded as operating in parallel" (p. 841) does not seem to me quite right, since it assumes that the time taken for one unit, **A**, to send information to the next unit up the line, **B**—that is, for **A** to provide data to **B**—is zero. If that is not so—and how could it be so?—then activation in **B** will begin after activation in **A** has begun, and so the two will be ordered temporally rather than operating in parallel. To be precise, the *onsets of activity* in the two modules will be ordered temporally: In real time, **A** will begin to operate before **B** begins to operate. In cascaded models, **A** will continue to operate after **B** has begun to operate, and hence the operation of **A** and **B** will overlap in time in the sense that there will be a period of time when both are operating. But if by "complete overlap" is meant that there is no period of time during which one of these is operating, and the other is not, I do not think that there are any cascaded models that possess this property.

Thresholded processing

A third and intermediate possibility is that the processing being done by **A** has to reach a certain level of maturity—but not full completion—before **A** communicates with **B**. For example, if **A** contains local representations of stimuli, communication from **A** to **B** might need to wait for some local representation in **A** to reach some critical level—that is, for it to reach some threshold (hence the term "thresholded processing": Besner & Roberts, 2003).[2] Note that even after **A** has communicated with **B** here, **A** will still continue to process its input further and will also still continue to communicate the results of this processing to **B**. The quality and/or nature of the information that **A** sends to **B** may thus change over time as processing in the whole system unfolds. Here there is a sense in which one can speak of the "duration" of the processing by **A**: It is the time that elapses between when **A** first receives input and when **A** first communicates information to **B**. However, "duration" here does not refer to how long **A** operates before it stops operating, since **A** continues to operate after it has first communicated information to **B**.

Sternberg (1998) considers a theoretical possibility like this, referring to it as "overlapping processes: partial overlap". Here, **A** starts when the stimulus is presented, **B** starts after a duration T1 has elapsed since **A** started, and **A** continues to operate even after **B** has started to operate.

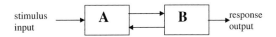

Figure 2. *A modular model with feedback.*

What is critical here is whether **B** continues to be provided with data from **A** even after **B** has started: In this case, "strictly speaking, we do not have a stages architecture" (Sternberg, 1998, p. 841). If this is so, then there will be an interval of processing (the interval when **B** has started but **A** has not stopped) when a variable that affects just **A** and a variable that affects just **B** will both have effects. This "could result in a failure of additivity" (Sternberg, 1998, p. 841). I have argued above that even fully cascaded models fall into this category of "overlapping processes: partial overlap", so would want to argue that this category covers both cascaded and thresholded models and sets the two apart from stage models, which by definition have no temporal overlap of the processing by their component modules.

Communication from B back to A

The transmission of information between two modules can be unidirectional or bidirectional. In Figure 1, this transmission is unidirectional: So we have a purely feedforward model, with no feedback. But if we allow for feedback from B to A—that is, bidirectional transmission of information—we must draw the model as shown in Figure 2.

Models where there is bidirectional communication between modules are called *interactive* models. Models where all communication between modules is unidirectional are called *feedforward* or *noninteractive* models.

Note that if the direction of an arrow were meant to signify the direction in which time operates, there would be something bizarre about this diagram: It would seem to be suggesting that **B** happens after **A** but that **B** also happens before **A**. But there is nothing odd about the diagram if

---

[2] Here the *output* from a module is thresholded. As pointed out to me by Claudio Mulatti, one can also imagine *input* thresholding: A module does not respond to input until the strength of that input exceeds some threshold value.

what the arrows represent is instead direction of flow of information: There is nothing odd about the suggestion that **A** sends information to **B**, and **B** also sends information to **A**, which is the scenario that the diagram depicts.

Interaction (feedback) can obviously be conceived of when communication from **A** to **B** is cascaded and also when it is thresholded, because, when **B** is first engaged, processing by **A** is not yet complete, and so processing of **A** could be assisted by feedback from **B**. But when communication from **A** to **B** is staged, feedback from **B** to **A** cannot be beneficial to **A** because feedback could not occur until the processing done by **A** has been fully completed. Hence there will not be any interactive staged models—that is, staged models that include feedback as it is conceived of in Figure 2.

It might be argued that the massive degree to which there is reentrant processing in the cortex is incompatible with any model that lacks feedback—even incompatible with nonstage models that eschew feedback, such as the Merge model of spoken word recognition (Norris, McQueen, & Cutler, 2000), the Levelt–Roelofs–Meyer model of spoken word production (Levelt, Roelofs, & Meyer, 1999), or the Burton–Bruce–Hancock model of face recognition (Burton, Bruce, & Hancock, 1999). But to make this argument, one would have to demonstrate that there are reentrant pathways in the cortex whose function is to deliver the type of feedback that a model denies. For example, if a brain region whose function was visual word recognition and a brain region whose function was letter identification were identified, and it was shown that there are neural pathways from the first region to the second, that would not rule out models of reading that claim that there is no feedback from the word level to the letter level. To establish that point, one would have to show that the neural pathways concerned had the function of activating a word's constituent letter representations when that word's orthographic lexical representations was active. That kind of cognitive–neuroscientific work has not been done in relation to any cognitive model in which the occurrence of

feedback is asserted or denied. Until it is, the occurrence of reentrant processing in the cortex does not bear on cognitive models.

TYPES OF MODULAR MODEL: AND MODELS THAT ARE NOT STAGE MODELS

Whether communication between modules is cascaded, thresholded, or staged is orthogonal to the property of interactivity versus noninteractivity (except that, as explained above, when there is staged processing there is no interactivity). So there are five in-principle-possible general classes of modular model of cognition. One of these five is the class of stage models.

Sternberg (2011) gives several examples of the application of the AF method to the study of cognition. For example, he discusses the results of Schuberth, Spoehr, and Lane (1981, Experiment 2), who found that when the three factors of test word legibility, semantic congruity of a word with a sentence context, and frequency of the test word were factorially varied in an experiment, with the dependent variable being lexical decision accuracy, the results supported "theories in which the three factors influence three different modular processes, all of which must succeed for a correct response" (Sternberg, 2011 this issue). So these results support a stage model. However, Sternberg does not then go on to say anything about the nature of this stage model—that is, he does not say anything about what these three different modular processes might be. This is in fact generally true of his paper: He does give some examples in which the AF method suggests that a stage model in some cognitive domain is correct, but he does not then go on to state what this model is—that is, he does not state what the functions of its individual modules are.

If the AF method is to be considered as having contributed substantially to cognitive psychology, we need examples of specific stage models of cognition that arose out of studies using the AF method—that is, specific examples where what Sternberg (2011) refers to as "module verification" has occurred—and Sternberg's paper contains few or no examples of this as far as cognitive models are concerned.

Furthermore, very many cognitive models that have been of interest in cognitive neuropsychology (and in cognitive science generally), in a wide range of domains of cognition, belong to one or other of the remaining four classes—that is, none of them are stage models. This is especially true of the modular models of cognition that have been used in cognitive neuropsychology. There have been very many modular models of cognition discussed in the pages of this journal since its inception in 1984. As far as I am aware, none of these have been stage models.

Here are some examples (the list is far from exhaustive) of domains of cognition where influential modular models of cognition that are not stage models have been proposed (and used in cognitive neuropsychology).

Visual word recognition

In the interactive activation and competition (IAC) model of visual word recognition (McClelland & Rumelhart, 1981) there are three modules—visual feature detection, letter identification, and word recognition. Communication between the modules is cascaded. There is cascaded feedback from the word recognition module to the letter identification module.

Reading aloud

In the dual-route cascaded (DRC) model of visual word recognition and reading aloud (Coltheart, Rastle, Perry, Langdon, & Ziegler, 2001), which is depicted in Figure 3, there are seven modules. Communication between the modules is cascaded. Most of the modules receive cascaded feedback from at least one other module.

Spelling

The dual-route computational model of spelling developed by Houghton and Zorzi (2003) is a fully cascaded model and also incorporates one form of feedback (self-feedback for units within the model's orthographic lexicon).

Spoken word recognition

The Merge model of spoken word recognition (Norris et al., 2000) explicitly excludes feedback—these authors deny that there is any evidence that feedback is used during the process of spoken word recognition—but the model is a fully cascaded one.

Spoken word production

The Levelt–Roelofs–Meyer model of spoken word production (see Levelt et al., 1999, Figure 1) possesses a mixture of thresholded and cascaded processing (and no feedback). One of the processes in this model is *lemma selection*: The lemma corresponding to the input word must be selected before the word's morphological and phonological representations are activated. The criterion for determining when lemma selection has occurred is the ratio of that lemma unit's activation to the summed activation of all the lemma units. Thus lemma selection is not a process that is completed after a fixed amount of time (as would be the case if lemma selection were a stage in the model) but instead completed after a certain level of activation is reached. Before that has happened, the lemma selection system contributes no activation to morphological and phonological subsystems of the model. In other words, communication from the lemma selection component of the model to other components of the model is thresholded. However, communication between some other modules of the model is cascaded—for example, communication from the conceptual (semantic) level to the lexical level.

Face recognition

In the Burton–Bruce–Hancock model of face recognition, "there are no thresholds for passing activation within the model. Instead activation is passed in a cascade fashion throughout" (Burton et al., 1999, p. 3). There is no feedback in this model.

Thus one is left wondering about two things here, as far as the AF method is concerned. The first question is: What particular contemporary models of cognition (especially those in cognitive neuropsychology) are stage models? The second question is: Given that many contemporary

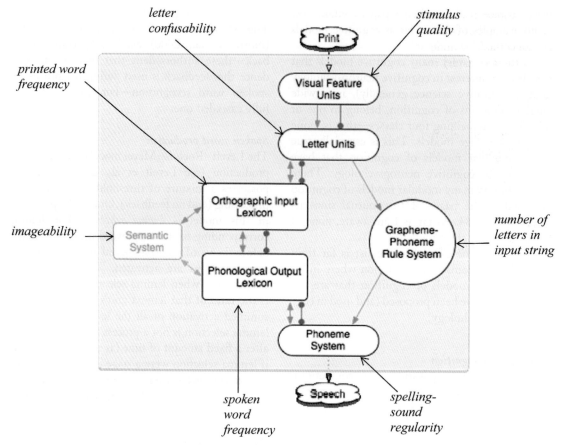

Figure 3. *The dual-route cascaded (DRC) model of visual word recognition and reading aloud, and factors directly affecting each of its modules. To view a colour version of this figure, please see the online issue of the Journal.*

models of cognition are not stage models, is the AF method of value for the investigation of such nonstage models? The critical issue here is what one can conclude about models that are not stage models from the observation of additivities or interactions of the effects of factors in factorial experiments.

IS ADDITIVITY OF EFFECTS COMPATIBLE WITH CASCADED (I.E., NONSTAGED) COMMUNICATION BETWEEN MODULES?

One might think that additivity of factors in experiments in some domain of cognition can

only be observed if the cognitive system in question is a system of stages. If that were so, then the finding of additive effects would be enough to rule out cascaded models, making the AF method an extremely powerful one. Unfortunately, matters are not so simple.

This issue has been discussed by Roberts and Sternberg (1993). They consider two alternatives to simple stage models: an alternate pathways model and the McClelland–Ashby cascade model. The former model is not relevant to the question being asked here, because it is still a kind of stage model, as Roberts and Sternberg (1993, p. 619) note. But the latter model is directly relevant to the question under consideration. Their investigations led Roberts and Sternberg (1993, p. 614) to conclude that "the cascade model approximates additivity with some parameter values but not others".

The conditions under which the McClelland–Ashby cascade model could show additive effects were as follows (Sternberg, 1998, p. 842):

1. The model's modules must be separately modifiable: that is, there are experimental variables (factors) that selectively influence the rate at which activations rise in modules;
2. These factors must not have any effect on the asymptotic values that activations in modules can reach—they must only influence rates of activation rise;
3. The model must contain at least one module in which activation rises very slowly relative to the rise of activation in other modules;
4. The rate at which activation rises in that slow module must be independent of the levels of the factors that are manipulated.

Thus it cannot be claimed that cascaded models can *never* yield additive effects, since there is one cascaded model that under certain circumstances does yield additive effects. However, the AF method would still be a powerful way of investigating cascaded models if we know exactly what properties cascaded models need to possess in order to generate additive effects because, if we knew that, and were investigating a cascaded model which did *not* possess these properties, we could take the observation of additive effects as evidence against the model.

Unfortunately, matters are not even this simple. We do not know what properties a nonstage model must have for it to be compatible with the observation of additive effects, and we do not know whether the properties (a) through (d) listed above are sufficient for *any* cascaded model to be compatible with additivity of effects. But what we would like to know is something much more general: We would like to know whether or not it is true for *every* cascaded model that there are circumstances under which such a model can produce additive effects. This greatly complicates attempts to use the AF method in the investigation of nonstage models such as cascaded models.

Given that no general statement can be made about additivity in relation to cascaded models, all that one can do is study additivity in relation to some specific cascaded model. When, as is usually the case, such models are expressed verbally, it can be difficult or impossible to decide whether they are compatible with additivity of effects. It is therefore unclear just how valuable the AF method could be here.

However, some cascaded models of cognition are expressed as computer programs—that is, are computational models—and it is possible, at least in principle, to determine for any computational model of cognition whether it is compatible with the observation of additive effects. One simply does a thorough exploration of the model's parameter space to see whether there is any set of parameters under which the model's behaviour exhibits additivity of effects. If there is not, then the observation of additivity in relevant experimental data is inconsistent with the model.

One such model is the DRC computational model of visual word recognition and reading aloud (Coltheart et al., 2001) as shown in Figure 3. This is a modular model: As Figure 3 shows, the model has seven modules (the semantic module will be included here even though as shown by its being greyed out in the figure it has not been computationally implemented yet). These are modules in the domain-specific sense since each has a specific domain of application (visual features, letters, whole-word orthographic representations, etc.).

This model's modules are also modules in the Sternbergian sense because, as Figure 3 shows, the modules of the DRC model possess the property of separate modifiability. For every module in the model, one can identify at least one property of printed letter strings that directly affects the operation of that particular module.

Because of this, one can investigate the DRC model by using AF-style factorial experiments to determine whether particular pairs of factors are additive or interactive (a) in human reading-aloud data and (b) in DRC model simulations of those data. If it is typically true that, when the modules of a model are in cascaded communication, a factor that selectively affects one of these modules will interact with a factor that selectively influences another of the model's modules, one would expect to find interactive effects in the simulations, which means that the model predicts interactive effects in the human data; such effects have been reported. For example, an interaction between written word frequency and spelling–sound regularity has been reported both in human data and DRC simulations: Reading-aloud reaction times (RTs) of humans and of the DRC model are slower for irregular words than for regular words, but only when these words are low in frequency (Coltheart et al., 2001).

However, there have been some cases where factors mentioned in Figure 3 have revealed additive effects in the human data, and that raises the question of whether such additivities are inconsistent with the DRC model. As mentioned above, additive effects can be yielded by at least one fully cascaded model, the McClelland–Ashby model, but unfortunately we do not know in general what properties a fully cascaded model must have in order to be compatible with additivity of effects, and so we cannot answer, from first principles, the question of whether additivity of effects on reading-aloud RTs in factorial experiments with human subjects is compatible with some particular cascaded model.

This would be a particularly difficult problem if the DRC model were not a computational model. But since it is, the problem can be explored by trying to determine whether there is a parameter set for the model under which the model's RTs show additive effects of factors that show additive effects in experiments with human readers.

Besner, O'Malley, and Robidoux (2010, Table 1) list some examples where human readers' RTs show additive effects. In some cases, the same materials as those used to test human subjects were run through the DRC model. Here the RTs of the model, when its default parameters were used, showed interactions between pairs of factors that exhibited additive effects on the RTs of human

readers. Attempts were made to find a different parameter set under which the model would show additivities, but no such set could be found. So even though this model is not a stage model, the AF method can nevertheless be used to collect data that challenge the model. But that is only possible because the model is a computational model.

Implementing the manipulation of stimulus quality (SQ) in computational models of reading aloud

It is perhaps striking that in every one of the examples given by Besner et al. (2010, Table 1) where a pair of factors exhibit additive effects on human RTs but interactive effects on the DRC model's RTs, stimulus quality (SQ) was always one of the pair of factors (SQ was manipulated by varying stimulus contrast). In experiments that measure reading-aloud RTs with human subjects, SQ has additive effects with word frequency, lexicality, regularity, repetition, neighbourhood size, and number of letters.[3] When SQ is manipulated in the DRC model by varying the strength with which the visual feature units activate the letter units, SQ has interactive effects with these other variables.

To the best of my knowledge, there are no factorial experiments on reading aloud in human subjects that have observed additive effects of any pair of the factors listed in Figure 1, except when one of these factors is SQ. So it is the case, at least at present, that additive effects of these factors have only been observed when one of those factors is SQ. Might this mean that there is something special about this particular factor? Since the module which SQ selectively affects is the visual feature units module, we are led to the question: Is there something special about this module?

There is. As astute circuit-diagram analysts will already have noted, this is the only module on the lexical route of the DRC model that does not receive feedback from any other module. Since, as noted earlier, a module that receives feedback from other modules cannot be a stage, the other

---

[3] Such additivities are seen only when at least some of the items in reading-aloud experiments are nonwords, a point to which I will return.

modules cannot be stages. But the visual feature units module, since it does not receive feedback, could be a stage. If it were, then modelling the SQ factor in terms of the strength with which the visual feature units module activates the letter units module in the DRC module is the wrong way to go. This would be wrong because this way of simulating SQ causes the strength of the output of the visual feature units model to vary as a function of this factor, and that is not what happens when a module is a stage. "Given its input, the output of a stage should be independent of factors influencing its duration" (Sternberg, 1969, p. 283). Instead, if the visual feature units module is a stage, varying SQ should be simulated by varying the *duration* of the visual feature units module—that is, the time that elapses between when the stimulus is presented and when the visual feature units module first sends any communication to the letter units module, with the strength or quality of that communication being independent of the level of the SQ factor.

First, though, we should consider why there is no feedback to the visual feature units module. For the DRC model, the answer is simple: It is because there is no such feedback in the IAC model, and the DRC model, in the spirit of nested modelling (Jacobs & Grainger, 1994), is required to incorporate the IAC model, of which it is a generalization. The question therefore is: Why was there no feedback from the letter units to the visual feature units in the IAC model?

Figure 1 of McClelland and Rumelhart (1981), describing a general interactive-activation framework for the processing of written and spoken language, does have feedback from the letter level to the feature level. But their Figure 2, which is the IAC model, does not. McClelland and Rumelhart explain that this was because the IAC model could simulate the data they wished to simulate when there was feedback only from word to letter level; feedback from letter to feature level was not required for this simulation to be successful, and furthermore the presence of this extra level of interaction "introduces an order of complexity that obscures comprehension" (McClelland &

Rumelhart, 1981, p. 378). Hence the absence of this form of feedback in the IAC model was the result of pragmatism, not of principle.

If the visual feature level is thought of as a stage, then it must be a module whose strength of output is not affected by the levels of any stimulus variable (such as SQ). Instead, what variation in SQ has to do if the visual feature level were a stage is to modulate the duration of that stage—that is, the time between when the stimulus is input to that module of the model and when that module generates an output to other modules of the model. The lower SQ is, the longer this duration would be, but what would be delivered to the rest of the system by the visual feature level would be independent of the level of SQ. If that were the case, the factor SQ would then be additive with any factor that affects any other module in the system, and that is what the data (so far) tell us is the case—at least in experiments where the items to be read aloud include nonwords.

Note that the way in which Besner et al. (2010) simulated the manipulation of SQ in the two computational models they studied involves *not* treating the visual features level as a stage, since their method of varying SQ in the model was to vary the strength of the output from the visual feature units module to the letter units module. The human data produced by use of the AF method suggest that SQ needs instead to be simulated in a way that is consistent with the visual feature units module being a stage. That requires that manipulation of SQ should be done by manipulating the duration of processing at the visual features level. The lower SQ is, the longer this processing should take. Communication from the visual features level to the letter identification level must not occur until after the visual features level has completed its job. And the quality of information sent from the former to the latter level must be the same regardless of the level of SQ.

Hence I investigated what would happen with DRC simulations if the actual stimuli used in papers reported in Table 1 of Besner et al. (2010) were run through the DRC model with variation in SQ simulated by varying the duration of processing at the visual features level, lowering

Table 1. *Reaction times of the DRC model for irregular words, regular words, and nonwords as SQ varies*

Duration of the visual feature stage, in cycles	Word			Effect	
	Irreg	*Reg*	*Nwd*	*Regularity*	*Lexicality*
1	104.39	72.28	140.89	32.11	68.61
5	108.39	76.28	144.89	32.11	68.61
10	113.39	81.28	149.89	32.11	68.61
20	123.39	91.28	159.89	32.11	68.61

Note: DRC = dual-route cascaded. SQ = stimulus quality. Irreg = irregular word. Reg = regular word. Nwd = nonword.

of SQ corresponding to increased duration of the visual features level, with no communication from visual features level to letter identification level until the prescribed duration of processing at the visual features level had elapsed. Two factorial manipulations were simulated: SQ by regularity and SQ by lexicality (the levels of the lexicality factor being regular words vs. nonwords). The results are shown in Table 1 here.

Here the model RTs show perfect additivity between SQ and regularity and perfect additivity between SQ and lexicality.

This is an example of using the AF method to achieve what Sternberg (2011 this issue) refers to as module verification and what I refer to as model evaluation, since there is a general conclusion to be drawn about the DRC model here. The conclusion is that a fully cascaded version of the DRC model may be inconsistent with the additivities reported by Besner et al. (2010). Instead, communication between the visual features module and the letter identification module has to be staged rather than cascaded—that is, the visual features module has to be a stage in the Sternbergian sense, even though the other modules of the model are not stages.[4] Hence the AF method can be of use in the evaluation of modular models of cognition even when most or all of the processing in such a model is conceived of as cascaded rather than staged, provided that the model is a computational model.

In this particular example, a problem remains for the DRC model, in that the additivities of

SQ with various other factors in reading-aloud experiments are only seen when at least some of the items to be read are nonwords (Besner et al., 2010, Table 1). When all are words, these additive effects become interactions. It is scarcely plausible to argue that the visual features level is a stage when the stimulus material includes at least some nonwords, but is cascaded when only words are present in the stimulus material. But that is a challenge to the model, not to the use of the AF method for evaluating the model.

In theory, one might propose here that the experimental list composition (just words, as against words plus nonwords or even just nonwords) has some influence on how the first level of the system (the visual features module) operates. But it scarcely seems plausible that so early a process in the system could be strategically manipulable.

Nevertheless, consider the results reported by Sternberg (1967). The task here was to decide whether a target digit was or was not a member of a previously memorized short set of digits. Two factors were manipulated: SQ and set size. Each subject was tested in two sessions, a week apart. A model with two stages was proposed: Stage 1 was stimulus encoding, and Stage 2 was memory scanning. That model predicts additivity of SQ with set size, and just such additivity occurred—but only in the second session. In the first session, the function relating RT to set size was steeper in the low-SQ condition than in the high-SQ condition. That interaction implies that

---

[4] Alternatively, it might be possible to capture the additive effects by making some other module of the DRC model—the letter identification level, for example—a stage, as Besner et al. (2010) have suggested.

in Session 1 the stimulus representation delivered by the stimulus encoding system to the memory-scanning system was of poorer quality when SQ was low than when it was high (so that each comparison in memory was slower when the stimulus had been low in SQ). But that means, for two reasons, that in Session 1 the stimulus encoding system was not operating as a stage:

1. The quality of information delivered by the stimulus encoding system to the memory scanning system was influenced by the level of the SQ factor.
2. Given that cleaning up the stimulus is a job that the stimulus encoding system is responsible for, in Session 1 the stimulus encoding system was passing on information before it had completed its cleaning-up job.

Thus early in practice (Session 1), the stimulus encoding system was not operating as a stage, whereas late in practice (Session 2), that system *was* operating as a stage. It is as if in Session 1 the stimulus encoding system passed information on to the memory scanning system before it was fully ready to do so, because of the emphasis on speed of responding. That would mean that whether a module acts as a stage or not can depend on level of practice.

Given that finding, perhaps it seems less implausible that the visual feature system—which is equivalent to the stimulus encoding system of Sternberg (1967)—might be allowed to communicate to the letter level prematurely under the easy condition (i.e., where the stimulus is known to be a real word) but required to complete its job—in other words, to act as a stage—under difficult conditions (i.e., where the stimulus may be an unknown letter string).

COGNITIVE NEUROPSYCHOLOGY

Even if (a) the mind is massively modular, and in addition (b) damage to the brain can impair mental information processing, that is not sufficient to allow the cognitive-neuropsychological method the possibility of achieving its aims

(these aims being evaluation of modular theories of cognition and the discovery of new mental modules). As mentioned above, what also needs to be the case is that distinct mental modules must at least to some degree map onto distinct regions of the brain. This is needed because, if cognitive neuropsychology is to succeed, brain damage must be able to exert selective influence on modular cognitive systems. If **A** and **B** are two modules of such a system, it needs to be the case that one kind of brain damage can impair the functioning of **A** but not of **B**, and another kind of brain damage can impair the functioning of **B** but not of **A**, so that the modules **A** and **B** are separately modifiable.

A criterion weaker than the criterion of selective influence is *differential influence* (Sternberg, 2011 this issue, Section 12.4). Suppose that instead of brain damage being able to exert selective influence on mental modules, what is instead the case is that one kind of brain damage can impair the functioning of **A** more than the functioning of **B**, and another kind of brain damage can impair the functioning of **B** more than the functioning of **A**. Here the modules **A** and **B** are not *separately* (i.e., completely independently) modifiable, but they are *differentially* modifiable. The distinction between selective influence and differential influence is standard in cognitive neuropsychology: It is the distinction (Shallice, 1988) between *classical* double dissociation (where performance on the better performed task is within the normal range) and *nonclassical* double dissociation (where performance on the better performed task is below the normal range but significantly better than performance on the worse performed task).

Seeking to demonstrate selective or differential influence of brain damage on cognition faces, according to Sternberg (2011 this issue, Section 11), two impediments.

The first is the difficulty in showing that a patient's performance on tasks tapping the putatively intact modules has indeed not been affected by the patient's brain damage. If one had predamage and postdamage performance measures on the relevant tasks, a within-subject comparison of satisfactory statistical power might be possible, but the patients investigated by cognitive neuropsychologists rarely come accompanied by prelesion data. So attempts to demonstrate that a patient's performance on tasks tapping the putatively intact modules has not been affected by the patient's brain damage rely on between-subject comparisons with a control group, where the control group performance is intended as an estimate of what the patient's performance would have been like if measured pre lesion. However, this could only be a problem when one is claiming a classical double dissociation; the point is not relevant to nonclassical double dissociations.

The second impediment is that one has to assume that brain damage does not have qualitative effects on modular cognitive systems—that it cannot, for example, add a new module to the system. This is widely recognized as an assumption in cognitive neuropsychology: Caramazza (1986) calls it the "subtractivity assumption" (i.e., the assumption that brain damage can subtract modules from a cognitive system but cannot add new modules to the system). Sternberg (2011 this issue) asserts that brain damage can sometimes have such qualitative effects, but he does not cite any evidence that this is so. He then suggests that the existence of these two impediments may justify the use within cognitive neuropsychology of the task-comparison approach rather then the process-decomposition approach, even though, on his view, the task-comparison approach has more limited goals than the process-decomposition approach. These limitations are discussed in his Section 9.

It is certainly true that cognitive neuropsychological investigations typically involve task comparisons, with the aim of documenting double dissociations between task pairs. Patient X is better (perhaps even normal) at Task 1 but impaired at Task 2, whereas Patient Y is better (perhaps even normal) at Task 2 but impaired at Task 1. From this it is inferred that the cognitive system used to perform Task 1 contains at least one module that is absent from the cognitive system used to perform Task 2, and also that the cognitive system used to perform Task 2 contains at least one module that is absent from the cognitive system

used to perform Task 1. These inferences can be used to evaluate existing modular theories or, where no such theory currently exists, to head towards the development of such a theory.

It is not at all clear to me why Sternberg (2011 this issue, Section 9) takes the view that "task comparison is inferior to process decomposition for discovering the modular subprocesses of a complex process or for investigating its properties. The interpretation usually requires a theory of the complex process in each task, and the method includes no test of such theories. In contrast, process decomposition requires a theory of only one task, and, as illustrated by the examples above, incorporates a test of that theory".

Suppose Task 1 is reading aloud of irregular words, and Task 2 is reading aloud of nonwords. There have been many reports of double dissociations between these two tasks. In *surface dyslexia* (Patterson, Marshall, & Coltheart, 1985), brain-damaged patients are less accurate at reading aloud irregular words than at reading aloud nonwords (accuracy on the latter task can even be normal: (Behrmann & Bub, 1992; McCarthy & Warrington, 1986). In *phonological dyslexia* (Coltheart, 1996), brain-damaged patients are less accurate at reading aloud nonwords than at reading aloud words (whether these be regular or irregular). But though we have two tasks here, it is not necessary, as Sternberg (2011 this issue) claims, to have two theories: The DRC model (Figure 3) is a single theory, which offers an explanation of how both of these tasks are performed (and also explanations of how various other tasks, such as visual lexical decision, are performed). Figure 3 proposes the existence of particular modular subprocesses of the complex process of reading, and the cognitive-neuropsychological evidence from Task 1 (reading aloud irregular words) and Task 2 (reading aloud nonwords) provides strong support for these proposals. Furthermore, the task comparison approach provides ways of directly testing the theory. For example, the theory says that a patient who is impaired at the visual lexical decision task cannot show normal accuracy at the task of reading aloud irregular words. So a task-comparison study that documented such a patient would be inconsistent with the theory.

CONCLUSION

I argue, then, that the task comparison approach as commonly used in cognitive neuropsychology is not inferior to the process decomposition approach for the purposes of module verification and module discovery. Both approaches have their strengths and their weaknesses. More generally, I argue that this is true of the AF method and the cognitive-neuropsychological method. And that is Sternberg's general view also: "What should be the relation between traditional cognitive neuropsychology (i.e., making inferences about normal cognitive processes from the effects of brain damage) and the process decomposition approach with normals? One goal they share is the identification of separately modifiable processes of the normal brain. I suggest that each can inform the other" (Sternberg, 2011 this issue).

REFERENCES

Behrmann, M., & Bub, D. (1992). Surface dyslexia and dysgraphia: Dual routes, single lexicon. *Cognitive Neuropsychology*, *9*(3), 209–251.

Besner, D., O'Malley, S., & Robidoux, S. (2010). On the joint effects of stimulus quality, regularity, and lexicality when reading aloud: New challenges. *Journal of Experimental Psychology: Learning, Memory and Cognition*, *36*, 750–764.

Besner, D., & Roberts, M. A. (2003). Reading nonwords aloud: Results requiring change in the dual route cascaded model. *Psychonomic Bulletin & Review*, *10*, 398–404.

Bowers, J. S., & Davis, C. J. (2004). Is speech perception modular or interactive? *Trends in Cognitive Sciences*, *8*, 3–5.

Burton, A. M., Bruce, V., & Hancock, P. J. B. (1999). From pixels to people: A model of familiar face recognition. *Cognitive Science*, *23*, 1–31.

Caramazza, A. (1986). On drawing inferences about the structure of normal cognitive systems from the analysis of patterns of impaired performance: The case for single-patient studies. *Brain & Cognition*, *5*, 41–66.

Coltheart, M. (Ed.). (1996). *Phonological dyslexia*. Hove, UK: Lawrence Erlbaum Associates.

Coltheart, M. (1999). Modularity and cognition. *Trends in Cognitive Sciences*, *3*, 115–120.

Coltheart, M., Inglis, L., Cupples, L., Michie, P., Bates, A., & Budd, B. (1998). A semantic subsystem specific to the storage of information about visual attributes of animate and inanimate objects. *Neurocase*, *4*, 353–370.

Coltheart, M., Rastle, K., Perry, C., Langdon, R., & Ziegler, J. (2001). DRC: A dual route cascaded model of visual word recognition and reading aloud. *Psychological Review*, *108*, 204–256.

Fodor, J. A. (1983). *The modularity of mind*. Cambridge, MA: Bradford Books.

Houghton, G., & Zorzi, M. (2003). Normal and impaired spelling in a connectionist dual-route architecture. *Cognitive Neuropsychology*, *20*, 135–162.

Jacobs, A. M., & Grainger, J. (1994). Models of visual word recognition: Sampling the state of the art. *Journal of Experimental Psychology: Human Perception and Performance*, *20*, 1311–1334.

Levelt, W. J. M., Roelofs, A., & Meyer, A. S. (1999). A theory of lexical access in speech production. *Behavioral & Brain Sciences*, *22*, 1–75.

Lipton, P. (1991). *Inference to the best explanation*. London, UK: Routledge.

McCarthy, R., & Warrington, E. K. (1986). Phonological reading: Phenomena and paradoxes. *Cortex*, *22*, 359–380.

McClelland, J. L. (1979). On the time relations of mental processes: An examination of systems of processing in cascade. *Psychological Review*, *86*, 287–330.

McClelland, J. L., & Rumelhart, D. E. (1981). An interactive activation model of context effects in letter perception: Part 1. An account of basic findings. *Psychological Review*, *88*, 375–407.

Norris, D., McQueen, J. M., & Cutler, A. (2000). Merging information in speech recognition: Feedback is never necessary. *Behavioral and Brain Sciences*, *23*, 299–325.

Patterson, K. E., Marshall, J. C., & Coltheart, M. (Eds.). (1985). *Surface dyslexia: Cognitive and neuropsychological studies of phonological reading*. Hove, UK: Lawrence Erlbaum Associates Ltd.

Pierce, C. S. (1997). P.A. Turrisi (Ed.), *Pragmatism as a principle and method of right thinking: The 1903 Harvard lectures on pragmatism*. Albany, NY: State University of New York Press. (Original work published 1903).

Roberts, S., & Sternberg, S. (1993). The meaning of additive reaction-time effects. In D. E. Meyer & S. Kornblum (Eds.), *Attention and Performance XIV: Synergies in experimental psychology, artificial intelligence and cognitive neuroscience—A silver jubilee* (pp. 611–653). Cambridge, MA: MIT Press.

Schuberth, R. E., Spoehr, K., & Lane, D. M. (1981). Effects of stimulus and contextual information on the lexical decision process. *Memory and Cognition, 9*, 68–77.

Shallice, T. (1988). *From neuropsychology to mental structure*. Cambridge, UK: Cambridge University Press.

Sternberg, S. (1967). Two operations in character recognition: Some evidence from reaction-time measurements. *Perception & Psychophysics, 2*, 45–53.

Sternberg, S. (1969). The discovery of processing stages: Extensions of Donders' method. *Acta Psychologica, 30*, 276–315.

Sternberg, S. (1998). Discovering mental processing stages: The method of additive factors. In D. Scarborough & S. Sternberg (Eds.), *An invitation to cognitive science: Vol. 4. Methods, models and conceptual issues* (pp. 703–864). Cambridge, MA: MIT Press.

Sternberg, S. (2011). Modular processes in mind and brain. *Cognitive Neuropsychology, 28*, 156–208.

COGNITIVE NEUROPSYCHOLOGY, 2011, 28 (3 & 4), 241–250

Modules and brain mapping

Karl J. Friston and Cathy J. Price

The Wellcome Trust Centre for Neuroimaging, University College London, London, UK

This review highlights the key role of modularity and the additive factors method in functional neuroimaging. Our focus is on structure–function mappings in the human brain and how these are disclosed by brain mapping. We describe how modularity of processing (and possibly processes) was a key point of reference for establishing functional segregation as a principle of brain organization. Furthermore, modularity plays a crucial role when trying to characterize distributed brain responses in terms of functional integration or coupling among brain areas. We consider additive factors logic and how it helped to shape the design and interpretation of studies at the inception of brain mapping, with a special focus on factorial designs. We look at factorial designs in activation experiments and in the context of lesion–deficit mapping. In both cases, the presence or absence of interactions among various experimental factors has proven essential in understanding the context-sensitive nature of distributed but modular processing and discerning the nature of (potentially degenerate) structure–function relationships in cognitive neuroscience.

Keywords: Additive factors; Modularity; Factorial; Connectivity; Degeneracy.

This review is essentially a narrative about how some of the fundaments of experimental design and interpretation of human brain mapping studies have developed over the past two decades. Its focus is on the role of modularity and additive factors logic in guiding these developments. This is a somewhat self-referential account, which allows us to describe how our earlier misconceptions gave way to more enduring perspectives— perspectives that help guide our current research into structure–function relationships in the brain.

This review comprises four sections. The first considers, briefly, the rationale for modularity and its place within distributed neuronal processing architectures. We consider evolutionary imperatives for modularity and then a slightly more abstract treatment that underpins the analysis of functional and effective connectivity. The second section is a short historical perspective that covers the rise and fall of cognitive subtraction and the emergence of factorial designs in neuroimaging. Our focus here is on the role of additive factors logic and the connection to conjunction analyses in neuroimaging. The third section pursues the importance of interactions in factorial designs—specifically, their role in disclosing context-sensitive interactions or coupling among modular brain areas. We illustrate this using the notion of dynamic diaschisis and psychophysiological interactions. The final section turns to

Correspondence should be addressed to Karl J. Friston, The Wellcome Trust Centre for Neuroimaging, Institute of Neurology, Queen Square, London WC1N 3BG, UK. (E-mail: k.friston@fil.ion.ucl.ac.uk).

This work was funded by the Wellcome Trust. We would like to thank Marcia Bennett for help preparing this manuscript.

http://www.psypress.com/cogneuropsychology   http://dx.doi.org/10.1080/02643294.2011.558835

lesion–deficit mapping and neuropsychology (in the sense of using lesions to infer functional architectures). Here, we review the concept of necessary and sufficient brain systems for a given task and how these led to the appreciation of degenerate structure–function mappings. Additive factors logic again plays a key role but, in this instance, the combination rule (Sternberg, 2011 this issue) becomes probabilistic and acquires a multiplicative aspect. We rehearse the importance of degenerate mappings in the context of multilesion–deficit analysis and conclude with some comments on the role of cognitive ontologies in making the most of neuroimaging data.

In defence of modularity

Most neurobiologists who are sensitive to the distributed and self-organized nature of neuronal dynamics tend to distance themselves from functionalist accounts of modularity. However, there is a growing appreciation of the importance of modularity in network theory (e.g., Bullmore & Sporns, 2009; He & Evans, 2010; Valencia et al., 2009) and the study of complex systems in general. The importance of modularity is usually cast in terms of robustness and evolvability in an evolutionary setting (e.g., Calabretta, 2007; Redies & Puelles, 2001). At first glance, robustness might appear to limit the evolvability of biological networks, because it reduces the number of genetic variations that are expressed phenotypically (and upon which natural selection can act; Sporns, 2010). However, neutral mutations, which are expressed in a phenotypically neutral way, can promote evolution by creating systems that are genetically varied but function equally well (i.e., degenerate, many-to-one mappings between genotype and functional phenotype). In brief, "robustness implies that many mutations are neutral and such neutrality fosters innovation" (Wagner, 2005 p. 1773). Both robustness and evolvability are enhanced by the modular organization of biological systems—from gene and protein networks to complex processes in development (e.g., Duffau, 2006). The dissociability or decomposability afforded by modularity is

characteristic of the brain's small world connectivity architecture, a feature that has received increasing empirical support from analyses of anatomical and functional connectivity (Bullmore & Sporns, 2009). In short, modularity may be an emergent characteristic of any biological network that has been optimized by selective pressure (irrespective of the particular constraints on adaptive fitness). Interestingly, these arguments about modularity have emerged in a field one might least expect—namely, network theory.

The role of network theory (and graph theory) is also central to the way that imaging neuroscience tries to assess functional brain architectures. In brief, the brain appears to adhere to two principles of organization: functional segregation and integration. Functional segregation refers to the specialization of brain regions for a particular cognitive or sensorimotor function, where that function is anatomically segregated within a cortical area or system. Functional integration refers to the coupling and interactions (message passing) among these areas (Friston, Frith, Liddle, & Frackowiak, 1993). The mathematical description of networks like the brain often appeals to graph theory, where the interactions among regions (nodes) are encoded by connections (edges). These connections imply a conditional dependency between the (usually hidden) states of each region. In the brain, these hidden states correspond to population or ensemble neuronal activity performing computations. The key point here is that, to understand the network, one has to identify where there are no connections. This may sound paradoxical but emphasizes the importance of conditional independencies. Conditional independence means that knowing the activity of one area tells you nothing about the activity of a second area, given the activity in all other areas. If this can be shown statistically, one can infer the absence of a connection between the two areas in question. This absence endows the graph with a sparsity structure and a specific sort of architecture. The very existence of conditional independencies induces modularity and becomes the ultimate aim of network and effective connectivity analyses in neuroimaging.

The importance of conditional independence is reflected in the first sentence of Sternberg (2011 this issue): "The first step in one approach to understanding a complex process is to attempt to divide into modules; parts that are independent in some sense." Mathematically, this "sense" is a conditional independence.

A key example of a connectivity analysis is dynamic causal modelling (DCM), in which one is trying to explain observed neuronal responses in terms of an underlying Bayesian dependency graph (Friston, Harrison, & Penny, 2003). In DCM, the dependencies are modelled in terms of the effective connectivity between hidden neuronal states in each brain area. Model selection is then used to identify the architecture that best explains the systems response, using Bayesian model selection. The very fact that one characterizes distributed responses in terms of a set of connected regions (nodes) speaks to the implicit modularity of processing within each node. See Figure 1 (and Seghier & Price, 2010) for an example of dynamic causal modelling in addressing the modular but distributed architectures underlying reading and object naming. It should be noted, however, that the dependencies can themselves be context sensitive. In other words, being modular does not mean responding to the same inputs in the same way all the time. Understanding this context sensitivity is one of the most important aspects of network and causal modelling, especially in cognitive

Connectivity through the putamen is modulated by reading more than naming

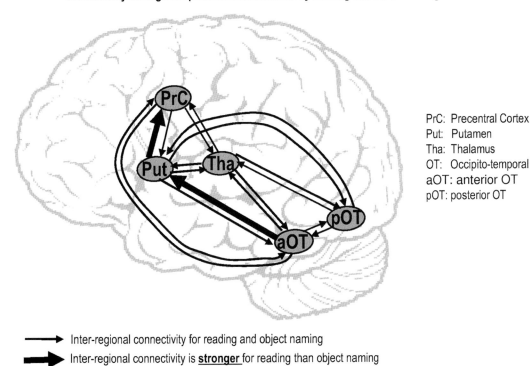

PrC: Precentral Cortex
Put: Putamen
Tha: Thalamus
OT: Occipito-temporal
aOT: anterior OT
pOT: posterior OT

→ Inter-regional connectivity for reading and object naming

➤ Inter-regional connectivity is **stronger** for reading than object naming

Figure 1. *An example of how dynamic causal modelling (DCM) can address modular and distributed architectures. This DCM includes five regions that are commonly activated during reading and picture naming. The results of the DCM analysis show that the connection from visual recognition areas (pOT/aOT) to articulatory areas (PrC), via the putamen, is stronger for reading than for object naming (Seghier & Price, 2010).*

neuroimaging (cf. McIntosh, 2004). We return to this later but first consider how the key regions (nodes) in casual modelling are identified in the first place.

Additive factors logic and context sensitivity

Prior to the inception of modern brain mapping, the principle of functional segregation was a hypothesis, based upon decades of careful electrophysiological and anatomical research (Zeki & Shipp, 1988). Within months of the introduction of whole-brain activation studies, the selective activation of functionally segregated brain areas was evident, and the hypothesis became a principle (e.g., Zeki et al., 1991). It is interesting to look back at how these activation maps were obtained experimentally: Most early brain mapping studies used an elaboration of Donder's subtractive method (e.g., Petersen, Fox, Posner, Mintun, & Raichle, 1988). Put simply, this entailed adding a process to a task and subtracting the evoked brain activity to reveal the activation due to the extra processing. Our first misconception was that one could associate the brain activation with the added process.

This interpretation of an activation rests upon the assumption of *pure insertion*—namely, that the extra process can be inserted purely without changing existing processes or eliciting new processes (or processing). The pure insertion assumption is very similar to the additivity assumption in the combination of factors in the additive factors method (Sternberg, 2011, this issue). In other words, it is necessary to exclude interactions between the old and new task factors before associating any brain activation with the new task component. To address this empirically, one needs a factorial design in which one can test for the interactions (Friston et al., 1996). The adoption of factorial designs—and the ability to assess interactions in neuroimaging experiments—was incredibly important and allowed people to examine the context-sensitive nature of the activations, in the sense of quantifying the dependency of the activation due to one factor on that of another. Factorial designs are now the mainstay

of experimental design in neuroimaging. Certainly, in our unit, it has been nearly a decade since we have used a design that had fewer than two factors. Indeed, at the time of writing, a search on PubMed.gov for "interaction AND brain AND (fMRI OR PET)" yielded 1,854 results, while a search for "subtraction AND brain AND (fMRI OR PET)" gave only 1,615. Figure 2a shows a simple example of a factorial design and a test for a regionally specific interaction, again focusing on the processes underlying reading and object naming.

Cognitive subtraction and process decomposition

As described carefully by Sternberg (2011, this issue), there is a key distinction between cognitive subtraction and process decomposition. In cognitive subtraction, one changes the task in a qualitative way to induce a new putative processing component. Conversely, in process decomposition, the task remains the same but the stimuli or context is changed in a multifactorial way. This circumvents the assumption of pure insertion, while affording the opportunity to test for interactions. As noted in Sternberg (2011 this issue) "with a composite measure factorial experiments are essential, to assess how the effects of the factors combine". Neuronal responses are, by their nature, composite, in the sense that they reflect the processing of multiple processing elements. Figure 2b provides an example of a factorial design where stimulus factors were varied parametrically to reveal an interaction or dependency between name frequency and stimulus modality (pictures or written names). Much of the additive factors method rests upon excluding an interaction to make inferences about the decomposition of the underlying processes: If two processes do not interact, they can be decomposed functionally. Exactly the same logic underpins cognitive conjunctions in neuroimaging (Price & Friston, 1997). In cognitive conjunction analyses, one tests for colocalized activation attributable to two or more factors *in the absence of an interaction*. Figure 2 provides a simple example of this

(a) **A simple 2x2 Factorial design.**

Factor 1: Task   **Factor 2: Stimuli**

Pictures   Written names

	Pictures	Written names
Naming :	**A**	**B**
Categorisation :	**C**	**D**

Main effect of task: [A+B] > [C+D]
Main effect of stimulus: [A+C] > [B+D]
Interaction of task & stimulus: [A-C] > [B-D]
Cognitive conjunction: [A-C] = [B-D]

(b) **Regionally specific effects.**

Interaction: [A-C] > [B-D]

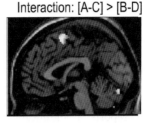

Conjunction: [A-C]=[B-D]

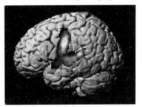

(c) **A factorial parametric design**

Factor 1:
Word frequency

Factor 2: Stimuli
Pictures   Written names

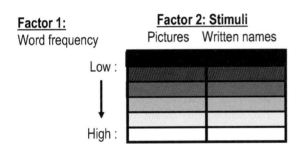

Low :

High :

(d) **Interaction showing the effect of frequency varies for picture naming and reading**

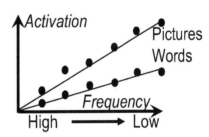

Figure 2. *Factorial designs in brain activation experiments. (a) An example of a simple factorial design that uses the interaction to identify regions where differences between naming and semantic categorization are greater for pictures of objects than for their written names. (b) Regions identified by the interaction and conjunction (unpublished data). (c) An example of a factorial parametric design that uses the interaction to identify regions where the effect of a parametric factor (e.g., word frequency) is stronger for naming than for reading. (d) Hypothetical data illustrating an interaction. To view a colour version of this figure, please see the online issue of the Journal.*

method, which has become popular—with 195 PubMed.gov results for (cognitive AND conjunction) AND (fMRI OR PET OR neuroimaging). However, in the context of brain mapping, interactions can be extremely informative about neuronal processing and are usually used to infer the integration of inputs from two or more modules (brain regions). This can be essential in understanding the coupling among brain regions and

the nature of hierarchical and recursive message passing among and within levels of sensory processing hierarchies. We pursue this theme in the context of changes in coupling below.

Context-sensitive coupling

In the same way that factorial designs disclose interactions in terms of regional processing, they can also inform the context-sensitive nature of coupling between brain areas. Interactions simply mean a difference in a difference (e.g., how a response to one factor depends upon the response to another). If we replace one (psychological) factor with the (physiological) activity in a seed or reference brain area, then the ensuing interaction becomes a psychophysiological interaction (PPI; Friston et al., 1997). Roughly speaking, this PPI reports a significant change in the (linear) influence of the seed region on any significant target region, with different levels of the psychological factor. Although a simple analysis, this has been exploited in a large number of neuroimaging studies to look at how coupling between brain areas can change with brain state or set—with 222 PubMed.gov results for (psychophysiological interaction OR PPI) AND (fMRI OR PET OR imaging). The notion that connectivity (and implicit modularity) is itself state and activity dependent is crucial for understanding the dynamic repertoire of real brain networks. Furthermore, it reiterates the importance of thinking about modular function in a context-sensitive way.

This becomes important in a pragmatic sense when one tries to understand the remote effect of brain lesions on brain activity and responses. This is usually referred to in terms of diaschisis (from Greek, meaning "shocked throughout"). A particular form of diaschisis can emerge when the remote effect of a lesion is itself context dependent—in other words, where there is an abnormality of evoked responses, due to a remote lesion that is revealed in, and only in, some specific tasks or brain states. This has been referred to as "dynamic diaschisis" (Price, Warburton, Moore, Frackowiak, & Friston, 2001) and underscores the subtleties in understanding highly context-dependent and nonlinear exchanges between modular brain regions. An example of dynamic diaschisis is shown in Figure 3. In the final section, we pursue the effect of brain lesions on evoked responses and look more closely at the notion of modularity and segregation, in the context of structure–function relationships.

Modularity, structure, and function

For many people, the goal of neuroimaging is to understand the functional architecture of the brain in relation to particular tasks or cognitive processing. This understanding entails knowledge of the mapping between the brain's structure and its function. An important complement to brain activation studies are lesion–deficit studies. Here brain imaging is used to define a regionally specific brain insult, and its implicit functional specialization is inferred from the associated behavioural deficit. Many people in neuroimaging have noted the importance of the complimentary contributions of functional and structural imaging. For example, identifying a regionally specific lesion, in the context of a behavioural deficit, suggests that this region was necessary for performance. Initially, it was hoped that a combination of lesion–deficit mapping and functional activation studies would identify necessary and sufficient brain regions for a particular task or process (Price, Mummery, Moore, Frackowiak, & Friston, 1999). However, this ambition quickly turned out to be misguided: This is because it overlooked the ubiquitous many-to-one (degenerate) mapping between structure and function in biological networks (Edelman & Gally, 2001). Put simply, this means that two or more areas could fulfil the same task requirements. Extending this notion to high-order combinatorics means that there may be no necessary brain area for any particular process and therefore no "necessary and sufficient brain area". This was a fundamental insight, which mandated a revision of (our) approaches to lesion–deficit mapping and activation studies (Price & Friston, 2002).

Crucially, the possibility of degenerate structure–function mappings brings us back to factorial designs and additive factors logic. One can see this simply by considering the difference between two structure–function relationships: In the first mapping, processing is distributed over two regions (nodes). This means that damage to the first or the second will produce a deficit. Now consider the degenerate case, where either

Left subcortical regions including left putamen (PUT) are activated in healthy subjects during our 4 conditions (A,B,C,D) but not in patient with left PUT damage

White: normal subcortical activation
(projected on the patient's brain)

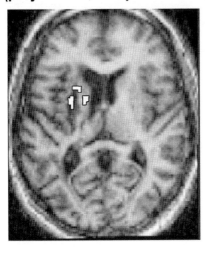

Relative activation in left PUT
(damaged in patient)

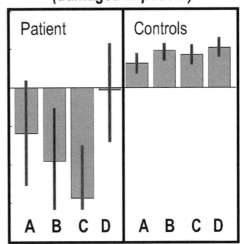

Dynamic Diaschisis
Left PUT damage lowers PrC activation during successful reading (B) but not during successful naming (A)

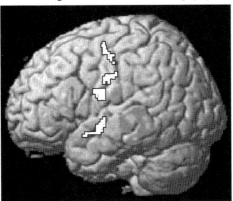

Relative activation in left PrC
(undamaged in patient)

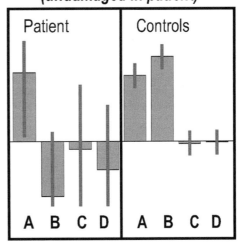

Figure 3. *An example of dynamic diaschisis (unpublished data). Following a lesion to the left putamen (see Figure 1), activation in the left precentral cortex (PrC in Figure 1) is abnormally low during successful reading but normally activated during successful object naming. This is consistent with the dynamic causal modelling (DCM) results reported in Figure 1 and suggests that PrC activation is driven by left putamen activation during reading but not naming. See Figure 2a for details of Conditions A, B, C, and D. To view a colour version of this figure, please see the online issue of the Journal.*

Degeneracy predicts:
Effect of lesion to X
depends on
presence or absence
of lesion to Y

Area X =
Putamen & insula:

(lesion = dark at
cross hairs)

Area Y=
Parietal white matter

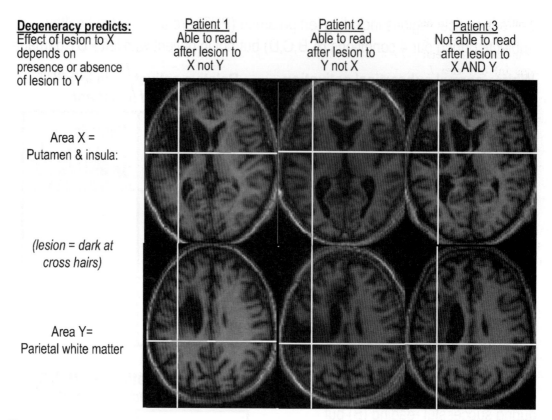

Patient 1
Able to read
after lesion to
X not Y

Patient 2
Able to read
after lesion to
Y not X

Patient 3
Not able to read
after lesion to
X AND Y

Figure 4. *An example of degeneracy. Reading is impaired following lesions that damage the left putamen, left insula, and left parietal cortex inclusively (Patient 3). However, damage to only one of these regions does not impair reading (Patients 1 and 2). The results suggest that reading can be supported either by a pathway that involves the parietal cortex or by a pathway that involves the putamen/insula. When one pathway is damaged, the other pathway can support reading. When both pathways are damaged, reading is impaired. This previously unpublished result is consistent with a study of reading aloud in healthy subjects (Seghier, Lee, Schofield, Ellis, & Price, 2008) that showed an inverse relationship (across participants) between activation in the left putamen and parietal cortex. Together, the results from patient studies (above) and healthy subjects (Seghier et al., 2008) suggest that the putamen and parietal cortex are components of different reading pathways and that either one or the other is needed for successful reading.*

node can support the function. Here, only a lesion to the first *and* second area will cause a deficit. If we assume that the deficit is a pure measure of the assumed process in question, then we have two fundamentally different (multiplicative) combination rules within additive factors logic. In the first situation (deficit following lesions to first or second area), the probability of a deficit $p(D|L)$ is equal to one minus the probability that they are both undamaged, which is the product of the probability that neither are lesioned.

$$p(D|L)=1-[1-p(L_1=1)][1-p(L_2=1)] \quad (1a)$$

Conversely, under the degenerate mapping, the probability of a deficit becomes the probability of a lesion in either area, leading to a very different combination rule:

$$p(D|L) = p(L_1 = 1)p(L_2 = 1) \quad (1b)$$

Crucially, in order to disambiguate between these two scenarios we need a factorial design, in which we can lesion (or obtain access to patients with lesions in) one area $L_1 = 1$ and the other area $L_2 = 1$. In short, we need a multilesion analysis. This provides an important and principled motivation for studying patients with different brain lesions (and has implications for traditional single-case studies in neuropsychology). Figure 4 shows an example of degeneracy inferred using this Boolean logic associated with degenerate structure–function mappings. Interestingly, a classical one-to-one structure–function mapping implies that $p(D_i|L) = p(L_i = 1) \Rightarrow p(D_i|L) = p(D_i|L_i)$, which means the deficit is conditionally independent of lesion $L_k \in \{0, 1\} : \forall k \neq i$ in all other areas.

There are many interesting issues that attend the analysis of multilesions studies. However, we close by noting that a truly inclusive approach to modularity and structure–function mappings in the human brain will account for both lesion–deficit data and functional activation studies. In short, our empirical and conceptual models of brain architecture have to explain both evoked responses due to experimental manipulations in activation studies and the behavioural deficits elicited by selective lesions. Clearly, these models entail a precise specification of the mapping between neuronal activity and cognitive function. This mapping is itself a holy grail of cognitive neuroscience, which has been referred to as a cognitive ontology (Poldrack, 2006; Price & Friston, 2005). Indeed, cognitive ontologies are now becoming a major focus of the brain imaging and cognitive neuroscience community, particularly with the advent of new neuroinformatics tools (Poldrack, Halchenko, & Hanson, 2009). One can see how the combination of data from different modalities and different patients acquires a principled motivation from the arguments above.

In conclusion, the arguments and developments discussed in this review rest explicitly on the notion of modular but coupled brain regions and the additive factors method (with linear or nonlinear combination rules), introduced by Sternberg (2011 this issue).

REFERENCES

Bullmore, E., & Sporns, O. (2009). Complex brain networks: Graph theoretical analysis of structural and functional systems. *Nature Reviews. Neuroscience*, *10*(3), 186–198.

Calabretta, R. (2007). Genetic interference reduces the evolvability of modular and non-modular visual neural networks. *Philosophical Transactions of the Royal Society of London. Series B, Biological Sciences*, *362*(1479), 403–410.

Duffau, H. (2006). Brain plasticity: From pathophysiological mechanisms to therapeutic applications. *Journal of Clinical Neuroscience*, *13*(9), 885–897.

Edelman, G. M., & Gally, J. A. (2001). Degeneracy and complexity in biological systems. *Proceedings of the National Academy of Sciences, USA*, *98*(24), 13763–13768.

Friston, K. J., Büchel, C., Fink, G. R., Morris, J., Rolls, E., & Dolan, R. J. (1997). Psychophysiological and modulatory interactions in neuroimaging. *NeuroImage*, *6*(3), 218–229.

Friston, K. J., Frith, C. D., Liddle, P. F., & Frackowiak, R. S. (1993). Functional connectivity: The principal-component analysis of large (PET) data sets. *Journal of Cerebral Blood Flow and Metabolism*, *13*(1), 5–14.

Friston, K. J., Harrison, L., & Penny, W. (2003). Dynamic causal modelling. *NeuroImage*, *19*(4), 1273–1302.

Friston, K. J., Price, C. J., Fletcher, P., Moore, C., Frackowiak, R. S., & Dolan, R. J. (1996). The trouble with cognitive subtraction. *NeuroImage*, *4*(2), 97–104.

He, Y., & Evans, A. (2010). Graph theoretical modeling of brain connectivity. *Current Opinion in Neurology*, *23*(4), 341–350.

McIntosh, A. R. (2004). Contexts and catalysts: A resolution of the localization and integration of function in the brain. *Neuroinformatics*, *2*(2), 175–182.

Petersen, S. E., Fox, P. T., Posner, M. I., Mintun, M., & Raichle, M. E. (1988). Positron emission tomographic studies of the cortical anatomy of single-word processing. *Nature*, *331*(6157), 585–589.

Poldrack, R. A. (2006). Can cognitive processes be inferred from neuroimaging data? *Trends in Cognitive Sciences*, *10*(2), 59–63.

Poldrack, R. A., Halchenko, Y. O., & Hanson, S. J. (2009). Decoding the large-scale structure of brain function by classifying mental states across individuals. *Psychology Science*, *20*(11), 1364–1372.

Price, C. J., & Friston, K. J. (1997). Cognitive conjunction: A new approach to brain activation experiments. *NeuroImage, 5*(4, Pt. 1), 261–270.

Price, C. J., & Friston, K. J. (2002). Degeneracy and cognitive anatomy. *Trends in Cognitive Sciences, 6*(10), 416–421.

Price, C. J., & Friston, K. J. (2005). Functional ontologies for cognition: The systematic definition of structure and function. *Cognitive Neuropsychology, 22,* 262–275.

Price, C. J., Mummery, C. J., Moore, C. J., Frackowiak, R. S., & Friston, K. J. (1999). Delineating necessary and sufficient neural systems with functional imaging studies of neuropsychological patients. *Journal of Cognitive Neuroscience, 11*(4), 371–382.

Price, C. J., Warburton, E. A., Moore, C. J., Frackowiak, R. S., & Friston, K. J. (2001). Dynamic diaschisis: Anatomically remote and context-sensitive human brain lesions. *Journal of Cognitive Neuroscience, 13*(4), 419–429.

Redies, C., & Puelles, L. (2001). Modularity in vertebrate brain development and evolution. *Bioessays, 23*(12), 1100–1111.

Seghier, M. L., Lee, H. L., Schofield, T., Ellis, C. L., & Price, C. J. (2008). Inter-subject variability in the use of two different neuronal networks for reading aloud familiar words. *NeuroImage, 42*(3), 1226–1236.

Seghier, M. L., & Price, C. J. (2010). Reading boosts connectivity through the putamen. *Cerebral Cortex, 20*(3), 570–582.

Sporns, O. (2010). *Networks of the brain.* Cambridge, MA: MIT Press.

Sternberg, S. (2011). Modular processes in mind and brain. *Cognitive Neuropsychology, 28,* 156–208.

Valencia, M., Pastor, M. A., Fernández-Seara, M. A., Artieda, J., Martinerie, J., & Chavez, M. (2009). Complex modular structure of large-scale brain networks. *Chaos, 19*(2), 023119. doi: 10.1063/1.3129783

Wagner, A. (2005). Robustness, evolvability and neutrality. *FEBS Letters, 579,* 1772–1778.

Zeki, S., & Shipp, S. (1988). The functional logic of cortical connections. *Nature, 335*(6188), 311–317.

Zeki, S., Watson, J. D., Lueck, C. J., Friston, K. J., Kennard, C., & Frackowiak, R. S. (1991). A direct demonstration of functional specialization in human visual cortex. *Journal of Neuroscience, 11*(3), 641–649.

COGNITIVE NEUROPSYCHOLOGY, 2011, 28 (3 & 4), 251–275

Complementary neural representations for faces and words: A computational exploration

David C. Plaut and Marlene Behrmann

Department of Psychology, Carnegie Mellon University, Pittsburgh, PA, USA

A key issue that continues to generate controversy concerns the nature of the psychological, computational, and neural mechanisms that support the visual recognition of objects such as faces and words. While some researchers claim that visual recognition is accomplished by category-specific modules dedicated to processing distinct object classes, other researchers have argued for a more distributed system with only partially specialized cortical regions. Considerable evidence from both functional neuroimaging and neuropsychology would seem to favour the modular view, and yet close examination of those data reveals rather graded patterns of specialization that support a more distributed account. This paper explores a theoretical middle ground in which the functional specialization of brain regions arises from general principles and constraints on neural representation and learning that operate throughout cortex but that nonetheless have distinct implications for different classes of stimuli. The account is supported by a computational simulation, in the form of an artificial neural network, that illustrates how cooperative and competitive interactions in the formation of neural representations for faces and words account for both their shared and distinctive properties. We set out a series of empirical predictions, which are also examined, and consider the further implications of this account.

Keywords: Prosopagnosia; Alexia; Neural substrate.

Two opposing theoretical perspectives have been offered to explain the manner by which biological structures, such as the ventral visual cortical regions, come to be functionally optimized for visual object recognition. The first approach argues that there are distinct cortical modules or subsystems, which mediate particular behavioural processes, such as face, word, and object recognition, in a domain-specific manner (for recent reviews, see Kanwisher, 2010; McKone & Robbins, 2011).[1] Consistent

---

Correspondence should be addressed to David C. Plaut, Department of Psychology, Carnegie Mellon University, Pittsburgh, PA 15213–3890, USA. (E-mail: plaut@cmu.edu).

This work was funded by National Science Foundation (NSF) Grant BCS0923763 to Behrmann and Plaut and by NSF Grant SBE-0542013 to the Temporal Dynamics of Learning Center, an NSF Science of Learning Center. We thank Jennifer Brace for her work in creating the stimuli used in the reported simulation.

---

[1] We use the terms "module" and "modular" not in the strict senses in which Fodor (1983) defined them, but to denote a general class of theoretical commitments in which domain-specific cognitive processes, such as face recognition, are each carried out by a neuroanatomically identifiable cortical area, such as the FFA. To the extent that multiple cortical areas are involved in a given cognitive process, it would mitigate against a modular account of that process but might still be consistent with modular accounts of localized subprocesses.

---

http://www.psypress.com/cogneuropsychology

http://dx.doi.org/10.1080/02643294.2011.609812

with this approach is the finding that different regions in extrastriate visual cortex respond selectively to domain-specific categories of visual stimuli: Many recent functional neuroimaging studies have shown, for example, that the fusiform face area (FFA) is activated in response to faces (e.g., Kanwisher, McDermott, & Chun, 1997; Puce, Allison, Gore, & McCarthy, 1995), the parahippocampal place area (PPA) to scenes (e.g., Epstein, Harris, Stanley, & Kanwisher, 1999; Epstein & Kanwisher, 1998; Sewards, 2011), the extrastriate body area (EBA) and fusiform body area (FBA) to human bodies and body parts (e.g., Downing, Jiang, Shuman, & Kanwisher, 2001; Peelen & Downing, 2005; Schwarzlose, Baker, & Kanwisher, 2005; Taylor, Wiggett, & Downing, 2010; Willems, Peelen, & Hagoort, 2010), and the visual word form area to orthographic inputs (e.g., Dehaene & Cohen, 2011). Indeed, in each of these regions, the cortical response for the preferred category is about twice that for the nonpreferred category, and this category selectivity can be consistently observed in most normal individuals, even across a range of very different experimental paradigms. All of this attests to the robustness of the evidence that these regions are specialized for, and perhaps even dedicated to, the recognition of particular object classes (Kanwisher, 2010; McKone & Robbins, 2011).

The second approach recognizes the apparent selectivity of neural systems for certain visual classes but argues that this selectivity need not implicate very specialized or dedicated modules per se. This theoretical account entails one or both of two possible brain–behaviour organizations: rather than a single region alone subserving processing of a particular input type (e.g., faces), multiple regions mediate the recognition of a particular object type, and/or an individual region mediates the neural representations of multiple object types. The claim, then, is that, under either of these scenarios, specialization is more graded, and regions may be optimized for, but not necessarily dedicated to, a particular cognitive function. Consistent with this alternative perspective, in addition to the FFA, multiple other cortical regions evince face selectivity, including the

occipital face area (OFA; Gauthier et al., 2000), the posterior superior temporal sulcus (Hoffman & Haxby, 2000), and the anterior temporal lobe (Kriegeskorte, Formisano, Sorge, & Goebel, 2007; Rajimehr, Young, & Tootell, 2009), and, indeed, multiple regions have sufficient neural information to discriminate between individual face exemplars (Nestor, Plaut, & Behrmann, 2011; for more extended review, see Avidan & Behrmann, 2009; Haxby, Petit, Ungerleider, & Courtney, 2000; Ishai, 2008). Furthermore, it is not simply that the distributed network is domain-specific as there are now many functional magnetic resonance imaging (fMRI) studies showing that even highly selective single regions, such as the FFA, evince a blood-oxygen-level-dependent (BOLD) response to different object classes, albeit with lesser degrees of activation than, for example, to faces (e.g., Grill-Spector, Sayres, & Ress, 2006; Hanson & Schmidt, 2011; Haxby et al., 2001; Haxby et al., 2000; Ishai, Schmidt, & Boesiger, 2005; Nestor et al., 2011; Norman, Polyn, Detre, & Haxby, 2006), and the same is true for the visual word form area (VWFA; Nestor, Behrmann, & Plaut, 2011; Price & Devlin, 2011).

In this paper, we compare and contrast the more modular and more distributed accounts with specific reference to two visual classes—faces and words. We choose these two classes not only because, intuitively, they appear to be diametrically opposed but also because they differ obviously along many other dimensions. Words and faces share little in common in their overt geometry, and so their image statistics share minimal, if any, overlap. Additionally, whereas face representations are acquired naturally over the course of experience, word recognition typically requires explicit instruction. Also, whereas faces are probably the most ecologically relevant visual stimuli, orthographies have only been around for a few thousand years, and so the evolutionary trajectories of these two visual classes differ greatly.

We start by reviewing the clear evidence for the separability of the underlying systems for words and faces. Thereafter, we present a proposal in which we argue that common principles may account for both the similarities and differences in the mechanisms underlying words and faces. We support this proposal with a computational simulation in which a common underlying mechanism, constrained by a putative set of computational principles, mediates both face and word recognition and demonstrates the types of functional specialization observed empirically. Although we address the correspondences between brain and behaviour in these two particular domains, the argument has applicability to other aspects of cognition and its neural correlates, as well, provided that these other cognitive behaviours place the same computational demands on the visual recognition system. We also return to this point in the final discussion.

Evidence for separability of word and face processing systems

On a modular account of brain–behaviour organization, words and faces engage separate psychological and neural mechanisms and are, essentially, unrelated and independent. Support for this view is substantial and is gleaned from functional imaging investigations, as well as from neuropsychological studies (Kleinschmidt & Cohen, 2006).

The visual word form area
Numerous functional imaging studies have demonstrated that the word module or "visual word form area" (VWFA; e.g., Cohen et al., 2000; Cohen et al., 2003; Dehaene & Cohen, 2011; Dehaene, Cohen, Sigman, & Vinckier, 2005) responds selectively to visually presented words and letter strings (e.g., Fiez, Balota, Raichle, & Petersen, 1999; Mechelli, Gorno-Tempini, & Price, 2003; Petersen & Fiez, 1993; Petersen, Fox, Snyder, & Raichle, 1990; Turkeltaub, Eden, Jones, & Zeffiro, 2002) to a greater degree than to digits (Polk et al., 2002) or pseudoletters (Allison, McCarthy, Nobre, Puce, & Belger, 1994; Cohen & Dehaene, 2004), but not to spoken words (Cohen & Dehaene, 2004). The VWFA activation is located in left extrastriate cortex (Talairach

coordinates: $x = -43$, $y = -54$, $z = -12$), is identifiable in single subjects (Puce, Allison, Asgari, Gore, & McCarthy, 1996), and is sensitive to the individual's experience—Hebrew readers show greater activation of this region for Hebrew than for English words and vice versa (Baker et al., 2007), and activation in this area is correlated with literacy (Dehaene & Cohen, 2007, 2011; Dehaene et al., 2010). The VWFA is situated anterior to retinotopic cortex, and, consistent with this, activation is relatively insensitive to retinal position and to the font, size, or case of the input (Polk & Farah, 2002). Activation of VWFA, as measured by event-related potentials (ERPs), is rapid, emerging around 150–200 ms after stimulus onset (McCandliss, Cohen, & Dehaene, 2003). In normal readers, the minimal increase in reaction time (RT) as a function of word length (Lavidor, Ellis, Shillcock, & Bland, 2001; Weekes, 1997) is attributed to the parallel processing of multiple letters (to the limits of foveal acuity, i.e., around 9 letters), and this parallel processing is ascribed to the functionality of the VWFA.

Further support for the circumscribed functionality of the VWFA comes from studies of premorbidly literate individuals with "pure alexia" (for review of cases, see Montant & Behrmann, 2000; Starrfelt & Behrmann, 2011). The lesion site in these cases is typically in the left occipitotemporal area along the fusiform and adjacent lingual gyrus, with possible incursion to the inferior longitudinal fasciculus (Cohen, Henry et al., 2004; Cohen et al., 2003; Feinberg, Schindler, Ochoa, Kwan, & Farah, 1994; Salvan et al., 2004) and overlaps the region of the VWFA activation reported above (Hasson, Levy, Behrmann, Hendler, & Malach, 2002; Petersen et al., 1990; Puce et al., 1996). The characteristic profile of pure alexia is a linear increase in RT as a function of the number of letters in the input (giving rise to the label "letter-by-letter reading"), and this is assumed to reflect the breakdown of parallel processing in the VWFA and the subsequent reliance on a serial, laborious left–right letter spelling strategy (McCandliss et al., 2003; Warrington & Shallice, 1980). The patients are not aphasic, typically showing intact production and comprehension of spoken language along with normal writing, all of which supports the circumscribed nature of the problem as a specific difficulty in processing visual word forms (but see Starrfelt & Behrmann, 2011, for discussion of high association with an impairment of number processing as well).

The fusiform face area

Just as in the case of the VWFA, there is substantial evidence for face-processing specificity gleaned from fMRI studies and from patient studies. Functional imaging studies have provided evidence that the region that is functionally specialized for faces, the "fusiform face area" (FFA; $x = 40, y = -55, z = -10$), is selectively activated by faces, especially upright faces, over other nonface objects (Kanwisher, 2010; Puce et al., 1995; Yovel & Kanwisher, 2005) and over animal or cartoon faces (e.g., Kanwisher, 2000; Kanwisher, McDermott, et al., 1997; Kanwisher, Woods, Iacoboni, & Mazziotta, 1997; Sergent, Ohta, & MacDonald, 1992; Spiridon, Fischl, & Kanwisher, 2006), and the magnitude of the activation is correlated with face identification ability (Furl, Garrido, Dolan, Driver, & Duchaine, 2010; Yovel, Tambini, & Brandman, 2008). FFA activation is situated anterior to retinotopic cortex, and, consistent with this, activation is relatively insensitive to retinal position and to size, colour, format (drawing or photographs), and viewpoint of input. The FFA is selectively activated for faces but abuts other cortical regions that are specialized for other visual categories, such as scenes, animals, and tools (e.g., Reddy & Kanwisher, 2006; Spiridon & Kanwisher, 2002; also, Puce et al., 1996; Puce et al., 1995; Tranel, Damasio, & Damasio, 1997).

Correspondingly, lesions to the FFA (Bouvier & Engel, 2006; Damasio, Damasio, & Tranel, 1986; Kleinschmidt & Cohen, 2006) result in prosopagnosia, a selective impairment in face recognition. The lesion in prosopagnosia is often bilateral, affecting the temporo-occipital cortex in the region of the FFA, but unilateral right-hemisphere lesions to this same region may suffice to give rise to this disorder (Barton, 2008; Bouvier & Engel, 2006), and prosopagnosia can also be congenital or developmental in the absence of a frank lesion (Behrmann & Avidan, 2005). The difficulty in recognizing faces can be dramatic, including failures to recognize friends or even close family members. Unlike normal observers, these individuals do not obviously exhibit the advantage for upright over inverted faces (occasionally even showing an inversion superiority effect; Farah, 1996; Farah, Tanaka, & Drain, 1995) and do not appear to process faces configurally, thus failing to evince the benefit from the presence of the whole face over just parts of the face (Barton, 2009; Barton, Cherkasova, Press, Intriligator, & O'Connor, 2004; Busigny & Rossion, 2010; Tanaka & Farah, 1993).

Taken together, these studies provide empirical support for the claim that there is specialized processing of faces and words associated with two distinct cortical modules, the FFA for faces and the VWFA for words, and that these two systems are separable and independent.

Not only differences but also commonalities

Although there is general consensus that the FFA and VWFA are tuned to faces and words, respectively, there are also intriguing empirical data that suggest that both their tuning and their hemispheric specialization is relative or graded. For example, it appears that both the VWFA and FFA can be activated by a wide range of stimuli, not just faces or words: The VWFA is strongly activated in response to chequerboards, pictured objects, and verb naming to pictures (Devlin, Jamison, Gonnerman, & Matthews, 2006; Murtha, Chertkow, Beauregard, & Evans, 1999; Price & Devlin, 2003, 2011) and even to nonvisual inputs such as Braille (Büchel, Price, & Friston, 1998; Reich, Szwed, Cohen, & Amedi, 2011), whereas the FFA is activated by a range of nonface stimuli, such as houses and cars, but also novel objects such as Greebles (Gauthier, Tarr, Anderson, Skudlarski, & Gore, 1999) and chess configurations (Bilalic, Langner, Ulrich, &

Grodd, 2011), although the full extent of the selectivity is still controversial (Gauthier et al., 1999; Grill-Spector et al., 2006; Haxby, 2006). Neither the FFA nor the VWFA, however, appears to be as strongly activated by these other stimuli as is the case when shown the "preferred" input type, reflecting perhaps the graded nature of the underlying representations. Recent imaging studies adopting multivariate methods applied to fMRI data of ventral visual cortex have begun to uncover the co-mingling of patterns of activation associated with different stimulus types (e.g., face and word representations) to an even greater degree than was revealed in earlier studies employing univariate analyses (for an example of a recent study using multivoxel pattern analysis, see Nestor et al., 2011). In these multivariate studies, it is not simply the magnitude of the activation that is crucial but the distribution of the neural information in the patterns of voxel activation.

Also relevant to the similarities across classes is the observation that almost all fMRI and ERP studies show bilateral activation for words and for faces, albeit with differential hemispheric asymmetry and greater scalp potential for the preferred stimulus type in the corresponding hemisphere—words on the left and faces on the right (e.g., see Hasson et al., 2002; Kanwisher, McDermott & Chun, 1997; Kronbichler et al., 2004; Price & Mechelli, 2005; Puce et al., 1996; Sergent et al., 1992; Tagamets, Novick, Chalmers, & Friedman, 2000). Moreover, the peak activation for words in VWFA and for faces in FFA (although coordinates differ a little across different studies) are very comparable in the two hemispheres (for example, Talairach coordinates for peak for words, $x = -43$, $y = -54$, $z = -12$, and for faces, $x = 40$, $y = -55$, $z = -10$). We also note that these coordinates roughly demarcate cortical sites that are anterior to retinotopic cortex but are situated in what would be the anterior extrapolation of the fovea (Hasson et al., 2002; Levy, Hasson, Hendler, & Malach, 2001). The localization of the functional regions in this cortical location is consistent with the invariance of face and word activation over retinal position of the inputs, but also with the fact that reliance on fine-grained visual discrimination is a necessary component of both face and word recognition.

Somewhat surprisingly, there has not been a systematic examination of the word recognition of prosopagnosic individuals and the face recognition of pure alexic individuals. There are some hints, however, that each hemisphere may play a dual, albeit graded, role in both face and word recognition. For example, it has been reported that the face recognition impairment is more severe following bilateral than unilateral lesions (Damasio et al., 1986; Gainotti & Marra, 2011), implicating both hemispheres to some extent, and that transcranial magnetic stimulation (TMS) of the right hemisphere (RH) even impairs reading in patients with left-hemisphere (LH) lesions (Coslett & Monsul, 1994).

Additionally, in a few case studies in which both stimulus classes have been examined, some prosopagnosic individuals show increased word length effects in reading aloud single words: For example, the slope of the reaction time in single word reading was 104 ms and 241 ms per additional letter for prosopagnosic patients S.M. and R.N., respectively, compared with the normal slope of about 10 ms for words 3 through 8 letters in length (Behrmann & Kimchi, 2003). In a complementary fashion, there have only been a few reports of pure alexic individuals who have difficulties with face recognition (also see Farah, 1991, 1992, 1999, for listing of co-occurrences of different forms of agnosia/alexia), although this is not always assessed in these cases. One recent relevant study documents a case with left occipital arteriovenous malformation in whom both pure alexia and prosopagnosia were evident (Liu, Wang, & Yen., 2011). Many studies do report abnormalities in the recognition of non-orthographic stimuli in pure alexia even after a unilateral lesion (Behrmann, Nelson, & Sekuler, 1998; Starrfelt & Behrmann, 2011), and so one might predict a decrement in face recognition in these cases, as well. As evident, closer scrutiny of the existing data, to the extent they are available, suggests that there may be more overlap in face and word processing in the preeminent face (right FFA) and word (left VWFA) regions than originally considered. To account for both the apparent differences and the similarities, we propose an account that differs from the strictly modular or domain-specific view.

An alternative proposal: Common constraints on faces and words

The theoretical proposal outlined in this paper adopts an alternative perspective with respect to the key systems engaged in face and word processing. The central idea is that visual object recognition (e.g., face and word recognition) is supported, not by highly specialized (or dedicated) modules per se, but by a distributed and interactive network of brain regions with similar computations but whose organization is strongly shaped and modified by experience. This view then incorporates both the claim that multiple cortical regions are engaged and that the nodes of this distributed network play a role in representing more than one stimulus type. Importantly, on this view, the functional specialization of brain regions is graded rather than absolute and reflects the consequences of a set of general principles and constraints on neural computation that operate throughout cortex but that nonetheless have distinct implications for different classes of stimuli. Note that, on this account, there is no appeal to prespecified modules, and, rather than claiming de facto sensitivity to different visual classes, the origin and emergence of these graded mechanisms is captured too. The novelty of this approach is not the principles themselves (see both Dehaene & Cohen, 2011, and Price & Devlin, 2011, for similar notions about the VWFA) but their integrated application to derive common consequences for cortical organization and behaviour for words and faces.

This alternative proposal takes as its starting assumptions three general principles of neural computation: that the neural system for face/word recognition is distributed, that knowledge is represented in this system by cooperation and competition between the processing units, and

that the organization of the system is constrained by topographical considerations, pressure for proximity, and the division of labour between the two hemispheres of the brain. We expand on these assumptions here.

Distributed representation and knowledge

We assume that the neural system for visual object recognition consists of a set of hierarchically organized cortical areas, ranging from local retinotopic information in V1 through more global, object-based, and semantic information in anterior temporal cortex (Grill-Spector & Malach, 2004). At each level, the visual stimulus is represented by the activity of a large number of neurons, and each neuron participates in coding a large number of stimuli. Generally, stimuli that are similar with respect to the information coded by a particular region evoke similar (overlapping) patterns of activity. The set of constraints on how activity at one level produces activity at the next level—that is, the knowledge of how features combine to form features at the next level—is encoded by the pattern of synaptic connections and strengths between and within the regions. Learning involves modifying these synapses in a way that alters the representations evoked by visual stimuli—typically in a way that captures the relevant information in the domain better and that supports more effective behavioural outcomes. With extended experience, expertise develops through the refinement, specialization, and elaboration of representations, requiring the recruitment of additional neurons and a larger region of cortex (Quartz & Sejnowski, 1997).

Representational cooperation and competition

As illustrated by artificial neural networks (e.g., McClelland & Rumelhart, 1985), a single pattern of synaptic connections can learn to encode the knowledge needed to represent many stimuli, but its ability to do so depends on the degree to which the relevant knowledge is consistent or systematic (i.e., similar representations at one level correspond to similar representations at another). In general, systematic domains benefit from highly overlapping neural representations that support generalization, whereas unsystematic, unrelated domains require largely nonoverlapping representations to avoid interference. Thus, if a cortical region represents one type of information, it is ill-suited to represent another type of information that requires unrelated knowledge, and so that information must be represented by a different region. On the other hand, effective cognitive processing requires the coordination of multiple levels of representation within a given domain, and often across multiple domains. Of course, representations can cooperate directly only to the extent they are connected—that is, there are synapses between the regions encoding the relevant knowledge of how they are related; otherwise, they must cooperate indirectly through mediating representations. In this way, the neural organization of cognitive processing is strongly constrained by available connectivity (see Mahon & Caramazza, 2011, for a similar argument regarding connectivity serving as an endogenous constraint on topographic organization in the ventral stream).

Topography, proximity, and hemispheric organization

Brain organization must permit sufficient connectivity among neurons to carry out the necessary information processing, but the total axonal volume must fit within the confines of the skull (for similar discussion, see Cowey, 1979). This constraint is severe: If the brain's 10^{11} neurons were placed on a sphere and were fully interconnected with 0.1-mm radius axons, accommodating the axon volume would require a sphere over 20 km in diameter (Nelson & Bower, 1990). If we think of brain organization as the result of a complex optimization process that minimizes "costs" associated with the degree to which various pressures or biases are violated, then clearly there is a strong pressure to keep connectivity as local as possible. Long-distance projections are certainly present in the brain but they are relatively rare and presumably play a sufficiently critical functional role to offset their cost in volume. In fact, the organization of human neocortex as a folded sheet can be understood as a

compromise between the spherical shape that would minimize long-distance axon length and the need for greater cortical area to support highly elaborated representations. The organization into two hemispheres is also relevant here, as interhemispheric connectivity is largely restricted to homologous areas and is thus vastly less dense than connectivity within each hemisphere. Even at a local scale, the volume of connectivity within an area can be minimized by adopting a topographic organization so that related information is represented in as close proximity as possible (Jacobs & Jordan, 1992). This is seen most clearly in the retinotopic organization of early visual areas, given that light falling on adjacent patches of the retina is highly likely to contain related information. Note that the dimensions of this topography are not in the Cartesian (x, y) coordinates that apply naturally to images, but something closer to polar (r, θ) coordinates, where eccentricity (central vs. peripheral) is coded along one axis, and rotational angle is coded along another (e.g., De Yoe et al., 1996; Grill-Spector & Malach, 2004; Sereno et al., 1995; Tootell et al., 1997). The relevant dimensions of similarity for higher level visual areas are, of course, far less well understood, but the local connectivity constraint is no less pertinent (Jacobs, 1997).

Despite these commonalities, the principles rule out using the very same cortical region to represent both faces and words because these stimuli require entirely distinct primitives to be represented as visual objects and typically have distinct consequences for cognition (faces designate individuals, whereas—apart from proper names—words designate objects, actions, properties, typically at a basic rather than individual level). Given the need for written words to interact with aspects of language that are left lateralized in most individuals (Cai, Lavidor, Brysbaert, Paulignan, & Nazir, 2008), it follows from representational competition and cooperation that visual word representations would be predominantly located in the dominant language hemisphere (Price & Devlin, 2011) whereas face representations would be located in the homologous region in the RH. Indeed, some data to support this competition/cooperation come from the observation that, with increasing literacy, there is a decrease in response to faces in the VWFA (Dehaene et al., 2010) and that, in four-year-olds, performance in identifying alphanumeric characters (digits and letters) is correlated with a decrease in left fusiform activity (Cantlon, Pinel, Dehaene, & Pelphrey, 2011). In both of these studies, however, the competition appears to be restricted to the left hemisphere, with the trading relations between faces and words manifesting in the left fusiform region. The hypothesis we propose, however, encompasses both the left and right hemispheres, with the competition and cooperation playing out for words and faces across both sides of cortex.

SIMULATION

To date, the majority of computational work on face recognition has an applied focus with only tangential relevance to the human cognitive and neural system—this includes approaches based on principal components analysis (e.g., Turk & Pentland, 1991), independent components analysis (e.g., Bartlett, Movellan, & Sejnowski, 2002), linear discriminant analysis (e.g., Etemad & Chellappa, 1997), kernel methods (e.g., Bach & Jordan, 2002; Yang, 2002), 3D morphable models (e.g., Blanz & Vetter, 2003), and Bayesian inference (e.g., Moghaddam, Jebara, & Pentland, 2000). Modelling efforts that explicitly address psychological and neuropsychological issues (e.g., Burton, Young, Bruce, Johnston, & Ellis, 1991; Farah, O'Reilly, & Vecera, 1993) have tended to focus on the interaction of higher level knowledge with rather less consideration of low- and intermediate-level visual representation and processing (although see Burton et al., 1999). More recently, Cottrell and colleagues (Dailey & Cottrell, 1999; Dailey, Cottrell, Padgett, & Adolphs, 2002; Hsiao, Shieh, & Cottrell, 2008; Kanan & Cottrell, 2010; Tong, Joyce, & Cottrell, 2008) have extended this work by coupling distributed network modelling with

more realistic assumptions about early visual processing.

A similar situation holds with regard to word recognition. Although some early cognitive and neuropsychological modelling employed hierarchical visual representations of letters and words (McClelland & Rumelhart, 1981; Mozer, 1991; Mozer & Behrmann, 1990), the vast majority of more recent work has emphasized higher level interactions of orthographic, phonological, and semantic knowledge (e.g., Coltheart, Rastle, Perry, Langdon, & Ziegler, 2001; Harm & Seidenberg, 1999, 2004; Perry, Ziegler, & Zorzi, 2007; Plaut, McClelland, Seidenberg, & Patterson, 1996; although see Plaut, 1999). Efforts to model orthographic representations per se (e.g., SOLAR, Davis, 1999; SERIOL, Whitney, 2001) have typically focused more narrowly on letter position effects in orthographic priming. One notable exception is the split-fovea model (Shillcock, Ellison, & Monaghan, 2000), which explicitly considers the representational implications of a divided visual field. Although this specific model runs into some empirical difficulties (see, e.g., Grainger, Granier, Farioli, Van Assche, & van Heuven, 2006), there is no doubt that the cortical representation of words is shaped in important ways by hemispheric organization and specialization (Cai et al., 2008).

Given the apparent lack (to date) of any proposed relationship between face and word processing, it is not surprising that our computational work is the first to address these domains together within a single model. Although the current implementation does not extend to the higher level knowledge involved in face and word recognition, the underlying principles are fully compatible with ongoing modelling work at these higher levels.

Perhaps the least familiar of our computational principles concerns the impact of local connectivity on learning. Thus, as an initial exploration of the impact of topographically constrained learning on cortical organization, we carried out a simulation in which an artificial neural network was trained to take retinotopic visual information as input and to map this via hemisphere-specific intermediate representations (corresponding to left and right occipitotemporal cortex) to recognize faces, words, and—as a commonly used contrasting category—houses. The topographic bias on learning, combined with the demands for high-acuity information for face and word recognition, should lead to these stimuli being represented in intermediate (fusiform) regions near central vision. The need for representational cooperation between words and language-related information, in conjunction with representational competition between faces and words (given their incompatibility as visual objects), is predicted to give rise to left-hemisphere specialization for words and right-hemisphere specialization for faces. Due to the graded nature of the learning constraints, this specialization should be only partial, with both regions participating in processing both types of stimuli to a certain degree. Houses are expected to be represented by more peripheral regions in fusiform cortex, analogous to the "parahippocampal place area" (PPA; Epstein & Kanwisher, 1998; Levy et al., 2001).

All simulations were developed within the Light Efficient Network Simulator (Lens; Version 2.63), developed by Doug Rohde and available for download at http://tedlab.mit.edu/∼dr/Lens.

Method

Stimuli

As the goals of the current work are to explore and illustrate the implications of a set of putative computational principles rather than to build a realistic model of visual face and word perception, the task and network architecture employed in the simulation were kept as simple as possible. The stimuli used in the simulation were derived from 32×32-bit schematic line drawings of faces, houses, and words that embodied critical differences in the demands of recognition of these classes of stimuli (see Figure 1). Each of 34 faces differed in terms of small changes in the positions or shapes of central features (e.g., separation and height of eyes, length of nose, height and width of mouth). Each of 40 three-letter (CVC, where C = consonant, V = vowel) words were created

from combinations of five possible letters for each position and, like faces, differed from each other only in terms of features within central vision. By contrast, each of nine houses differed in terms of properties that varied across the entire visual field (e.g., size of windows, number of eaves, presence of porch, size of base). Note that these rather small differences place high demands on fine visual acuity to ensure accurate discrimination between exemplars.

Each item was presented at nine different scales, ranging from 1.0 to 0.6 in steps of 0.05, for a total of 747 input patterns. For each pattern, retinotopic input activation was generated by smoothing the original bit patterns by convolving them with a Gaussian ($SD = 0.5$) and then transforming the resulting values into polar coordinates (r, θ), such that eccentricity r varied along the horizontal axis (with central information on the left and peripheral information on the right), and visual angle θ varied along the vertical axis (see Figure 2 for examples).

As the current work is concerned only with the nature of the visual representations of various stimulus classes, no attempt was made to approximate the structure of higher level information that such representations provide access to, beyond the need to identify (individuate) each unique face, word, and house (despite changes in scale). Accordingly, the output representations used in the simulation consisted of individual "localist" units for each of the 34 faces, 40 words, and 9 houses. We recognize, of course, that this is implausible as the actual output of the human system.

Network architecture

The network architecture is depicted in Figure 3. In the model, 32×32 retinotopic visual input to each hemisphere (in polar coordinates) is mapped via 64 (32×2) intermediate units in each hemisphere (corresponding to fusiform cortex) onto a set of 83 "identity" units (one for each unique word, face, and house). In addition, to approximate the influence of a left-hemisphere specialization for language, word inputs were also trained to activate one of a set of 40 "language" units

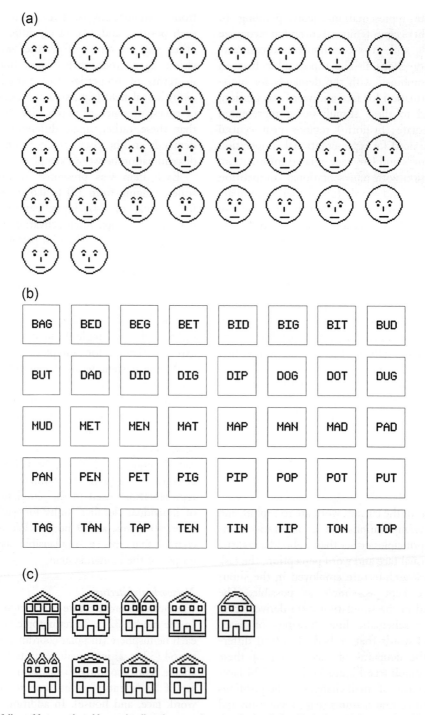

Figure 1. *The full set of face, word, and house stimuli used to create inputs to the simulation. Each picture defines a unique identity; the actual inputs to the network were generated by smoothing and transforming into polar coordinates (see Figure 2 for examples).*

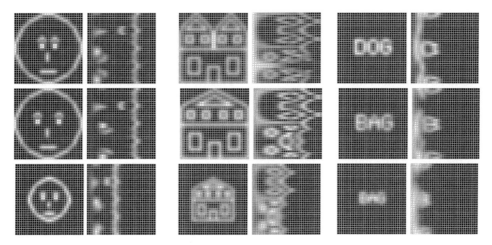

Figure 2. *Example face, house, and word stimuli after Gaussian smoothing. For each stimulus class, the left three panels show stimuli in x−y coordinates; the corresponding right panel shows the same stimulus in polar coordinates—the form actually presented to the network as input. Also, for each class, the top two rows differ in identity; the bottom two rows differ only in scale.*

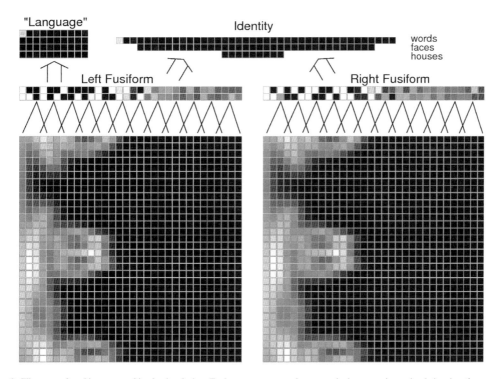

Figure 3. *The network architecture used in the simulation. Each square corresponds to a particular processing unit. Activations for a particular example input are depicted by the greyscale value of the square (black = 0.0; white = 1.0). Sets of connections are depicted by lines/arrows but are not shown in detail. For each of the two retinotopic input layers, activations toward the left encode central visual information, whereas activations toward the right encode more peripheral information. The projections from the two input layers to the left and right intermediate (fusiform) layers are subject to a horizontal topographic bias favouring short connections.*

that receive input solely from the left-hemisphere intermediate units. Finally, the input-to-intermediate connections were subject to strong topographic bias during learning. Although this bias is assumed to be enforced in the brain by the relative density of synapses as a function of distance, the small scale of the simulation made it more appropriate to implement this bias slightly differently. Specifically, the input units were fully connected to the intermediate units, but the efficacy of learning decreased as a Gaussian function ($SD = 3.0$) of the distance between the connected units (Plaut, 2002). As we were primarily concerned with the impact of eccentricity on learning, this metric considered only horizontal distance in the simulation (i.e., all units in the same column in Figure 2 were considered to have the equivalent functional position). Thus, in practical terms, learning was effective on connections from inputs directly "below" a given intermediate unit, but increasingly ineffective on connections from units with progressively different horizontal positions. For similar reasons, although we would claim that all connectivity in the brain is subject to a topographic bias, we did not apply this bias to any of the intermediate-to-output connections because we had no hypothesis concerning the relative proximity of semantic or identity information (beyond the left-lateralization of language information). The important consequence of this is that the identity units for faces, words, and houses are equivalent in their connectivity with the intermediate units, and thus any distinction in the specialization of the intermediate units must arise solely from properties of the inputs. Finally, the simulation employed a feedforward architecture, without lateral (within-layer) or top-down connections, solely for computational convenience.

Training and testing

When presented with a scaled version of each face, word, or house, the network was trained to activate the correct identity unit (and, for words, the correct "language" unit). Back-propagation (Rumelhart, Hinton, & Williams, 1986) was used to calculate how to change each connection weight in the network to reduce the discrepancy between the output activation pattern generated by the network and the correct pattern. Although not biologically plausible in literal form, back-propagation is functionally equivalent to more plausible procedures such as contrastive Hebbian learning (see, e.g., O'Reilly, 1996). The topographic bias on learning at the intermediate layer was implemented by scaling these weight changes by a decreasing (Gaussian) function of the horizontal distance between the connected input and intermediate units. Following training, the network was considered to be correct if, for a given input, the correct identity unit was more active than any other.

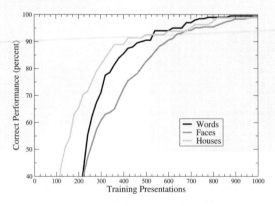

Figure 4. *Correct performance of the network in identifying faces, words, and houses as a function of the number of presentations of the entire set of 747 example patterns received by the network during training.*

262 COGNITIVE NEUROPSYCHOLOGY, 2011, 28 (3 & 4)

The primary basis for establishing specialization in the network was its performance following lesions restricted to spatially contiguous areas of either the left or right intermediate (fusiform) layer. Lesions were administered by removing three adjacent columns (6 units in total) from one of these layers and evaluating the performance of the damaged network for each of the 747 input patterns (83 identities × 9 scales). The horizontal position of these lesions was varied systematically in order to evaluate the relative specialization of each intermediate layer for each stimulus class as a function of visual eccentricity.

Results and discussion

After 1,000 training presentations of each pattern, the network is fully accurate at recognizing instances of each face, word, and house (see Figure 4). Over the course of acquisition, performance on houses is better than on the other stimulus classes because there are fewer of them to differentiate. Performance on words is better than on faces in part because the latter involve more subtle featural distinctions and, in part, because the extra demands of activating "language" information for words provide additional error (and therefore learning). By the end of training, however, performance on all three classes is equivalent and at ceiling.

To illustrate the effects of the topographic bias on learning in the network, Figure 5 shows examples of the "receptive" and "projective" fields learned by two intermediate units. The left display is for a unit that has a receptive field in central vision (i.e., toward the left of the retinotopic input) and has output that is largely selective for faces (third and fourth rows in the top group of units). By contrast, the right display is for a unit that has a more peripheral receptive field (i.e., toward the centre or right of the input) and is largely selective for houses (last row in the top group). These weight diagrams illustrate

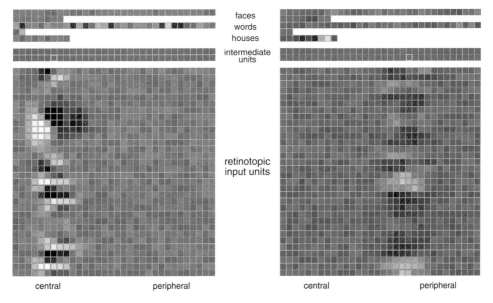

Figure 5. *Example receptive (input-to-intermediate) and projective (intermediate-to-output) fields for two units in the right-hemisphere intermediate layer. Each square shows the value of the weight (lighter for positive weights; darker for negative weights) from that unit either into or out of the depicted unit (outlined in the middle layer). The top group of units are output units; the first two rows are for words, the next two rows are for faces, and the last row is for houses.*

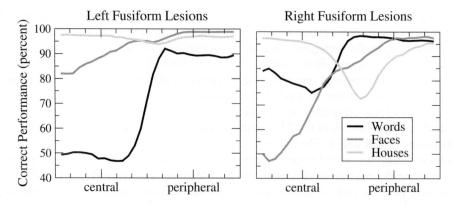

Figure 6. *Correct performance on faces, words, and houses following focal lesions to either the left or the right intermediate (fusiform) layer in the network, as a function of the horizontal position of the lesion (ranging from central to peripheral moving left to right within each hemisphere).*

the impact of the topographic constraint on learning and provide indirect evidence for learned category specificity of intermediate units as a function of their eccentricity.

More direct evidence for topographic specialization comes from the effects of localized lesions to the network. Figure 6 shows the performance of the network for each category of stimuli as a function of the horizontal position of lesions to three adjacent columns of units in either the left or right intermediate (fusiform) layer. Left-hemisphere lesions to the region of the fusiform near central visual information (analogous to the VWFA) produce a marked impairment in word recognition, but also a milder impairment in face recognition (relative to house recognition). By contrast, lesions to the corresponding region in the right hemisphere (analogous to the FFA) impair face recognition most, but also word recognition to a lesser extent. Finally, lesions to the right fusiform adjacent to more peripheral visual information (analogous to the PPA) produce the greatest impairment on houses and a milder impairment on faces (relative to words). These findings are in qualitative agreement with existing observations (Epstein, Deyoe, Press, Rosen, & Kanwisher,

2001) and our derived predictions for graded functional specialization.[2]

This small-scale simulation provides a simple but clear demonstration of the impact of a topographic constraint on learning on the organization of representations mediating face, word, and house recognition. The reliance of face and word recognition on central, high-acuity information leads to selectivity in the intermediate (fusiform) units closest to this information (Hasson et al., 2002; Levy et al., 2001; Levy, Hasson, & Malach, 2004). Competition between inconsistent information (and cooperation between word representations and language-related information) leads to substantial but still graded hemispheric specialization, with words represented primarily on the left and faces primarily on the right.

GENERAL DISCUSSION

This paper takes at its starting point a debate about the manner in which the brain is organized in the service of behaviour. One longstanding view is that different parts of the brain are specialized for, and perhaps even dedicated to, different cognitive

---

[2] Although not reported here in detail, these qualitative results are stable over changes to nonessential aspects of the network architecture and training methods, including variations (within reasonable limits) in random initial weights, learning parameters, and numbers of hidden units.

functions. An alternative account is one in which there is no unique, one-function one-region correspondence; rather, a single region subserves many different tasks, and/or a single task is mediated by many different regions. We have explored this latter, distributed perspective in the context of the ventral visual cortex and its organizational structure, taking as a model the case of face and word recognition. This is a particularly good domain in which to explore these different theoretical accounts as there are considerable empirical data on both the psychological and neural mechanisms involved in these functions, derived primarily from neuroimaging and neuropsychological investigations. We note, however, that the theoretical proposal is more general and applies to other visual domains that have the same computational demands as do words and faces.

The computational account we propose puts forward the theoretical claim that the representations of faces and words, albeit so apparently different in their surface characteristics and their underlying neural substrate, are the product of the same computational principles. Specifically, the visual recognition system has at its core three general principles, all of which have profound implications for both the commonalities and differences in the neural organization and functionality of face/word processing. The key principles are:

1. *Distributed representation and knowledge:* Visual objects are represented by distributed patterns of neural activity within a hierarchically organized system, where learning involves modifying the pattern of synaptic connectivity between neurons within and between regions on the basis of experience.
2. *Representational cooperation and competition:* Effective cognitive processing requires the coordination of related information across multiple levels of representation, whereas unrelated or incompatible information must be represented over separate regions to avoid interference.
3. *Topography, proximity, and hemispheric organization:* Representational cooperation must be

accomplished with largely local connectivity between topographically organized brain regions, and with limited connectivity between hemispheres, so that total axonal volume fits within the confines of the skull.

These constraints have a fundamental impact on how faces and words are represented and processed within the visual system.

Here, we show that a small-scale simulation that is trained to recognize faces, words, and houses in a manner consistent with these principles illustrates how a topographic constraint on learning can give rise to learned category specificity of intermediate units as a function of their eccentricity. This topographic constraint is further anchored by the reliance on fine-grained visual processing for discriminating subtle visual differences among words and among faces. Specifically, left-hemisphere lesions to the region of the intermediate layer near central visual information (analogous to the VWFA) produce a marked impairment in word recognition, but also a milder impairment in face recognition (relative to house recognition). By contrast, lesions to the corresponding region in the right hemisphere (analogous to the FFA) impair face recognition most, but also word recognition to a lesser extent. These findings are in qualitative agreement with existing observations and our derived predictions for graded functional specialization.

The results of the simulation provide an existence proof of a system in which face and word recognition are subject to the same computational constraints but in which relative specialization, by virtue of other competing pressures (to restrict connection length specifically with language areas, see Cai et al., 2008; Price & Devlin, 2011) also demonstrates some functional specialization. The idea that there are both many similarities as well as differences among the mechanisms supporting face and word recognition is endorsed by the existing neuroimaging studies (many or even most of which reflect bilateral activation for faces and words) and some neuropsychological studies, which show dual impairment following a unilateral hemispheric lesion.

Converging evidence

There are some additional considerations that favour a common-mechanism perspective. Both face and word recognition are domains with which most individuals have extensive experience and expertise. Both classes place demands on high-acuity information to encode subtle but critical visual information, and, thus, the fact that the cortical regions that are selective for face and word processing are located adjacent to the central visual information within the highest level of retinotopic representation (Hasson et al., 2002; Levy et al., 2001) can be understood as a natural consequence of topography and the constraint on local connectivity. Furthermore, the cortical regions selective for these stimuli come to be located adjacent to retinotopic regions coding foveal information, but in different hemispheres, with words in the left to permit coordination with other language-related knowledge. Additionally, the VWFA and FFA are both insensitive to low-level input variations (e.g., letter font; viewpoint for faces) suggesting that both regions reflect functional specialization of higher order visual cortex.

A further commonality is that lesions to each region render the individual reliant on a more piecemeal or segmental approach rather than one in which the configural or whole is accessible. Just as VWFA lesions result in a laborious letter-by-letter sequential decoding of the individual letters, lesions resulting in prosopagnosia give rise to a similar sequential process with greater reliance on some features of the face (e.g., mouth, see example in Bukach, Le Grand, Kaiser, Bub, & Tanaka, 2008) and a laborious encoding of the features as reflected in eye movement patterns (e.g., see Stephan & Caine, 2009). Also, just as VWFA activation is affected by experience (Baker et al., 2007; Wong et al., 2005), so adult-like face processing in the FFA also emerges with age and experience, and both regions evince a protracted developmental trajectory with signs of specificity emerging roughly when children are in elementary school (Brem, Bach et al., 2010; Brem, Bucher et al., 2006; Cohen Kadosh & Johnson, 2007; Cohen Kadosh et al., 2010; Golarai et al., 2007; Golarai, Liberman, Yoon, & Grill-Spector, 2010; Joseph, Gathers & Bhatt, 2011; Scherf, Behrmann, Humphreys, & Luna, 2007).[3] Finally, both regions are rather plastic: The VWFA can be acquired in the RH after left occipital resection in childhood (Cohen, Lehericy, et al., 2004), and there may also be a shift to the right in patients following acquired LH lesions (Cohen, Lehericy, et al., 2004; Cohen et al., 2003). Relatedly, there are no apparent differences in the face recognition deficits of individuals with unilateral lesions in infancy that impacted either the LH or the RH (de Schonen et al., 2005).

One apparent challenge to our emphasis on the role of visual experience in shaping the cortical organization of face and word processing is the recent observation by Reich et al. (2011) that the VWFA, as localized in sighted individuals, is also the location of peak activation in congenitally blind individuals reading Braille words (compared to nonsense Braille control stimuli). It should be noted, however, that Reich et al. found reliable differences in the entire left ventral occipitotemporal cortex all the way to V1, consistent with earlier findings by Noppeney, Friston, and Price (2003) that were attributed to recruitment of these areas for semantic processing. Reich et al.'s only evidence for (tactile) word-form representations per se was that activation differences were larger for Braille reading than for auditory verb generation, but this comparison was possibly dubious as it involved separate and unrelated control tasks. Moreover, the fact that activation differences peaked in the same location in blind and sighted individuals may arise because of intrinsic

---

[3] The exact nature of the change over developmental time remains somewhat controversial with some studies showing changes in the volume of activation for one category over another and others showing a change in functional/effective connectivity over the course of development. The studies are also not entirely consistent with each other (see Cantlon et al., 2011, showing adult-like activation to faces as well as sensitivity to alphanumeric symbols in four-year-olds although volume/cluster size was not evaluated in this study). These empirical discrepancies remain to be resolved.

patterns of connectivity between early visual cortex and parietal structures involved in spatial attention (Greenberg et al., 2011), and this inherent white matter arrangement biases where activation peaks are likely to be observed in functional imaging studies.

Where do hemispheric differences come from?

Our account presupposes that the hemispheric differences and asymmetries emerge over the course of experience, during which time the connectivity and topography constraints play out. There are, however, other theoretical stances, which interpret the emergent hemispheric differences as arising from a different origin. One such account is that the left-hemisphere (LH) processes input in an analytical or part-based way (hence its role with words) whereas the right-hemisphere (RH) processes input more holistically (hence its role with faces; see also Farah 1991, 1992). A second view attributes the word/face distinction to the distinction between linguistic (LH) and spatial (RH) processing. Yet a further view is that the face/word difference arises from differential frequency sensitivity (Robertson & Ivry, 2000) with the RH and LH responding to relatively low and high spatial frequency information, respectively, and the former critical for faces (RH), and the latter for words (LH). A final possibility is that the face/word differences arise from the differential predisposition to process inputs categorically (LH words) versus by coordinate relations (RH faces; Kosslyn et al., 1989). These accounts all suggest that it is the fundamental (perhaps even hardwired or innately specified) properties of the two hemispheres that play a role in shaping the underlying computational differences between words and faces, but how and to what extent this is so remains to be determined.

Our approach is not mutually exclusive with these process-based accounts but it emphasizes the importance of expertise in shaping cortical organization and function (Gauthier & Bukach, 2007; Gauthier & Nelson, 2001), although

expertise alone cannot explain why the FFA and VWFA are located where they are, nor why other types of expertise (namely, those not demanding high-acuity visual information) do not engage these areas. It also shares the fundamental assumption of Malach and colleagues (Levy et al., 2001; Levy et al., 2004) regarding pressure for foveal acuity and cortical topography, but goes beyond this by implementing the ideas in explicit simulations, enabling the testing of specific predictions concerning the relationship of face and word processing. There remain, of course, complex questions about why the left hemisphere is language dominant in the majority of the population and the source of this organizational pattern. Such issues are beyond the scope of this paper but are intriguing and remain to be addressed, too.

Predictions

A full assessment of the tractability of our account remains to be undertaken, and, in particular, there are a number of predictions that can be tested. Much of our work, thus far, has focused on the need for representational cooperation between words and the language-related output, as the key pressure that drives the left-hemisphere specialization. But this cooperation occurs in conjunction with representational competition between faces and words (given their incompatibility as visual objects), and this competition, too, motivates the hemispheric distinctions with left and right biased for words and faces, respectively. A prediction of this trading relations view is that individuals who have greater asymmetries for faces (e.g., relative to baseline, greater performance advantage for faces presented to left than to right visual field, or greater activation in the right hemisphere in imaging) should show the converse for words on an individual-by-individual basis, depending on how the cooperation and competition play our during the course of development and experience. We also anticipate that some individuals will have more bilaterally graded representation and that there will be a large range of individual differences across the population. This prediction is eminently testable through half-field studies, as well as functional imaging investigation, and we are currently undertaking such explorations including examining hemispheric asymmetries for faces and words within individual and across groups of young children, adolescents, and young adults (Dundas, Plaut, & Behrmann, 2011).

A further rather obvious prediction is that individuals with damage to the left VWFA and presenting with pure alexia might also be impaired at face recognition, relative to normal participants, albeit to a lesser extent than individuals with prosopagnosia following a lesion to the right FFA. The converse is also predicted: Individuals with a lesion to the right FFA and presenting with prosopagnosia might also be impaired at word recognition, relative to controls, albeit to a lesser extent than individuals with pure alexia following a lesion to the left VWFA. We have examined these predictions in a small group of individuals, all of whom were premorbidly normal and have acquired unilateral ventral cortex lesions (Behrmann & Plaut, 2011). In this study, we used the same series of face and word experiments to evaluate the performance of three adults with circumscribed unilateral right-hemisphere lesions and prosopagnosia and four pure alexic adults with circumscribed unilateral left-hemisphere lesions. Control participants matched to the two groups were also tested. In addition to the expected impairment in face recognition, the prosopagnosic individuals showed abnormal word recognition relative to the controls, albeit not as marked as in the pure alexics, and, in complementary fashion, the pure alexic individuals showed abnormal face recognition relative to the controls, albeit to a lesser extent than in the prosopagnosics (for related findings, see Buxbaum, Glosser, & Coslett, 1996, 1999). These empirical findings anchor a key prediction of our account, which is that hemispheric asymmetries for face and word recognition are graded and not fully and independently segregated.

Limitations and extensions

The computational simulation presented here was intentionally kept as simple as possible in order to provide the clearest illustration of the consequences of our putative computational principles for graded specialization of the neural representations of faces and words (and, to a more limited extent, houses). The most obvious limitations of the simulation are that it used a small set of highly schematized stimuli, a strictly feed-forward network architecture without lateral and top-down interactions within or between hemispheres, a lack of separate excitatory and inhibitory unit populations, and a biologically implausible learning procedure. Although we claim that the core findings regarding learned functional specialization do not depend critically on any of these simplifications, it is important to validate these findings in more realistic follow-up simulations. Such follow-up versions should use realistic stimuli, employ a more biologically plausible learning procedure (e.g., contrastive Hebbian learning; see O'Reilly, 1996), and permit only excitatory connections between layers by using a separate population of local inhibitory units within each layer. We do not anticipate that these elaborations will alter the basic operation of the model but they will bring it into much closer alignment with the operation of real neural systems.

CONCLUSION

Our central hypothesis is that the commonalities in the neural mechanisms of face and word processing are not merely coincidental, as modular theories are left to conclude, but, rather, are the signature consequences of a set of general principles and constraints on neural computation that operate throughout cortex. We note that these principles themselves are not intended to be novel; in fact, we take them to be largely noncontroversial. Instead, the novelty derives from their common consequences for cortical organization and behaviour in two seemingly unrelated domains, specifically, in the context of words and faces,

Critically, when instantiated in explicit computational terms, these principles provide insight into why each of these properties is partial rather than absolute. This is because the principles and constraints are inherently graded—adherence to the forces of cooperation, competition, and proximity in the process of learning cortical representations is a matter of degree as these constraints trade off against each other, and thus the consequences for neural and behavioural specialization are also graded. As a result, the implications of graded constraints go beyond explaining why neither pure alexia nor prosopagnosia is entirely "pure" and why, across a host of imaging studies, the FFA and VWFA show substantial responses to stimuli other than faces and words, respectively. They also imply that the functional and anatomical division between face and word recognition should be graded—despite the clear differences between the two domains, the FFA should be partially involved in word recognition, and the VWFA should be partially involved in face recognition. In this way, our theoretical perspective leads to important and otherwise unexpected predictions concerning the partial comingling of face and word processing, including face recognition impairments in pure alexia, word recognition impairments in prosopagnosia, graded participation of the FFA and VWFA in face/word recognition in normal observers, and a number of other implications that remain to be tested.

REFERENCES

Allison, T., McCarthy, G., Nobre, A. C., Puce, A., & Belger, A. (1994). Human extrastriate visual cortex and the perception of faces, words, numbers and colors. *Cerebral Cortex, 5,* 544–554.

Avidan, G., & Behrmann, M. (2009). Functional MRI reveals compromised neural integrity of the face processing network in congenital prosopagnosia. *Current Biology, 19,* 1146–1150.

Bach, F. R., & Jordan, M. I. (2002). Kernel independent component analysis. *Journal of Machine Learning Research, 3,* 1–48.

Baker, C. I., Liu, J., Wald, L. L., Kwong, K., Benner, T., & Kanwisher, N. (2007). Visual word processing and experiential origins of functional selectivity in human extrastriate cortex. *Proceedings of the National Academy of Sciences, USA, 104,* 9087–9092.

Bartlett, M. S., Movellan, J. R., & Sejnowski, T. J. (2002). Face recognition by independent component analysis. *IEEE Transactions on Neural Networks, 13,* 1450–1464.

Barton, J. J. S. (2008). Structure and function in acquired prosopagnosia: Lessons from a series of 10 patients with brain damage. *Journal of Neuropsychology, 2,* 197–225.

Barton, J. J. S. (2009). What is meant by impaired configural processing in acquired prosopagnosia? *Perception, 38,* 242–260.

Barton, J. J., Cherkasova, M. V., Press, D. Z., Intriligator, J. M., & O'Connor, M. (2004). Perceptual functions in prosopagnosia. *Perception, 33,* 939–956.

Behrmann, M., & Avidan, G. (2005). Congenital prosopagnosia: Face-blind from birth. *Trends in Cognitive Science, 9,* 180-187.

Behrmann, M., & Kimchi, R. (2003). What does visual agnosia tell us about perceptual organization and its relationship to object perception? *Journal of Experimental Psychology: Human Perception and Performance, 29,* 19–42.

Behrmann, M., Nelson, J., & Sekuler, E. (1998). Visual complexity in letter-by-letter reading: "Pure" alexia is not so pure. *Neuropsychologia, 36,* 1115–1132.

Behrmann, M., & Plaut, D. C. (2011). *Faces and words: Flip sides of the same brain*, Manuscript submitted for publication.

Bilalic, M., Langner, R., Ulrich, R., & Grodd, W. (2011). Many faces of expertise: Fusiform face area in chess experts and novices. *Journal of Neuroscience, 31,* 10206–10214.

Blanz, V., & Vetter, T. (2003). Face recognition based on fitting a 3D morphable model. *IEEE Transactions on Pattern Analysis and Machine Intelligence, 25,* 1063–1074.

Bouvier, S. E., & Engel, S. A. (2006). Behavioral deficits and cortical damage loci in cerebral achromatopsia. *Cerebral Cortex, 16,* 183–191.

Brem, S., Bach, S., Kucian, K., Guttorm, T. K., Martin, E., Lytinen, H., Brandeis, D., & Richardson, U. (2010). Brain sensitivity to print emerges when children learn letter-sound correspondences. *Proceedings of the National Academy of Science USA, 107,* 7939–7944.

Brem, S., Bucher, K., Halder, P., Summers, P., Dietrich, T., Martin, E., et al. (2006). Evidence for developmental changes in the visual word processing network beyond adolescence. *NeuroImage, 29,* 822–837.

Büchel, C., Price, C., & Friston, K. (1998). A multimodal language region in the ventral visual pathway. *Nature, 394*, 274–277.

Bukach, C., Le Grand, R., Kaiser, M. D., Bub, D. N., & Tanaka, J. W. (2008). Preservation of mouth region processing in two cases of prosopagnosia. *Journal of Neuropsychology, 2*, 227–244.

Burton, M. A., Bruce, V., & Hancock, P. J. B. (1999). From pixels to people: A model of familiar face recognition. *Cognitive Science, 23*, 1–31.

Burton, M. A., Young, A. W., Bruce, V., Johnston, R. A., & Ellis, A. W. (1991). Understanding covert recognition. *Cognition, 39*, 129–166.

Busigny, T., & Rossion, B. (2010). Acquired prosopagnosia abolishes the face inversion effect. *Cortex, 46*, 965–981.

Buxbaum, L., Glosser, G., & Coslett, H. B. (1996). Relative sparing of object recognition in alexia–prosopagnosia. *Brain and Cognition, 32*, 202–205.

Buxbaum, L. J., Glosser, G., & Coslett, H. B. (1999). Impaired face and word recognition without object agnosia. *Neuropsychologia, 37*, 41–50.

Cai, Q., Lavidor, M., Brysbaert, M., Paulignan, Y., & Nazir, T. A. (2008). Cerebral lateralization of frontal lobe language processes and lateralization of the posterior visual word processing system. *Journal of Cognitive Neuroscience, 20*, 672–681.

Cantlon, J. F., Pinel, P., Dehaene, S., & Pelphrey, K. A. (2011). Cortical representations of symbols, objects, and faces are pruned back during early childhood. *Cerebral Cortex, 21*, 191–199.

Cohen, L., & Dehaene, S. (2004). Specialization within the ventral stream: The case for the visual word form area. *NeuroImage, 22*(1), 466–476.

Cohen, L., Dehaene, S., Naccache, L., Lehericy, S., Dehaene-Lambertz, G., Henaff, M. A., et al. (2000). The visual word form area: Spatial and temporal characterization of an initial stage of reading in normal subjects and posterior split-brain patients. *Brain, 123*, 291–307.

Cohen, L., Henry, C., Dehaene, S., Martinaud, O., Lehericy, S., Lemer, C., et al. (2004). The pathophysiology of letter-by-letter reading. *Neuropsychologia, 42*, 1768–1780.

Cohen, L., Lehericy, S., Henry, C., Bourgeois, M., Larroque, C., Sainte-Rose, C., et al. (2004). Learning to read without a left occipital lobe: Right-hemispheric shift of visual word form area. *Annals of Neurology, 56*, 890–894.

Cohen, L., Martinaud, O., Lemer, C., Lehericy, S., Samson, Y., Obadia, M., et al. (2003). Visual word recognition in the left and right hemispheres: Anatomical and functional correlates of peripheral alexias. *Cerebral Cortex, 13*, 1313–1333.

Cohen Kadosh, K., Cohen Kadosh, R., Dick, F., & Johnson, M. H. (2010). Developmental changes in effective connectivity in the emerging core face network. *Cerebral Cortex, 21*, 1389–1394.

Cohen Kadosh, K., & Johnson, M. H. (2007). Developing a cortex specialized for face perception. *Trends in Cognitive Science, 11*, 367–369.

Coltheart, M., Rastle, K., Perry, C., Langdon, R., & Ziegler, J. (2001). DRC: A dual route cascaded model of visual word recognition and reading aloud. *Psychological Review, 108*, 204–256.

Coslett, H. B., & Monsul, N. (1994). Reading with the right hemisphere: Evidence from transcranial magnetic stimulation. *Brain and Language, 46*, 198–211.

Cowey, A. (1979). Cortical maps and visual perception. The Grindley Memorial Lecture. *Quarterly Journal of Experimental Psychology, 31*, 1–17.

Dailey, M. N., & Cottrell, G. W. (1999). Organization of face and object recognition in modular neural networks. *Neural Networks, 12*, 1053–1074.

Dailey, M. N., Cottrell, G. W., Padgett, C., & Adolphs, R. (2002). EMPATH: A neural network that categorizes facial expressions. *Journal of Cognitive Neuroscience, 14*, 1158–1173.

Damasio, A., Damasio, H., & Tranel, D. (1986). Prosopagnosia: Anatomic and physiological aspects. In H. D. Ellis, M. A. Jeeves, F. Newcombe, & A. Young (Eds.), *Aspects of face processing* (pp. 279–290). Dordrecht, The Netherlands: Martinus Nijhoff.

Davis, C. J. (1999). *The self-organizing lexical acquisition and recognition (SOLAR) model of visual word recognition*, Unpublished doctoral dissertation, University of New South Wales, Sydney, Australia.

Dehaene, S., & Cohen, L. (2007). Cultural recycling of cortical maps. *Neuron, 56*, 384–398.

Dehaene, S., & Cohen, L. (2011). The unique role of the visual word form area in reading. *Trends in Cognitive Science, 15*, 254–262.

Dehaene, S., Cohen, L., Sigman, M., & Vinckier, F. (2005). The neural code for written words: A proposal. *Trends in Cognitive Science, 9*, 335–341.

Dehaene, S., Pegado, F., Braga, L. W., Ventura, P., Filho, G. N., Jobert, A., et al. (2010). How learning to read changes the cortical networks for vision and language. *Science, 330*, 1359–1364.

de Schonen, S., Mancini, J., Camps, R., Maes, E., & Laurent, A. (2005). Early brain lesions and face-processing development. *Developmental Psychobiology, 46,* 184–208.

Devlin, J. T., Jamison, H. L., Gonnerman, L. M., & Matthews, P. M. (2006). The role of the posterior fusiform gyrus in reading. *Journal of Cognitive Neuroscience, 18,* 911–922.

De Yoe, E. A., Carman, G. J., Bandettini, P., Glickman, S., Wieser, J., Cox, R., et al. (1996). Mapping striate and extrastriate visual areas in human cerebral cortex. *Proceedings of the National Academy of Sciences, 93,* 2382–2386.

Downing, P. E., Jiang, Y., Shuman, M., & Kanwisher, N. (2001). A cortical area selective for visual processing of the human body. *Science, 293,* 2470–2473.

Dundas, E., Plaut, D. C., & Behrmann, M. (2011). *The joint development of hemispheric lateralization for words and faces.* Submitted for publication.

Epstein, R. A., Deyoe, E. A., Press, D. Z., Rosen, A. C., & Kanwisher, N. (2001). Neuropsychological evidence for a topographical learning mechanism in parahippocampal cortex. *Cognitive Neuropsychology, 18,* 481–508.

Epstein, R. A., Harris, A., Stanley, D., & Kanwisher, N. (1999). The parahippocampal place area: Recognition, navigation, or encoding? *Neuron, 23,* 115–125.

Epstein, R. A., & Kanwisher, N. (1998). A cortical representation of the local visual environment. *Nature, 392,* 598–601.

Etemad, K., & Chellappa, R. (1997). Discriminant analysis for recognition of human face images. *Journal of the Optical Society of America A, 14,* 1724–1733.

Farah, M. J. (1991). Patterns of co-occurrence among the associative agnosias: Implications for visual object recognition. *Cognitive Neuropsychology, 8,* 1–19.

Farah, M. J. (1992). Is an object an object an object? Cognitive and neuropsychological investigations of domain specificity in visual object recognition. *Current Directions in Psychological Science, 1,* 164–169.

Farah, M. J. (1996). Is face recognition "special"? Evidence from neuropsychology. *Behavioural Brain Research, 76,* 181–189.

Farah, M. J. (1999). Relations among the agnosias. In G. W. Humphreys (Ed.), *Case studies in the neuropsychology of vision* (pp. 181–200). Hove, UK: Psychology Press.

Farah, M. J., O'Reilly, R. C., & Vecera, S. P. (1993). Dissociated overt and covert recognition as an emergent property of a lesioned neural network. *Psychological Review, 100,* 571–588.

Farah, M. J., Tanaka, J. W., & Drain, H. M. (1995). What causes the face inversion effect? *Journal of Experimental Psychology: Human Perception and Performance, 21,* 628–634.

Feinberg, T. E., Schindler, R. J., Ochoa, E., Kwan, P. C., & Farah, M. J. (1994). Associative visual agnosia and alexia without prosopagnosia. *Cortex, 30,* 395–412.

Fiez, J. A., Balota, D. A., Raichle, M. E., & Petersen, S. E. (1999). Effects of lexicality, frequency, and spelling-to-sound consistency on the functional anatomy of reading. *Neuron, 24,* 205–218.

Fodor, J. (1983). *The modularity of mind.* Cambridge, MA: MIT Press.

Furl, N., Garrido, L., Dolan, R. J., Driver, J., & Duchaine, B. (2010). Fusiform gyrus face selectivity relates to individual differences in facial recognition ability. *Journal of Cognitive Neuroscience, 23,* 1723–1740.

Gainotti, G., & Marra, C. (2011). Differential contribution of right and left temporo-occipital and anterior temporal lesions to face recognition disorders. *Frontiers in Human Neuroscience, 5,* 1–11.

Gauthier, I., & Bukach, C. (2007). Should we reject the expertise hypothesis? *Cognition, 103,* 322–330.

Gauthier, I., & Nelson, C. A. (2001). The development of face expertise. *Current Opinion in Neurobiology, 11,* 219–224.

Gauthier, I., Tarr, M. J., Anderson, A. W., Skudlarski, P., & Gore, J. C. (1999). Activation of the middle fusiform "face area" increases with expertise in recognizing novel objects. *Nature Neuroscience, 2,* 568–573.

Gauthier, I., Tarr, M. J., Moylan, J., Skudlarski, P., Gore, J. C., & Anderson, A. W. (2000). The fusiform "face area" is part of a network that processes faces at the individual level. *Journal of Cognitive Neuroscience, 12,* 495–504.

Golarai, G., Ghahremani, D. G., Whitfield-Gabrieli, S., Reiss, A., Eberhardt, J. L., Gabrieli, J. D., et al. (2007). Differential development of high-level visual cortex correlates with category-specific recognition memory. *Nature Neuroscience, 10,* 512–522.

Golarai, G., Liberman, A., Yoon, J. M., & Grill-Spector, K. (2010). Differential development of the ventral visual cortex extends through adolescence. *Frontiers in Human Neuroscience, 3,* 80.

Grainger, J., Granier, J. P., Farioli, F., Van Assche, E., & van Heuven, W. (2006). Letter position information and printed word perception: The relative-position priming constraint. *Journal of Experimental Psychology: Human Perception and Performance, 32,* 865–884.

Greenberg, A., Verstynen, T., Chiu, Y.-V., Yantis, S., Schneider, W., & Behrmann, M. (2011). *Spatiotopic structural connectivity underlying visual attention,* Manuscript submitted for publication.

Grill-Spector, K., & Malach, R. (2004). The human visual cortex. *Annual Review of Neuroscience, 27,* 649–677.

Grill-Spector, K., Sayres, R., & Ress, D. (2006). High-resolution imaging reveals highly selective non-face clusters in the fusiform face area. *Nature Neuroscience, 9,* 1177–1185.

Hanson, S. J., & Schmidt, A. (2011). High-resolution imaging of the fusiform face area (FFA) using multivariate non-linear classifiers shows diagnosticity for non-face categories. *NeuroImage, 54,* 1715–1734.

Harm, M. W., & Seidenberg, M. S. (1999). Phonology, reading acquisition, and dyslexia: Insights from connectionist models. *Psychological Review, 106,* 491–528.

Harm, M. W., & Seidenberg, M. S. (2004). Computing the meanings of words in reading: Cooperative division of labor between visual and phonological processes. *Psychological Review, 111,* 662–720.

Hasson, U., Levy, I., Behrmann, M., Hendler, T., & Malach, R. (2002). Center-biased representation for characters in the human ventral visual stream. *Neuron, 34,* 479–490.

Haxby, J. V. (2006). Fine structure in representations of faces and objects. *Nature Neuroscience, 9,* 1084–1086.

Haxby, J. V., Gobbini, M. I., Furey, M. L., Ishai, A., Schouten, J. L., & Pietrini, P. (2001). Distributed and overlapping representations of faces and objects in ventral temporal cortex. *Science, 293,* 2425–2429.

Haxby, J. V., Petit, L., Ungerleider, L. G., & Courtney, S. M. (2000). Distinguishing the functional roles of multiple regions in distributed neural systems for visual working memory. *NeuroImage, 11,* 380–391.

Hoffman, E. A., & Haxby, J. V. (2000). Distinct representations of eye gaze and identity in the distributed human neural system for face perception. *Nature Neuroscience, 3,* 80–84.

Hsiao, J., Shieh, D., & Cottrell, G. W. (2008). Convergence of the visual field split: Hemispheric modeling of face and object recognition. *Journal of Cognitive Neuroscience, 20,* 2298–2307.

Ishai, A. (2008). Let's face it: It's a cortical network. *NeuroImage, 40,* 415–419.

Ishai, A., Schmidt, C. F., & Boesiger, P. (2005). Face perception is mediated by a distributed cortical network. *Brain Research Bulletin, 67,* 87–93.

Jacobs, R. A. (1997). Nature, nurture and the development of functional specializations: A computational approach. *Psychonomic Bulletin and Review, 4,* 299–309.

Jacobs, R. A., & Jordan, M. I. (1992). Computational consequences of a bias toward short connections. *Journal of Cognitive Neuroscience, 4,* 323–336.

Joseph, J. E., Gathers, A. D., & Bhatt, R. S. (2011). Progressive and regressive developmental changes in neural substrates for face processing: Testing specific predictions of the interactive specialization account. *Developmental Science, 14,* 227–241.

Kanan, C. M., & Cottrell, G. W. (2010). Robust classification of objects, faces, and flowers using natural image statistics. In *Proceedings of the IEEE Conference on Computer Vision and Pattern Recognition (CVPR-2010).* Washington DC: IEEE Computer Society.

Kanwisher, N. (2000). Domain specificity in face perception. *Nature Neuroscience, 3,* 759–763.

Kanwisher, N. (2010). Functional specificity in the human brain: A window into the functional architecture of the mind. *Proceedings of the National Academy of Sciences, USA, 107,* 11163–11170.

Kanwisher, N., McDermott, J., & Chun, M. M. (1997). The fusiform face area: A module in human extrastriate cortex specialized for face perception. *The Journal of Neuroscience, 17,* 4302–4311.

Kanwisher, N., Woods, R. P., Iacoboni, M., & Mazziotta, J. C. (1997). A locus in human extrastriate cortex for visual shape analysis. *Journal of Cognitive Neuroscience, 9,* 133–142.

Kleinschmidt, A., & Cohen, L. (2006). The neural bases of prosopagnosia and pure alexia: Recent insights from functional neuroimaging. *Current Opinion in Neurology, 19,* 386–391.

Kosslyn, S. M., Koenig, O., Barrett, A., Cave, C. B., Tang, J., & Gabrieli, J. D. E. (1989). Evidence for two types of spatial representations: Hemispheric specialization for categorical and coordinate relations. *Journal of Experimental Psychology: Human Perception and Performance, 15,* 723–735.

Kriegeskorte, N., Formisano, E., Sorge, B., & Goebel, R. (2007). Individual faces elicit distinct response patterns in human anterior temporal cortex. *Proceedings of the National Academy of Sciences, USA, 104,* 20600–20605.

Kronbichler, M., Hutzler, F., Wimmer, H., Mair, A., Staffen, W., & Ladurner, G. (2004). The visual word form area and the frequency with which words are encountered: Evidence from a parametric fMRI study. *NeuroImage, 21,* 946–953.

Lavidor, M., Ellis, A. W., Shillcock, R., & Bland, T. (2001). Evaluating a split processing model of visual word recognition: Effects of word length. *Cognitive Brain Research, 12,* 265–272.

Levy, I., Hasson, U., Hendler, T., & Malach, R. (2001). Center-periphery organization of human object areas. *Nature Neuroscience, 4,* 533–539.

Levy, I., Hasson, U., & Malach, R. (2004). One picture is worth at least a million neurons. *Current Biology, 14,* 996–1001.

Liu, Y. C., Wang, A. G., & Yen, M. Y. (2011). "Seeing but not identifying": Pure alexia coincident with prosopagnosia in occipital arteriovenous malformation. *Graefe's Archive of Clinical and Experimental Ophthalmology, 248,* 1087–1089.

Mahon, B. Z., & Caramazza, A. (2011). What drives the organization of knowledge in the brain. *Trends in Cognitive Sciences, 15,* 97–103.

McCandliss, B. D., Cohen, L., & Dehaene, S. (2003). The visual word form area: Expertise for reading in the fusiform gyrus. *Trends in Cognitive Science, 7,* 293–299.

McClelland, J. L., & Rumelhart, D. E. (1981). An interactive activation model of context effects in letter perception: Part 1. An account of basic findings. *Psychological Review, 88,* 375–407.

McClelland, J. L., & Rumelhart, D. E. (1985). Distributed memory and the representation of general and specific information. *Journal of Experimental Psychology: General, 114,* 159–188.

McKone, E., & Robbins, R. (2011). Are faces special? In A. J. Calder, G. Rhodes, J. V. Haxby, & M. H. Johnson (Eds.), *Oxford handbook of face perception* (pp. 149–176). Oxford, UK: Oxford University Press.

Mechelli, A., Gorno-Tempini, M. L., & Price, C. J. (2003). Neuroimaging studies of word and pseudoword reading: Consistencies, inconsistencies, and limitations. *Journal of Cognitive Neuroscience, 15,* 260–271.

Moghaddam, B., Jebara, T., & Pentland, A. (2000). Bayesian face recognition. *Pattern Recognition, 33,* 1771–1782.

Montant, M., & Behrmann, M. (2000). Pure alexia: Review of cases. *Neurocase, 6,* 265–294.

Mozer, M. C. (1991). *The perception of multiple objects: A connectionist approach.* Cambridge, MA: MIT Press.

Mozer, M. C., & Behrmann, M. (1990). On the interaction of selective attention and lexical knowledge: A connectionist account of neglect dyslexia. *Journal of Cognitive Neuroscience, 2,* 96–123.

Murtha, S., Chertkow, H., Beauregard, M., & Evans, A. (1999). The neural substrate of picture naming. *Journal of Cognitive Neuroscience, 11,* 399–423.

Nelson, M. E., & Bower, J. M. (1990). Brain maps and parallel computers. *Trends in Neurosciences, 13,* 403–408.

Nestor, A., Behrmann, M., & Plaut, D. C. (2011). *The neural basis of visual word form processing—a multivariate investigation,* Manuscript submitted for publication.

Nestor, A., Plaut, D. C., & Behrmann, M. (2011). Unraveling the distributed neural code of facial identity through spatiotemporal pattern analysis. *Proceedings of the National Academy of Science USA, 108,* 9998–10003.

Noppeney, U., Friston, K. J., & Price, C. J. (2003). Effects of visual deprivation on the organization of the semantic system. *Brain, 126,* 1620–1627.

Norman, K. A., Polyn, S. M., Detre, G. J., & Haxby, J. V. (2006). Beyond mind-reading: Multi-voxel pattern analysis of fMRI data. *Trends in Cognitive Science, 10,* 424–430.

O'Reilly, R. C. (1996). Biologically plausible error-driven learning using local activation differences: The generalized recirculation algorithm. *Neural Computation, 8,* 895–938.

Peelen, M. V., & Downing, P. E. (2005). Selectivity for the human body in the fusiform gyrus. *Journal of Neurophysiology, 93,* 603–608.

Perry, C., Ziegler, J. C., & Zorzi, M. (2007). Nested incremental modeling in the development of computational theories: The CDP+ model of reading aloud. *Psychological Review, 114,* 273–315.

Petersen, S. E., & Fiez, J. (1993). The processing of single words studies with positron emission tomography. *Annual Review of Neurosciences, 16,* 509–530.

Petersen, S., Fox, P. T., Snyder, A., & Raichle, M. E. (1990). Activation of extrastriate and frontal cortical areas by visual words and word-like stimuli. *Science, 249,* 1041–1044.

Plaut, D. C. (1999). A connectionist approach to word reading and acquired dyslexia: Extension to sequential processing. *Cognitive Science, 23,* 543–568.

Plaut, D. C. (2002). Graded modality-specific specialization in semantics: A computational account of optic aphasia. *Cognitive Neuropsychology, 19,* 603–639.

Plaut, D. C., McClelland, J. L., Seidenberg, M. S., & Patterson, K. (1996). Understanding normal and impaired word reading: Computational principles in quasi-regular domains. *Psychological Review, 103,* 56–115.

Polk, T. A., & Farah, M. J. (2002). Functional MRI evidence for an abstract, not perceptual, word-form area. *Journal of Experimental Psychology: General, 131,* 65–72.

Polk, T. A., Stallcup, M., Aguirre, G. K., Alsop, D. C., D'Esposito, M., Detre, J. A., et al. (2002). Neural specialization for letter recognition. *Journal of Cognitive Neuroscience, 14,* 145–159.

Price, C. J., & Devlin, J. T. (2003). The myth of the visual word form area. *NeuroImage, 19,* 473–481.

Price, C. J., & Devlin, J. T. (2011). The interactive account of ventral occipitotemporal contributions to reading. *Trends in Cognitive Science, 15,* 246–253.

Price, C. J., & Mechelli, A. (2005). Reading and reading disturbance. *Current Opinion in Neurobiology, 15,* 231–238.

Puce, A., Allison, T., Asgari, M., Gore, J. C., & McCarthy, G. (1996). Differential sensitivity of human visual cortex to faces, letter strings, and textures: A functional magnetic resonance imaging study. *The Journal of Neuroscience, 16,* 5205–5215.

Puce, A., Allison, T., Gore, J. C., & McCarthy, G. (1995). Face-sensitive regions in human extrastriate cortex studied by functional MRI. *Journal of Neurophysiology, 74,* 1192–1199.

Quartz, S. R., & Sejnowski, T. J. (1997). The neural basis of cognitive development: A constructivist manifesto. *Behavioral and Brain Sciences, 20,* 537–596.

Rajimehr, R., Young, J. C., & Tootell, R. B. (2009). An anterior temporal face patch in human cortex, predicted by macaque maps. *Proceedings of the National Academy of Sciences, USA, 106,* 1995–2000.

Reddy, L., & Kanwisher, N. (2006). Coding of visual objects in the ventral stream. *Current Opinion in Neurobiology, 16,* 408–414.

Reich, L., Szwed, M., Cohen, L., & Amedi, A. (2011). A ventral visual stream reading center independent of visual experience. *Current Biology, 21,* 363–368.

Robertson, L. C., & Ivry, R. (2000). Hemispheric asymmetries: Attention to visual and auditory primitives. *Current Directions in Psychological Science, 9,* 59–64.

Rumelhart, D. E., Hinton, G. E., & Williams, R. J. (1986). Learning representations by back-propagating errors. *Nature, 323,* 533–536.

Salvan, C. V., Ulmer, J. L., DeYoe, E. A., Wascher, T., Mathews, V. P., Lewis, J. W., et al. (2004). Visual object agnosia and pure word alexia: Correlation of functional magnetic resonance imaging and lesion localization. *Journal of Computer Assisted Tomography, 28,* 63–67.

Scherf, K. S., Behrmann, M., Humphreys, K., & Luna, B. (2007). Visual category-selectivity for faces, places and objects emerges along different developmental trajectories. *Developmental Science, 10,* 15–30.

Schwarzlose, R. F., Baker, C. I., & Kanwisher, N. (2005). Separate face and body selectivity on the fusiform gyrus. *Journal of Neuroscience, 25,* 11055–11059.

Sereno, M. I., Dale, A. M., Reppas, J. B., Kwong, K. K., Belliveau, J. W., Brady, T. J., et al. (1995). Borders of multiple visual areas in humans revealed by functional magnetic resonance imaging. *Science, 268,* 889–893.

Sergent, J., Ohta, S., & MacDonald, B. (1992). Functional neuroanatomy of face and object processing. *Brain, 115,* 15–36.

Sewards, T. V. (2011). Neural structures and mechanisms involved in scene recognition: A review and interpretation. *Neuropsychologia, 49*(3), 277–298.

Shillcock, R., Ellison, M. T., & Monaghan, P. (2000). Eye-fixation behavior, lexical storage and visual word recognition in a split processing model. *Psychological Review, 107,* 824–851.

Spiridon, M., Fischl, B., & Kanwisher, N. (2006). Location and spatial profile of category-specific regions in human extrastriate cortex. *Human Brain Mapping, 27*(1), 77–89.

Spiridon, M., & Kanwisher, N. (2002). How distributed is visual category information in human occipitotemporal cortex? An fMRI study. *Neuron, 35*(6), 1157–1165.

Starrfelt, R., & Behrmann, M. (2011). Number reading in pure alexia: A review. *Neuropsychologia, 49*(9), 2283–2298.

Stephan, B. C., & Caine, D. (2009). Aberrant pattern of scanning in prosopagnosia reflects impaired face processing. *Brain and Cognition, 69,* 262–268.

Tagamets, M. A., Novick, J. M., Chalmers, M. L., & Friedman, R. B. (2000). A parametric approach to orthographic processing in the brain: An fMRI study. *Journal of Cognitive Neuroscience, 12,* 281–297.

Tanaka, J. W., & Farah, M. J. (1993). Parts and wholes in face recognition. *Quarterly Journal of Experimental Psychology, 46A,* 225–245.

Taylor, J. C., Wiggett, A. J., & Downing, P. E. (2010). fMRI-adaptation studies of viewpoint tuning in the extrastriate and fusiform body areas. *Journal of Neurophysiology, 103,* 1467–1477.

Tong, M. H., Joyce, C. A., & Cottrell, G. W. (2008). Why is the fusiform face area recruited for novel categories of expertise? A neurocomputational investigation. *Brain Research, 1202,* 14–24.

Tootell, R. B. H., Mendola, J., Hadjikhani, H., Ledden, P., Liu, A., Reppas, J., et al. (1997). Functional analysis of V3a and related areas in human visual cortex. *Journal of Neuroscience, 71,* 7060–7078.

Tranel, D., Damasio, H., & Damasio, A. R. (1997). A neural basis for the retrieval of conceptual knowledge. *Neuropsychologia, 35,* 1319–1328.

Turk, M., & Pentland, A. (1991). Eigenfaces for recognition. *Journal of Cognitive Neuroscience, 3,* 71–86.

Turkeltaub, P. E., Eden, G. F., Jones, K. M., & Zeffiro, T. A. (2002). Meta-analysis of the functional neuroanatomy of single-word reading: Method and validation. *NeuroImage, 16,* 765–780.

Warrington, E. K., & Shallice, T. (1980). Word-form dyslexia. *Brain, 103,* 99–112.

Weekes, B. S. (1997). Differential effects of number of letters on word and nonword naming latency. *Quarterly Journal of Experimental Psychology, 50A,* 439–456.

Whitney, C. (2001). How the brain encodes the order of letters in a printed word: The SERIOL model and selective literature review. *Psychonomic Bulletin and Review, 8,* 221–243.

Willems, R. M., Peelen, M. V., & Hagoort, P. (2010). Cerebral lateralization of face-selective and body-selective visual areas depends on handedness. *Cerebral Cortex, 20,* 1719–1725.

Wong, A. C., Gauthier, I., Woroch, B., DeBuse, C., & Curran, T. (2005). An early electrophysiological response associated with expertise in letter perception. Cognitive, *Affective and Behavioral Neuroscience, 5,* 306–318.

Yang, M.-H. (2002). Face recognition using kernel methods. In T. Diederich, S. Becker, & Z. Ghahramani (Eds.), *Advances in neural information processing systems* (Vol. 14, pp. 1457–1464). Cambridge, MA: MIT Press.

Yovel, G., & Kanwisher, N. (2005). The neural basis of the behavioral face-inversion effect. *Current Biology, 15,* 2256–2262.

Yovel, G., Tambini, A., & Brandman, T. (2008). The asymmetry of the fusiform face area is a stable individual characteristic that underlies the left-visual-field superiority for faces. *Neuropsychologia, 46,* 3061–3068.

COGNITIVE NEUROPSYCHOLOGY, 2011, 28 (3 & 4), 276–287

When modularization fails to occur:
A developmental perspective

Dean D'Souza and Annette Karmiloff-Smith

Birkbeck Centre for Brain & Cognitive Development, University of London, London, UK

We argue that models of adult cognition defined in terms of independently functioning modules cannot be applied to development, whether typical or atypical. The infant brain starts out highly interconnected, and it is only over developmental time that neural networks become increasingly specialized—that is, relatively modularized. In the case of atypical development, even when behavioural scores fall within the normal range, they are frequently underpinned by different cognitive and neural processes. In other words, in neurodevelopmental disorders the gradual process of relative modularization may fail to occur.

Keywords: Modularity; Child development; Developmental disorders; Developing brain; Neonate start state; Adult neuropsychology.

Sternberg discusses an approach to understanding complex neural and cognitive processes by dividing them into modules. The concept of modularity—that is, the notion that cognitive processes are controlled by subsystems that operate largely independently from one another—is widely invoked in the cognitive sciences to explain perceptual processes and, often, high-level cognitive processes. On this view, behaviour emanates from minimally interactive modules or independent functional subsystems in the (adult) brain. These are realized in discrete anatomical systems, whereby selective damage to one system results in an associated loss of cognitive function, and by the same token, the loss of a specific cognitive function is indicative of damage to an associated brain region(s). This adult neuropsychological model of independently functioning modules is frequently used to understand brain,

cognition, and behaviour and has been especially fruitful in research into processes such as reading and writing (e.g., Damasio, 1977).

Arguments from brain modularity in adult neuropsychological patients have also been applied to development (e.g., Temple, 1997), particularly to the understanding of neurodevelopmental disorders (e.g., Pinker, 1999). However, it is critical to recall that the adult brain represents the consolidated end state of a developmental process. In other words, the adult brain has become specialized over time. But this in no way entails that it started out with the same degree of specialization. In other words, we should not invoke the concept of end-state modularity to infer the start-state of development, nor can the end state be used to shed light on the gradual *process* of relative modularization, which involves the complex dynamics of

Correspondence should be addressed to Annette Karmiloff-Smith, University of London—Centre for Brain and Cognitive Development, 32 Torrington Square, London WC1E 7JL, UK. (E-mail: a.karmiloff-smith@bbk.ac.uk).

http://www.psypress.com/cogneuropsychology   http://dx.doi.org/10.1080/02643294.2011.614939

ontogenetic change (Karmiloff-Smith, 1992, 1997, 1998; Paterson, Brown, Gsödl, Johnson, & Karmiloff-Smith, 1999).

In this paper, we use the concept of progressive modularization and present examples from atypical development in which relative modularization may fail to occur. In so doing, we highlight the importance of taking development seriously. First, we discuss the role of modular thinking in adult neuropsychology and how it has been applied to typical and atypical development. We then use examples from face processing and language to demonstrate how the modularity thesis has, in our view, been erroneously generalized to account for neurodevelopmental disorders. Finally, we argue that a more dynamic model is needed to fully understand neural and cognitive processes as they change over developmental time.

The role of modular thinking in adult neuropsychology

The evidence for modules has its roots in studies of adult neuropsychological patients (e.g., Butterworth, 1999; Temple, 1997; see discussion in Shallice, 1988). Neuropsychologists derive hypothetical modules by correlating brain lesions in humans and animals with losses of cognitive function. For example, individuals with sudden brain trauma may lose the ability to recognize familiar faces (prosopagnosia) or to use syntax and morphology (agrammatism), while the rest of their cognitive system (including the ability to recognize familiar objects or to use strings of vocabulary items) seems to remain unaffected. Cases such as these are taken as evidence that cognitive processes are controlled by subsystems that operate independently from one another, and have led theorists to conceive of the mind in the form of a box-and-arrow model, where one or several boxes have a cross through them while the others remain intact. The consideration of cognitive functions as independent and dissociated in the adult brain has

led many researchers to assume that they were like this from the start and remained so throughout development (Temple, 1997).

The box-and-arrow analogy has been applied to children with genetic disorders, by positing impaired modules as the cause of poor task performance. So, when an individual with a developmental disorder presents with an uneven cognitive profile, s/he is considered to have intact modules for domains in which behaviour falls within the normal range and impaired modules for domains in which behaviour falls below the normal range. Take, for example, individuals with specific language impairment (SLI) and individuals with Williams syndrome[1] (WS). Those with SLI present with serious deficits in language development, but their nonverbal ability falls within the normal range. By contrast, those with WS display poor performance on nonverbal tasks, but relatively strong performance on language tasks. Pinker, for example, assumes a modular interpretation of these findings: "overall, the genetic double dissociation is striking. . . . The genes of one group of children [SLI] *impair* their grammar while *sparing* their intelligence; the genes of another group of children [WS] *impair* their intelligence while *sparing* their grammar" (Pinker, 1999, p. 262, italics added). The very notion of "sparing" suggests that development plays no role in the phenotypic outcome and that intelligence has no effect on language at any age.

So, if one applies modular thinking to children with neurodevelopmental disorders, then it has to be assumed (a) that specific brain substrates underlie dissociable functions from the outset; (b) that there are no cross-domain interactions; (c) that there is one-to-one mapping between genotype and impaired cognitive modules; (d) that the genetic mutation can impair a limited number of functions but leave the rest of the system totally unaffected; and (e) that experience plays little role. We argue that these assumptions are unjustified.

---

[1] WS is a rare genetic syndrome caused by a hemizygous microdeletion on chromosome 7q23.11 of some 26–28 genes (Donnai & Karmiloff-Smith, 2000).

Gradual process of relative modularization

The lesion method works by assuming that cognitive functions involve specific regions in the brain, and that when those regions are structurally altered or destroyed by injury or disease, the cognitive functions that correspond to them are affected. Therefore, a correlation between a loss of cognitive function and a specific brain lesion is used to infer the existence of a causal relationship between that particular phenotype and site of injury. But this assumption ignores the dynamic and complex interactions of multiple, emerging systems that characterize the developing brain, as well as functional flexibility (Moses & Stiles, 2002). In fact, the human brain does not start out modular. The infant brain is anatomically and functionally significantly less differentiated and less modular than the adult brain, and it is initially highly interconnected (Huttenlocher & Dabholkar, 1997; Huttenlocher & de Courten, 1987; Neville, 2006). It only gradually becomes specialized and localized (i.e., relatively modularized) during ontogenesis (Johnson, 2001; Karmiloff-Smith, 1992). For instance, in typical infant development, faces are initially treated like objects, and neither stimulus type shows an inversion effect. Later, once the processing of faces has become relatively modularized, it is subject to an inversion effect, whereas the processing of objects is not. Progressive modularization also occurs within the context of an environment, which plays a key role in the developmental process and is characterized by interactivity (Karmiloff-Smith, 1998; Kuhl, 2004; Majdan & Schatz, 2006; Meaney & Szyf, 2005). In other words, the adult neuropsychological model ignores the process of development, and yet the roots of development are often critical for understanding the end state (Piaget, 1926). To illustrate these points, we now examine concrete examples from studies of face processing and language.

Face processing

Newborn babies are sensitive to face-like patterns (Johnson, 2005). This has been interpreted by some researchers as evidence that neonates have a face-processing module—that is, that they possess innate representations of faces (e.g., Kanwisher, McDermott, & Chun, 1997). On this view, evolution has endowed the human infant brain with a module dedicated to face processing. However, infant sensitivity to face-like patterns is not controlled neurally in the same way as in adult-like cortical structures—that is, predominantly the fusiform face area (FFA), but at least in part by subcortical visuomotor pathways (Johnson, 2011). By ensuring that the infant frequently orients to faces in the environment, this system enables cortical microcircuits to gradually develop representations for processing this particular class of stimuli. Thus, rather than the neural representations for face processing being innately specified, many scientists now agree that they emerge from interactions between the infant and its environment, and from the gradual reconfiguration of cortical circuitry. This has been demonstrated in several studies comparing 6- and 12-month-old infants' progressively changing neural processing of faces, using high-density event-related potentials (Johnson, 2005). In the early months, multiple regions are initially activated to process face stimuli, but the properties of some regions (type of neuron, neuronal density, etc.) are more relevant to the processing of faces than others and eventually win out (Elman et al., 1996; Karmiloff-Smith, 1992, 1998). For instance, face processing in 6-month-old infants is bilateral (Johnson, 2005). However, the microcircuitry of the right hemisphere lends itself better to the configural processing of faces than does the left hemisphere (de Schonen & Deruelle, 1994)—that is, it is more relevant (Karmiloff-Smith, 1998, 2007)—and during the second half of the first year, the right hemisphere begins to dominate the processing of faces (Johnson, 2005). By one year of age, face processing is predominantly localized in the right hemisphere in regions more characteristic of the adult brain (de Haan, Humphreys, & Johnson, 2002; Johnson, 2001, 2005). In other words, the developing brain is neither localized nor specialized at birth, but gradually *becomes* localized/specialized over developmental time. In sum, the neonate brain does not come preequipped with a dedicated face-processing module with representational content; rather, face specialization gradually emerges from experience and competition across different brain regions.

Why is the process of development so important? Why would evolution not build into the human brain a prespecified face-processing module, since recognizing conspecifics is so critical to our social lives? One reason is that having to *develop* a capacity makes the brain more flexible. Indeed, there is a trade-off between hyperspecialization and flexibility, with species the most distant from humans having the greatest degree of prespecification and those closest to humans the least prespecification (Quartz & Sejnowski, 1997). A further advantage for having cortical circuits develop over time, rather than being prespecified, may be to ensure that the microcircuitry is appropriately shaped by the specifics of the relevant input.

Another argument against a prespecified face-processing module is the existence of learning and specialization even in the adult brain. Thus, if an individual is trained to become an expert in identifying a category of artificial objects (e.g., "greebles"; Gauthier, Skudlarski, Gore, & Anderson 2000; Gauthier, Tarr, Anderson, Skudlarski, & Gore, 1999), then this too will result in specialized activation of the FFA. This suggests that the FFA is activated for faces in adults, not because the region was prespecified to process faces, but because its properties are relevant to visual expertise and that it has become specialized through the individual's massive experience with that class of stimuli.

However, the existence of genetic syndromes in which IQ is low but face processing is particularly good would seem to argue in favour of the existence of a dedicated face-processing module. In fact, individuals with Williams syndrome perform within the normal range on standardized tasks, such as the Benton Face Recognition Task (Bellugi, Lichtenberger, Jones, Lai, & St George, 2000; Bellugi, Wang, & Jernigan, 1994) and the Rivermead Face Memory Task (Udwin & Yule,

1991). This has been interpreted as evidence of an "intact", innately specified face-processing module (e.g., Bellugi et al., 1994). However, studies have since shown that the WS behavioural proficiency is actually underpinned by atypical cognitive processes (e.g., Deruelle, Macini, Livet, Casse-Perrot, & de Schonen, 1999; Karmiloff-Smith, 1997, 1998; Karmiloff-Smith et al., 2004; Rossen, Jones, Wang, & Klima, 1996; but see Tager-Flusberg, Plesa-Skwerer, Faja, & Joseph, 2003) and atypical neural processes (Grice et al., 2003; Grice et al., 2001; Mills et al., 2000). For example, studies using event-related potentials have shown that the brains of typically developing (TD) individuals process cars differently from human faces and monkey faces, whereas individuals with WS show the same brain signature for both cars and faces (Grice et al., 2003). Moreover, adults with WS do not display the normal hemispheric dominance for processing upright faces as compared to inverted faces (Karmiloff-Smith et al., 2004). In other words, although individuals with WS can achieve normal behavioural scores on standardized face-processing tasks, the WS brain fails to specialize and localize. Consequently, even though individuals with WS are drawn to faces and gain much experience of them, a finely tuned face-processing module fails to emerge over developmental time in the WS brain.

Language

Two brain regions in the left hemisphere are thought to be strongly associated with language functions—Broca's area and Wernicke's area—and lesions in hitherto normal adult brains to either of these areas giving rise to double dissociations have been interpreted as evidence of the existence in the brain of language-specific modules. An alternative view is that the pattern of synaptic connectivity within the cortical microcircuitry that gives rise to language-specific representations emerges from the *gradual* process of ontogenetic development (Karmiloff-Smith, 1992; Karmiloff-Smith, Plunkett, Johnson, Elman, & Bates, 1998). Indeed, children presenting with perinatal lesions to these so-called "language areas" can still acquire language. For example, most children with left hemispherectomy early in life subsequently fall within the normal range on language tests and attend age-appropriate schools (Stiles, Bates, Thal, Trauner, & Reilly, 2002). Notable is the fact that they perform significantly better than adults with left-hemisphere brain damage to language areas, suggesting that the child brains have found an alternative developmental route to fluent language, whereas the adult suffers damage to an already consolidated brain in terms of localization of language functions. This attests to the greater plasticity of the developing brain in contrast to the vulnerability of the developed brain (Karmiloff-Smith, 2010; Neville, 2006).

To falsify the view that language-specific representations emerge from the gradual process of ontogenetic development, the scientist needs to present examples of a single, pure impairment, present throughout development, in an otherwise totally normal child brain. However, to our knowledge, no such evidence is actually forthcoming when examined in depth. It is true that one developmental disorder is, by definition, usually characterized as a single impairment in an otherwise normal brain—that is, specific language impairment (SLI). However, recent research has shown that disorders such as SLI are likely to stem from lower level deficits and are accompanied by subtle impairments in parts of the brain that were initially thought to be "intact" (Benasich & Spitz, 1999; Bishop, 1997, 2002; Botting, 2005; Chiat, 2001; Choudhury & Benasich, 2011; Gou, Choudhury, & Benasich, 2011; Norbury, Bishop, & Biscoe, 2002).

Furthermore, even when the performance IQs of children with SLI fall within the normal range, they often turn out to be significantly lower than those of their siblings (Botting, 2005), suggesting that the SLI brain may be characterized by a more general, albeit subtle, impairment irrespective of "normal" nonverbal scores. Indeed, a magnetic resonance imaging (MRI) study that set out to investigate the entire SLI brain found that affected children had significantly more (above 10%) white matter distributed throughout cerebral cortex than did controls (Herbert et al., 2003). This pattern was just as apparent in nonlanguage areas of the brain as in the language areas, which led the authors to conclude that their participants had a general impairment that was more relevant to language but affected other areas albeit more subtly.

In contrast, according to Fonteneau and van der Lely (2008), language-specific impairments in SLI do exist. In an event-related potential study, individuals with so-called grammatical-SLI (G-SLI) heard sentences containing syntactic or semantic violations. The authors found that the syntactic violations failed to elicit the early left-anterior negative electrophysiological response (ELAN), found in healthy controls and which is considered to be specific to grammatical processing. Yet, the syntactic violations did elicit a normal P600, which is associated with the reanalysis of syntactic structure or syntactic integration. Moreover, the semantic violations did elicit a normal N400 response. This led the authors to claim "that grammatical neural circuitry underlying language is a *developmentally unique system* in the functional architecture of the brain, and this complex higher cognitive system can be selectively impaired" (Fonteneau & van der Lely, 2008, p. 1, italics added).

However, it should be recalled that Fonteneau and van der Lely (2008) found a domain-specific deficit in adolescents with G-SLI, with the receptive vocabulary of children half their chronological age. In other words, the single targeted age of the participants in their study merely represents a snapshot of development at the time of adolescence. Their data do not lend themselves to claims about cognitive or neural modularity over *developmental time*. Pivotal to Fonteneau and van der Lely's argument against the neuroconstructivist approach are two claims: (a) that this is a purely grammatical deficit, and (b) that in their adolescents they detected no lower level impairments in auditory processing (their measure was "processing speed") and found all other functions to be "normal". But neither of these "facts" can be invoked. First, the lexical levels of their adolescents were seriously below chronological age, so the deficit is not confined to grammar. Second, normal processing speed by the time an individual reaches adolescence does not constitute evidence of a lack of low-level perceptual problems at an earlier phase of development when such timing may have been critical, something that individuals could have overcome by adolescence (Karmiloff-Smith, 1998). This stresses how important ontogenetic timing is when trying to explain neurodevelopmental disorders.

Furthermore, the fact that the receptive vocabulary (measured using the British Picture Vocabulary Scale) of the adolescents with SLI was so delayed (reported as at a level half of their chronological age) is already indicative of atypical functioning. The syntactic violations elicited an N400 electrophysiological response in the participants—evidence that the neural circuitry that supported their semantic processing may have been compensating for their problems with the processing of information. Also, whereas the P600 was equally distributed on anterior sites across all the groups, in the G-SLI group it was maximally distributed on (and reached greater amplitude at) anterior sites *on the right*. This could indicate subtle quantitative and qualitative differences between the SLI group and the healthy controls. To resolve these questions, which are essentially developmental questions, it is critical to investigate such processes in the same individuals across time. Indeed, whereas the N400 response to semantic violations was distributed bilaterally in the posterior areas in the G-SLI and chronological age (CA)-matched participants, it was maximally negative in the right hemisphere of the younger language-matched children. This suggests that the neural substrates that give rise to the N400 are dynamic, not static, across developmental time.

An alternative interpretation of the SLI data is that one (or more) lower level deficits in early infancy have affected language at a critical time in development and more than any other domain. Language emerges from a number of lower level abilities, such as inter alia the ability to share attention, to understand communicative intentions, to segment and detect patterns in the speech stream, to make phonetic and phonemic discriminations, and to increase speed of speech processing (Choudhury & Benasich, 2011; Fernald, Pinto, Swingley, Weinverg, & McRoberts, 1998; Jusczyk, Pisoni, Reed, Fernald, & Myers, 1983; Tomasello, 2003). A lower level deficit in any one of these processes could disrupt development to such an extent that the emergence of higher level processes like language comprehension and production becomes seriously compromised. Indeed, some studies have shown that children with SLI have problems with detecting patterns in the speech stream, specifically with the processing of rapid sequences of auditory–verbal information, necessary for processing the flow of connected speech (Choudhury & Benasich, 2011; Tallal, 2000). Furthermore, morphological markers are frequently of low salience in the speech stream and are often a problem for individuals with SLI (Leonard et al., 2003). Finally, children with SLI, like other children with neurodevelopmental disorders, also have poor auditory working memory (Bishop, North, & Donlan, 1996; Conti-Ramsden, 2003; Gathercole & Baddeley, 1990).

Differences in brain function between children and adults must also be taken into account. For example, if we consider what is known about adult aphasia, then delays in vocabulary ought to be most pronounced in children with damage to posterior sites in the left hemisphere. Yet in actual fact, comprehension deficits turn out to be more common in children with right-hemisphere damage (Bates & Roe, 2001; Stiles et al., 2002; Stiles & Thal, 1993). In other words, regions responsible for language *learning* in young children are not necessarily the same regions as those responsible for language *use* in the adult. It is critical to recall that in the developing brain, other brain regions can compensate for damage (Guzzetta et al., 2008; Liégeois et al., 2004). The brains of the congenitally deaf provide a further indication of the plasticity of the developing brain. A lack of auditory input to the deaf brain results in the emergence of visual functions in otherwise normal auditory areas, and vice versa for the congenitally blind (Neville & Bavelier, 2002).

Language systems are shaped by experience. Studies of phoneme perception, word learning, and reading indicate that in typically developing children, the language system becomes progressively specialized and localized—increasingly modularized—over developmental time. For example, infants can discriminate a wide range of speech sounds at 6 months of age, but because of perceptual narrowing, by 10 months of age their ability becomes increasingly restricted to the speech sounds from their own native language (Werker & Polka, 1993). Furthermore, the more words a child learns, the more focally distributed their brain activity is when presented with known and unknown words (Mills & Conboy, 2009). In addition, the visual word form area, which shows a preferential response to visual words compared to other complex visual stimuli, is activated bilaterally in beginning readers, but becomes more focalized during ontogenesis to the left hemisphere (Schlaggar et al., 2002).

While gradual modularization of language function occurs over time in typically developing children, this is not always the case in atypically developing individuals even, paradoxically, when behavioural scores fall within the normal range. Indeed, as was the case for face processing, individuals with Williams syndrome display proficient language behaviourally. However, studies of WS brains have shown that, unlike typical controls, individuals with WS do not gradually shift over developmental time from bilateral to left-hemisphere processing (Mills et al., 2000). So proficient behaviour in a genetic disorder cannot be used to argue in favour of an "intact module". Despite its fluency, and contrary to the case of typical development, the language of individuals with WS does not seem to become progressively modularized.

In summary, the neural substrates of language are shaped over developmental time by language input from the spoken and written word. From the neuroconstructivist stance, we argue that regions of the left temporal lobe are likely to be more relevant to processing speech and language. But other regions can also support this function, albeit with subtle differences, if typical development goes awry.

Modularity of brain function versus the modularity of cognitive function

This discussion has been directed at both the modularity of brain function and the modularity of cognitive function. In our view, cognition and neural circuitry are necessarily linked, so both levels of description need to be consistent with one another because cognition arises from, and is therefore necessarily constrained by, the brain. In turn, the manifestation of cognitive processes (i.e., in behaviour) constantly changes the brain by fine-tuning neural connectivity. Furthermore, because initially the brain is so interconnected, changes in one system will necessarily affect other systems, at different levels, even if only subtly. As a consequence, neuroconstructivists challenge Marr's (1982) proposal for the independence of levels of description. Even if behaviour is best explained at the cognitive level, the cognitive theory ought be constrained by the levels of description below it (Mareschal et al., 2007).

To put our case more strongly, commitment to functionally independent and specialized modules, as defined by Fodor (1983), is no longer useful – at least, not with respect to the developing brain, despite the fact that it has been a very popular explanatory concept with some developmental psychologists (Hermer & Spelke, 1996; Leslie, 1994; Spelke, 2000; Wellman & Gelman, 1998). Modularity entails that behaviour is the product of independent, functional components, realized in discrete physical systems, and that these components are minimally interactive. But this concept leaves no room for the process of *ontogenetic development*. In our view, modules (both cognitive and neural) are the end product of an ontogenetic process, not its starting point. Because the process of specialization and localization of function (relative modularization) involves the active processing of environmental input, it makes no sense to speak of modules as being present at birth. Indeed, a "module" as crucial for survival as face processing none the less takes some 12 months of massive input before it begins to look like an adult one. And even when some adults appear to possess a face-processing module, as in the case of adults with Williams syndrome, empirical evidence suggests that they actually do not (Grice et al., 2001).

Although we have argued throughout that development involves a gradual process of relative modularization, in fact, even the evidence for true modularity in the adult brain remains ambiguous (Marslen-Wilson & Tyler, 1987; Stein & Stanford, 2008). For example, it used to be thought that multimodal processing is hierarchical, with low-level unimodal sensory areas projecting to higher order heteromodal regions for analysis. However, studies now show that the processing of multiple modalities occurs in parallel throughout the human cerebral cortex, including primary projection areas such as the primary auditory cortex (Stein & Stanford, 2008). For example, lip-reading activates the primary auditory cortex and surrounding auditory areas, even in the absence of auditory input (Bernstein, Auer, Moore, Ponton, & Don, 2002; Pekkola et al., 2006; Pekkola et al., 2005). Furthermore, the processing of sensory information is often modulated by a forward feedback and backward feedback mechanism: "talk" between systems. For instance, the processing of auditory information in the auditory cortex is modulated by projections from the visual cortex, as well as by projections from the superior temporal sulcus (STS; Besle et al., 2008; Calvert, Campbell, & Brammer, 2000). It is clear that the adult system is highly interconnected—neural circuits are not (in general) "minimally" interactive (i.e., they are not strictly modular), so the notion of neural modularity loses its explanatory power. But what about cognitive modularity? Single "cognitive" behaviours are almost always associated with distributed networks of brain areas. For instance, neuroimaging studies show that several cortical regions are activated when a face is processed. The region that is associated with the most activity is the fusiform face area (FFA), but even this area is activated (albeit less so) for objects. This suggests that there is a mismatch in granularity, perhaps even in ontology—brain function primitives may not actually look like cognitive primitives.

The challenge now is to move away from debates on what constitutes a module, and instead develop a causal framework that will allow investigators to study how the complex and highly interconnected self-organizing system in adults has developed from infancy onwards.

Conclusions

We have seen that a static model of the adult end state is often applied to development. Yet we need to draw a clear distinction between the *developed* brain and the *developing* brain (Karmiloff-Smith, 2010). The adult neuropsychological model assumes that the developing brain/mind can be viewed as a number of intact and impaired, independently functioning modules, where damage to one module will have little or no effect on the other modules. But we have argued throughout that it cannot be assumed that the adult structure reflects the start state. Individuals with neurodevelopmental disorders should not be viewed as having normal brains with parts impaired and parts spared, but as brains that are developing differently. Behavioural scores in the normal range do not necessarily imply normal underlying cognitive or neural processes. To the extent that the mind/brain is modular, it is, we argue, the *outcome* of a dynamic developmental process, mediated by experience. Thus, the application of modular thinking to development cannot answer key questions such as: (a) why certain brain regions take on and support the functions that they do, (b) when these regions fail, why some regions can compensate by supporting the same functions, while others cannot, (c) from what domain-relevant processes do domain-specific processes emerge, (d) whether a brain region *starts out* atypical or *becomes* atypical as a result of atypical processing, or (e) what factors constrain or shape development and give rise to individual differences? These developmental questions will remain intractable for as long as strictly modular thinking dominates the typical and atypical development literature. Future work in developmental neuroscience must move beyond the box-and-arrow model and place the process of development at the centre of its research programme.

The implications of taking development seriously are numerous. First, it is worth recalling that several cortical regions of recent evolutionary expansion are particularly immature in the human neonate (lateral temporal, parietal, and frontal regions) compared to other species (Hill, et al., 2010). It thus seems that, to develop a flexible mind that can generalize across domains, it may well be beneficial for parts of the brain to remain less mature at birth to enhance the influence of postnatal experience on neural circuitry. Second, if synaptic pruning occurs too early in ontogenesis, then the brain may specialize before the microcircuitry has been appropriately shaped by the relevant input. This could lead to a system that processes too few input types (Oliver, Johnson, Karmiloff-Smith, & Pennington, 2000). If pruning occurs too late, or does not occur at all, then the brain may fail to specialize, and this could impact the system's ability to multitask (Mackinlay, Charman, & Karmiloff-Smith, 2006). These and similar considerations arise from abandoning the classical box-and-arrow metaphor of the developing brain, with its impaired and spared modules, in favour of taking the complex dynamics of development and the gradual process of relative modularization more seriously. To understand how high-level functions (such as face processing and language) emerge, and indeed how they might come to differ in typically and atypically developing brains, they must be traced back to their low-level origins in infancy (Karmiloff-Smith, 1998, 2007). A tiny impairment in a basic process may have a huge cascading impact over developmental time, affecting some functions strongly and others more subtly. In sum, neurodevelopmental disorders must be understood within the dynamic context of development, rather than as damaged parts to an innately constituted modular system.

REFERENCES

Bates, E., & Roe, K. (2001). Language development in children with unilateral brain injury. In C. A. Nelson & M. Luciana (Eds.), *Handbook of developmental cognitive neuroscience* (pp. 281–307). Cambridge, MA: MIT Press.

Bellugi, U., Lichtenberger, L., Jones, W., Lai, Z., & St George, M. (2000). The neurocognitive profile of Williams syndrome: A complex pattern of strengths and weaknesses. *Journal of Cognitive Neuroscience, 12*(Suppl.), 7–29.

Bellugi, U., Wang, P. P., & Jernigan, T. L. (1994). Williams syndrome: An unusual neuropsychological profile. In S. H. Broman & J. Grafman (Eds.), *Atypical cognitive deficits in developmental disorders: Implications for brain function* (pp. 23–56). Hillsdale, NJ: Lawrence Erlbaum Associates.

Benasich, A. A., & Spitz, R. V. (1999). Insights from infants: Temporal processing abilities and genetics contribute to language impairment. In K. Whitmore, H. Hart, & G. Willems (Eds.), *A neurodevelopmental approach to specific learning disorders* (pp. 191–210). London, UK: MacKeith Press.

Bernstein, L. E., Auer, E. T., Moore, J. K., Ponton, C. W., & Don, M. (2002). Visual speech perception without primary auditory cortex activation. *Neuroreport, 13*, 311–315.

Besle, J., Fischer, C., Bidet-Caulet, A., Lecaignard, F., Bertrand, O., & Giard, M.-H. (2008). Visual activation and audiovisual interactions in the auditory cortex during speech perception: Intracranial recordings in humans. *The Journal of Neuroscience, 28*, 14301–14310.

Bishop, D. V. M. (1997). *Uncommon understanding: Developmental and disorders of language comprehension in children.* Hove, UK: Psychology Press.

Bishop, D. V. M. (2002). Motor immaturity and specific speech and language impairment: Evidence for a common genetic basis. *American Journal of Medical Genetics: Neuropsychiatric Genetics, 114*, 56–63.

Bishop, D. V. M., North, T., & Donlan, C. (1996). Nonword repetition as a behavioural marker for inherited language impairment: Evidence from a twin study. *Journal of Child Psychology and Psychiatry, 37*, 391–403.

Botting, N. (2005). Non-verbal cognitive development and language impairment. *Journal of Child Psychology and Psychiatry, 46*, 317–326.

Butterworth, B. (1999). *The mathematical brain.* London, UK: Macmillan.

Calvert, G. A., Campbell, R., & Brammer, M. J. (2000). Evidence from functional magnetic resonance imaging of crossmodal binding in the human heteromodal cortex. *Current Biology, 10*, 649–657.

Chiat, S. (2001). Mapping theories of developmental language impairment: Premises, predictions and evidence. *Language & Cognitive Processes, 16*, 113–142.

Choudhury, N., & Benasich, A. A. (2011). Maturation of auditory evoked potentials from 6–48 months: Prediction to 3 and 4 year language and cognitive abilities. *Clinical Neurophysiology, 122,* 320–338.

Conti-Ramsden, G. (2003). Processing and linguistic markers in young children with specific language impairment (SLI). *Journal of Speech, Language, and Hearing Research, 46,* 1029–1037.

Damasio, A. R. (1977). Varieties and the significance of the alexias. *Archives of Neurology, 34,* 325–326.

de Haan, M., Humphreys, K., & Johnson, M. H. (2002). Developing a brain specialized for face perception: A converging methods approach. *Developmental Psychobiology, 40,* 200–212.

Deruelle, C., Macini, J., Livet, M. O., Casse-Perrot, C., & de Schonen, S. (1999). Configural and local processing of faces in children with Williams syndrome. *Brain and Cognition, 41,* 276–298.

de Schonen, S., & Deruelle, C. (1994). Pattern and face recognition in infancy: Do both hemispheres perceive objects in the same way? In A. Vyt, B. Henriette, & M. H. Bornstein (Eds.), *Early child development in the French tradition: Contributions from current research* (pp. 35–54). Hillsdale, NJ: Lawrence Erlbaum Associates.

Donnai, D., & Karmiloff-Smith, A. (2000). Williams syndrome: From genotype through to the cognitive phenotype. *American Journal of Medical Genetics, 97,* 164–171.

Elman, J. L., Bates, E., Johnson, M. H., Karmiloff-Smith, A., Parisi, D., & Plunkett, K. (1996). *Rethinking innateness: A connectionist perspective on development.* Cambridge, MA: MIT Press.

Fernald, A., Pinto, J. P., Swingley, D., Weinberg, A., & McRoberts, G. W. (1998). Rapid gains in speed of verbal processing by infants in the 2nd year. *Psychological Science, 9*(3), 228–231.

Fodor, J. A. (1983). *Modularity of mind: An essay on faculty psychology.* Cambridge, MA: MIT Press.

Fonteneau, C., & van der Lely, H. J. K. (2008). Electrical brain responses in language-impaired children reveal grammar-specific deficits. *PLoS ONE, 3,* e1832, 1–6. doi:10.1371/journal.pone.0001832.

Gathercole, S. E., & Baddeley, A. D. (1990). Phonological memory deficits in language disordered children: Is there a causal connection? *Journal of Memory & Language, 29,* 336–360.

Gauthier, I., Skudlarski, P., Gore, J. C., & Anderson, A. W. (2000). Expertise for cars and birds recruits brain areas involved in face recognition. *Nature Neuroscience, 3,* 191–197.

Gauthier, I., Tarr, M. J., Anderson, A. W., Skudlarski, P., & Gore, J. C. (1999). Activation of the middle fusiform "face area" increases with expertise in recognizing novel objects. *Nature Neuroscience, 2,* 568–573.

Gou, S., Choudhury, N., & Benasich, A. A. (2011). Resting frontal gamma power at 16, 24 and 36 months predicts individual differences in language and cognition at 4 and 5 years. *Behavioural Brain Research, 220,* 263–270.

Grice, S. J., de Haan, M., Halit, H., Johnson, M. H., Csibra, G., Grant, J., et al. (2003). ERP abnormalities of visual perception in Williams syndrome. *Neuroreport, 14,* 1773–1777.

Grice, S., Spratling, M. W., Karmiloff-Smith, A., Halit, H., Csibra, G., de Haan, M., et al. (2001). Disordered visual processing and oscillatory brain activity in autism and Williams syndrome. *Neuroreport, 12,* 2697–2700.

Guzzetta, A., Pecini, C., Biagi, L., Tosetti, M., Brizzolara, D., Chilosi, A., et al. (2008). Language organisation in left perinatal stroke. *Neuropediatrics, 39,* 157–163.

Herbert, M. R., Ziegler, D. A., Makris, N., Bakardjiev, A., Hodgson, J., Adrien, K. T., et al. (2003). Larger brain and white matter volumes in children with developmental language disorder. *Developmental Science, 6,* F11–F22.

Hermer, L., & Spelke, E. (1996). Modularity and development: The case of spatial reorientation. *Cognition, 61,* 195–232.

Hill, J., Inder, T., Neil, J., Dierker, D., Harwell, J., & Van Essen, D. (2010). Similar patterns of cortical expansion during human development and evolution. *PNAS, 107,* 13135–13140.

Huttenlocher, P. R., & Dabholkar, A. S. (1997). Regional differences in synaptogenesis in human cerebral cortex. *Journal of Comparative Neurology, 387,* 167–178.

Huttenlocher, P. R., & de Courten, C. (1987). The development of synapses in striate cortex of man. *Human Neurobiology, 6,* 1–9.

Johnson, M. H. (2001). Functional brain development in humans. *Nature Reviews Neuroscience, 2,* 475–483.

Johnson, M. H. (2005). Sub-cortical face processing. *Nature Reviews Neuroscience, 6,* 766–774.

Johnson, M. H. (2011). *Developmental cognitive neuroscience* (3rd ed.). Chichester, UK: Wiley-Blackwell.

Juszcyk, P., Pisoni, D. B., Reed, M. A., Fernald, A., & Myers, M. (1983). Infants' discrimination of the duration of a rapid spectrum change in nonspeech signals. *Science, 222*(4620), 175–177.

Kanwisher, N., McDermott, J., & Chun, M. M. (1997). The fusiform face area: A module in human extrastriate cortex specialized for face perception. *Journal of Neuroscience, 17,* 4302–4311.

Karmiloff-Smith, A. (1992). *Beyond modularity: A developmental perspective on cognitive science.* Cambridge, MA: MIT Press.

Karmiloff-Smith, A. (1997). Crucial differences between developmental cognitive neuroscience and adult neuropsychology. *Developmental Neuropsychology, 13,* 513–524.

Karmiloff-Smith, A. (1998). Development itself is the key to understanding developmental disorders. *Trends in Cognitive Sciences, 2,* 389–398.

Karmiloff-Smith, A. (2007). Atypical epigenesis. *Developmental Science, 10,* 84–88.

Karmiloff-Smith, A. (2010). Neuroimaging of the developing brain: Taking "developing" seriously. *Human Brain Mapping, 31,* 934–941.

Karmiloff-Smith, A., Plunkett, K., Johnson, M. H., Elman, J. L., & Bates, E. A. (1998). What does it mean to claim something is innate? Response to Clark, Harris, Lightfoot and Samuels. *Mind and Language, 13,* 588–597.

Karmiloff-Smith, A., Thomas, M., Annaz, D., Humphreys, K., Ewing, S., Brace, N., et al. (2004). Exploring the Williams syndrome face processing debate: The importance of building developmental trajectories. *Journal of Child Psychology and Psychiatry, 45,* 1258–1274.

Kuhl, P. K. (2004). Early language acquisition: Cracking the speech code. *Nature Reviews Neuroscience, 5,* 831–843.

Leonard, L., Deevy, P., Miller, C., Rauf, L., Charest, M., & Kurtz, R. (2003). Surface forms and grammatical functions: Past tense and passive participle use by children with specific language impairment. *Journal of Speech, Language, and Hearing Research, 46,* 43–55.

Leslie, A. M. (1994). ToMM, ToBY, and Agency: Core architecture and domain specificity. In L. A. Hirschfeld & S. A. Gelman (Eds.), *Mapping the mind: Domain specificity in cognition and culture* (pp. 119–148). Cambridge, UK: Cambridge University Press.

Liégeois, F., Connelly, A., Cross, J. H., Boyd, S. G., Gadian, D. G., Vargha-Khadem, F., et al. (2004). Language reorganisation in children with early-onset lesions of the left hemisphere: An fMRI study. *Brain, 127,* 1229–1236.

Mackinlay, R., Charman, T., & Karmiloff-Smith, A. (2006). High functioning children with autistic spectrum disorder: A novel test of multi-tasking. *Brain and Cognition, 61,* 14–24.

Majdan, M., & Schatz, C. J. (2006). Effects of visual experience on activity-dependent gene regulation in cortex. *Nature Neuroscience, 9,* 650–659.

Mareschal, D., Johnson, M. H., Sirois, S., Spratling, M. W., Thomas, M. S. C., & Westermann, G. (2007). *Neuroconstructivism: Vol. I. How the brain constructs cognition.* Oxford, UK: Oxford University Press.

Marr, D. (1982). *Vision.* San Francisco, CA: W. H. Freeman.

Marslen-Wilson, W. D., & Tyler, L. K (1987). Against modularity. In J. L. Garfield (Ed.), *Modularity in knowledge representation and natural language understanding* (pp. 37–62). Cambridge, MA: MIT Press.

Meaney, M. J., & Szyf, M. (2005). Environmental programming of stress responses through DNA methylation: Life at the interface between a dynamic environment and a fixed genome. *Dialogues Clinical Neuroscience, 7,* 103–123.

Mills, D., Alvarez, T., St George, M., Appelbaum, L., Bellugi, U., & Neville, H. (2000). Electrophysiological studies of face processing in Williams syndrome. *Journal of Cognitive Neuroscience, 12*(Suppl. 1), 47–64.

Mills, D., & Conboy, B. (2009). Early communicative development and the social bra. In M. DeHaan (Ed.), *Handbook of social developmental neuroscience* (pp. 175–207). New York, NY: Guilford Press.

Moses, P., & Stiles, J. (2002). The lesion methodology: Contrasting views from adult and child studies. *Developmental Psychobiology, 40,* 266–277.

Neville, H. J. (2006). Flexibility and plasticity in cortical development. In Y. Munakata & M. H. Johnson (Eds.), *Attention and Performance XXI* (pp. 287–314). Oxford, UK: Oxford University Press.

Neville, H. J., & Bavelier, D. (2002). Specificity and plasticity in neurocognitive development in humans. In M. H. Johnson, Y. Munakata, & R. Gilmore (Eds.), *Brain development and cognition: A reader* (2nd ed., pp. 251–270). Oxford, UK: Blackwell.

Norbury, C. F., Bishop, D. V. M., & Briscoe, J. (2002). Does impaired grammatical comprehension provide evidence for an innate grammar module? *Applied Psycholinguistics, 23,* 247–268.

Oliver, A., Johnson, M. H., Karmiloff-Smith, A., & Pennington, B. (2000). Deviations in the emergence of representations: A neuroconstructivist framework for analysing developmental disorders. *Developmental Science, 3*, 1–23.

Paterson, S., Brown, J., Gsödl, M., Johnson, M. H., & Karmiloff-Smith, A. (1999). Cognitive modularity and genetic disorders. *Science, 286*, 2355–2358.

Pekkola, J., Laasonen, M., Ojanen, V., Autti, T., Jäskeläinen, I. P., Kujala, T., et al. (2006). Perception of matching and conflicting audiovisual speech in dyslexic and fluent readers: An fMRI study at 3T. *NeuroImage, 29*, 797–807.

Pekkola, J., Ojanen, V., Autti, T., Jäskeläinen, I. P., Mottonen, R., Tarkiainen, A., et al. (2005). Primary auditory cortex activation by visual speech: An fMRI study at 3 Tesla. *Neuroreport, 16*, 125–128.

Piaget, J. (1926). *The Language and Thought of the Child*. London, UK: Kegan Paul, Trench, Trübner & Co.

Pinker, S. (1999). *Words and rules*. London, UK: Weidenfeld & Nicolson.

Quartz, S., & Sejnowski, T. J. (1997). The neural basis of cognitive development. *Behavioral and Brain Sciences, 20*, 537–556.

Rossen, M. L., Jones, W., Wang, P. P., & Klima, E. S. (1996). Face processing: Remarkable sparing in Williams syndrome [Special issue]. *Genetic Counseling, 6*, 138–140.

Schlaggar, B. L., Brown, T. T., Lugar, H. L., Visscher, K. M., Miezin, F. M., & Petersen, S. E. (2002). Functional neuroanatomical differences between adults and school-age children in the processing of single words. *Science, 296*, 1476–1479.

Shallice, T. (1988). *From neuropsychology to mental structure*. Cambridge, UK: Cambridge University Press.

Spelke, S. (2000). Core knowledge. *American Psychologist, 55*, 1233–1243.

Stein, B. E., & Stanford, T. R. (2008). Multisensory integration: Current issues from the perspective of the single neuron. *Nature Reviews Neuroscience, 9*, 255–266.

Stiles, J., Bates, E., Thal, D., Trauner, D., & Reilly, J. (2002). Linguistic and spatial cognitive development in children with pre- and perinatal focal brain injury: A ten-year overview from the San Diego Longitudinal Project. In M. H. Johnson, Y. Munakata, & R. Gilmore (Eds.), *Brain development and cognition: A reader* (pp. 643–664). Oxford, UK: Blackwell.

Stiles, J., & Thal, D. (1993). Linguistic and spatial cognitive development following early focal brain injury: Patterns of deficit and recovery. In M. H. Johnson (Ed.), *Brain development and cognition: A reader* (pp. 643–664). Oxford, UK: Blackwell.

Tager-Flusberg, Plesa-Skwerer, Faja, & Joseph (2003). People with Williams syndrome process faces holistically. *Cognition, 89*, 11–24.

Tallal, P. (2000). Experimental studies of language learning impairments: From research to remediation. In D. V. M. Bishop & L. B. Leonard (Eds.), *Speech and language impairments in children: Causes, characteristics, intervention and outcome* (pp. 131–155). Hove, UK: Psychology Press.

Temple, C. M. (1997). *Developmental cognitive neuropsychology*. Hove, UK: Psychology Press.

Tomasello, M. (2003). *Constructing a language: A usage-based theory of language acquisition*. Cambridge, MA: Harvard University Press.

Udwin, O., & Yule, W. (1991). A cognitive and behavioural phenotype in Williams syndrome. *Journal of Clinical and Experimental Neuropsychology, 13*, 232–244.

Wellman, H. M., & Gelman, S. A. (1998). Knowledge acquisition in foundational domains. In W. Damon (Series Ed.) & D. Kuhn & R. Siegler (Vol. Eds.), *Handbook of child psychology: Vol. 2. Cognition, perception, and language* (5th ed., pp. 523–573). New York, NY: Wiley.

Werker, J. F., & Polka, L. (1993). Developmental changes in speech perception: New challenges and new directions. *Journal of Phonetics, 21*, 83–101.

COGNITIVE NEUROPSYCHOLOGY, 2011, 28 (3 & 4), 288–303

What can individual differences tell us about the specialization of function?

Cristina D. Rabaglia, Gary F. Marcus, and Sean P. Lane

Department of Psychology, New York University, New York, NY, USA

Can the study of individual differences inform debates about modularity and the specialization of function? In this article, we consider the implications of a highly replicated, robust finding known as positive manifold: Individual differences in different cognitive domains tend to be positively inter-correlated. Prima facie, this fact, which has generally been interpreted as reflecting the influence of a domain-general cognitive factor, might be seen as posing a serious challenge to a strong view of modularity. Drawing on a mixture of meta-analysis and computer simulation, we show that positive manifold derives instead largely from between-task neural overlap, suggesting a potential way of reconciling individual differences with some form of modularity.

Keywords: Individual differences; Functional specialization; Cognitive architecture; Positive manifold.

The notion of cognitive and neural modularity has been of considerable interest to cognitive science. Indeed, the field's dominant metaphor for the human mind—the modern computer—is characterized by modular structure, having both a domain-general central processing unit (itself constructed out of modular subcomponents) and a wide variety of specialized circuits dedicated to specific domains like graphics generation or sound. Many biological structures are similarly modular, at physiological and genetic levels (Beldade & Brakefield, 2003; Gerhart, Kirschner, & Moderbacher, 1997; Patthy, 2003; Schlosser & Wagner, 2004; Wagner, Pavlicev, & Cheverud, 2007); in fact, the human body as a whole includes a large number of specialized systems devoted to tasks such as circulation, digestion, and respiration.

Accordingly, influential perspectives in cognitive science hold that mental and neural structures might also be modular[1] in their make-up (Fodor, 1983; Lenneberg, 1967; Marr, 1982) and that such modularity might be an essential or highly probable result of the evolution of complex systems, at both cognitive (Barrett & Kurzban, 2006; Cosmides & Tooby, 1994; Marcus, 2006;

Correspondence should be addressed to Cristina D. Rabaglia, New York University, Department of Psychology, 6 Washington Place, Room 304, New York, NY 10003, USA. (E-mail: rabaglia@nyu.edu).

---

[1] Modularity and domain specificity are two closely related but not identical notions. One could, for example, have domain-specific knowledge (e.g., about the rules of chess) in an architecture like Newell and Simon's General Problem Solver, in which the rules of inference are fully domain general. Conversely, a single computational algorithm (e.g., for performing spectral analysis) could be modular in its implementation but be used in multiple domains (e.g., in both vision and audition). Although in most accounts modules are presumed domain specific, and vice versa, we do not here consider the terms to be fully interchangeable.

---

http://dx.doi.org/10.1080/02643294.2011.609813

Pinker, 1997) and neural levels (Calabretta, Ferdinando, Wagner, & Parisi, 2003; Calabretta, Nolfi, Parisi, & Wagner, 2000; Redies & Puelles, 2001).

Yet, the extent to which neural and cognitive modularity accurately characterize the human mind has remained deeply controversial. There are ongoing discussions regarding the basic definition of modules (Carruthers & Chamberlain, 2000; Coltheart, 1999), and there have been prolonged and well-known debates about the empirical evidence for modular systems within domains such as sentence processing (Ferreira & Clifton, 1986; Spivey, Tanenhaus, Eberhard, & Sedivy, 2002; Tanenhaus, Spivey-Knowlton, Eberhard, & Sedivy, 1995), reading (Coltheart, 1999; Shatil & Share, 2003), music (Peretz & Coltheart, 2003; Peretz & Zatorre, 2005), and face processing (Kanwisher, 2000; Tarr & Gauthier, 2000).

Although perhaps less well known to experimental cognitive psychologists, another sizeable psychological literature also wrestles with these issues of domain specificity versus domain generality. For the past 100 years, individual differences psychology has been highly influenced by a simple finding: When a range of distinct cognitive tasks are administered to a sample of individuals, the correlations between individuals' scores on these tasks is nearly always positive. Individuals who are high scoring in one cognitive domain tend to be high scoring on other cognitive domains. Termed the "positive manifold", this pattern of positive correlation was first noted over 100 years ago (Spearman, 1904) and is repeatedly observed in nearly every large-scale individual differences study.

To the extent that the mind consists of a collection of distinct, adaptively specialized components for different tasks, the existence of positive manifold might initially seem surprising. If different aspects of cognition were genuinely independent, one might, other things being equal, anticipate little or no intercorrelation between individual differences in diverse cognitive domains. Moreover, to the extent that investment and experience in one domain may trade off with that in another, one might even anticipate *negative* correlations—for example, that people who have trained heavily in mathematics might have little time to develop their verbal skills, and vice versa. Empirically, however, the evidence for positive manifold is robust; literally hundreds of studies have pointed to positive correlations between ostensibly distinct cognitive abilities (Carroll, 1993).

Yet, discussion of individual differences—and their potential implications for modularity—is relatively rare within the broader cognitive science community. In the words of one researcher, "differential psychologists may note that a datum of non trivial significance to their field appears to be absent from the picture that emerges from the mainstream practice of evolutionary psychology . . . positive manifold . . . if human cognitive abilities can be broken down into modules of independent origin and functionality, why is it that a diverse battery of mental tests administered to a large and representative sample of a human population always shows a covariance matrix with all-positive entries?" (Lee, 2007, p. 253). In essence, if the mind is made up of a collection of independent, domain-specific, and specialized abilities, why isn't variability in these abilities completely independent ?

How strong a challenge does the existence of positive manifold pose to modularity, and what sort of mechanisms might account for the existence of positive manifold in the first place? These are the questions we address in this paper.

Conceptions of positive manifold

Positive manifold as a "general factor" of intelligence
In the first discussion of positive manifold—Spearman's (1904) article "General Intelligence, Objectively Determined and Measured"—positive correlations between cognitive domains were conceptualized as stemming from some domain-general common mental resource—a "*general intelligence*"—that was recruited for the performance of nearly all cognitive tasks. By hypothesis, to the extent that this factor varied between individuals and played a role in each domain, individuals' performance on cognitive domains, relative to other people, would be positively correlated.

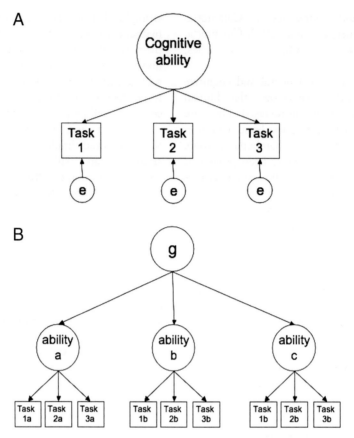

Figure 1. *Structural equation models. Panel A. Structural equation model representing tasks (represented by squares) thought to tap into a single latent cognitive ability (represented as a circle), with error terms unique to each task (represented as smaller circles). Panel B. A modern hierarchical instantiation of a g-factor model in which a higher order general factor (g) influences observed task performance through task-specific latent abilities.*

Over a century later, Spearman's (1904) general viewpoint continues to have broad currency. It has been pivotal in most theories of what human intelligence, itself, is,[2] and some form of the general resource perspective has arguably been the predominant view of individual differences in cognition for the past century.

Before evaluating the plausibility of this conception of positive manifold, it is important to begin with a clear understanding of the statistical technique known as structural equation modelling, which is central to most contemporary analyses of cognitive individual differences (see Figure 1).

In this type of analysis, individual cognitive tasks are conceptualized as imperfect indicators of unmeasurable, "true" cognitive ability in different cognitive domains. The presumption is that although it would be impossible to create an individual cognitive task that is a "pure" indicator of an underlying ability, underlying abilities can be captured by means of the shared variance between several tasks hypothesized to draw on the same

---

[2] As noted later, however, positive manifold (which is true at the population level, or *between* individuals), sometimes also referred to as psychometric g, is conceptually distinct from g as in general intelligence (a hypothesized construct *within* an individual): The former is a statistical phenomenon, and the other is a hypothesized cognitive ability or resource.

cognitive domain. Correspondingly, individual tasks are represented as comprising two parts: a portion reflecting the underlying cognitive ability of interest (the portion that is shared between that task and other tasks hypothesized to tap into the same construct) and a portion representing measurement error (Figure 1a).

In the modern structural equation models that derive from a typical application of the general resource perspective, individual differences in a collection of cognitive domains are fit with models similar to that depicted in Figure 1b: A latent "general" factor is hypothesized to influence performance on several cognitive domains, which in turn each influence performance on cognitive tasks belonging to those domains. Although formed primarily as a means for exploring and interpreting individual differences data, these models at their core could be seen as representing formal hypotheses about the structure of human cognition. For example, the model depicted (Figure 1b) explicitly represents the hypothesis that (a) there can be individual differences that are specific to individual domains, but that (b) there is also a general resource that is recruited by multiple task domains.

Models such as these generally fit data from individual differences studies very well, as has been documented in literally hundreds of data sets (Carroll, 1993). Further, the characteristics of the fits of these statistical models are sometimes interpreted as suggesting that a large portion of performance on cognitive tasks is due to differences between individuals that are completely domain general. Deary, Penke, and Johnson (2010), for instance, report that in data sets comprising individuals' performance in a variety of domains, a general factor "almost always accounts for 40% or more of the total variance" (p. 210). If the cause of these cognitive intercorrelations is conceptualized as stemming from a common shared psychological resource, the implication from the magnitude of these estimates is not only that a domain-general factor may influence *some* of cognitive life (i.e., the mind has *some* components that are not specialized for function) but, rather, that domain-general mechanisms are responsible for a *substantial* portion of cognitive function and hence might be taken prima facie as

conflicting with views that heavily emphasize specialization of function. For example, to the extent that a factor such as abstract reasoning ability might span a broad range of cognitive domains, the apparent success of the general-factor enterprise could pose a challenge to modularist hypotheses (e.g., Cosmides & Tooby, 1992) that posit that human reasoning might proceed in highly domain-specific way with narrow-grained heuristics such as rules for detecting cheaters, rather than abstractly specified formal logics. Indeed, some individual differences researchers have argued that, "results from differential psychology studies have shown that it is inappropriate to assume that performing any cognitive task involves only one relevant mental module (or faculty)" (Deary et al., 2010, p. 202).

At the same time, despite the apparent quality of the fit of *g*-factor models, there is little consensus on what—mechanistically—a "general factor" would actually correspond to. One common view is that intercorrelations between cognitive domains might reflect variation in a lower level biological property of the cognitive system as a whole, such as processing speed or grey matter volume. However, available empirical evidence suggests that these types of variables (including white matter volume, grey matter volume, sheer brain volume, or nerve conduction velocity) alone cannot account for the magnitude of the positive manifold, as they account for, typically, at best 1 to 25% of the variance in cognition represented at the general level (for a review, see Chabris, 2006). Instead, many contemporary theories ascribe Spearman's "general factor" to some truly domain-general *psychological* resource, such as abstract reasoning ability (Gustafsson, 1984) or working memory (Colom, Rebollo, Palacios, Juan-Espinosa, & Kyllonen, 2004; Kyllonen, 2002). There is no definitive evidence, however, to show that any of these proposed psychological sources, individually or collectively, could account for the apparent magnitude of positive manifold.

An alternative interpretation
Given the lack of a clear mechanistic consensus on what Spearman's (1904) general factor might map onto, it is worth considering an alternative

possibility, potentially less in conflict with theories of modularity: that the appearance of a general factor is to some (large) extent a statistical artefact. It has long been noted that even though some of the variance in individual differences across cognitive domains can be captured in a single latent dimension (g), it is not necessarily the case that this reflects the operation of a unitary or domain-general entity within an individual (e.g., see: Bartholomew, Deary, & Lawn, 2009; Borsboom & Dolan, 2006; Penke et al., in press; Van Der Maas et al., 2006).

In fact, the idea that the positive manifold may not necessarily reflect the workings of a general factor was first raised by a contemporary of Spearman's, Godfrey Thomson (1916; see also Bartholomew, Deary, & Lawn 2009). Instead, it is theoretically possible that individual differences in performance on cognitive domains tend to be intercorrelated not because of a specific, unitary shared mechanism or resource, but simply because different domains draw from a common set of neural resources. Along similar lines,[3] though suggested for independent reasons, several recent theories have emphasized the role of exaptation or "neural reuse" (Anderson, 2010), "neuronal recycling" (Dehaene & Cohen, 2007), or "descent with modification" (Marcus, 2006), according to which neural mechanisms that were originally developed in one domain take on—in ontogeny or phylogeny—new functions in other domains. Here we consider the extent to which such repurposing might provide an alternative explanation of the apparent existence of a general factor, and what that might mean for modularity.

Neural overlap and g

From modern neural science, we know there is both anatomical structure—the adult human neocortex, for example, contains a large number (52 by Brodmann's count) of "areas" that can be distinguished cytoarchitectonically in terms of connection patterns and distributions of cell types—and reasonable (albeit not perfect) consistency in imaging results, such that certain brain areas tend to be reliably associated with certain cognitive domains. To investigate the extent to which it is plausible that positive manifold might derive primarily from neural overlap in the way it is understood by modern neuroscience, we describe below a two-pronged approach, the first part empirical and meta-analytic, the other computational.

Empirical results from brain-based meta-analyses

In an initial examination of this hypothesis, we (Rabaglia, Lane, & Marcus, 2011) used meta-analytic techniques to derive quantitative inferences about the magnitude of the contribution of neural overlap to positive manifold. Our starting point was the largest extant meta-analysis of the Brodmann areas recruited by different cognitive task domains (Cabeza & Nyberg, 2000). Beginning with the set of cognitive domains (for example, selective attention and face perception) that were included in Cabeza and Nyberg's meta-analysis, we used keyword (corresponding to each cognitive domain) searches in PubMed and the journal Intelligence to obtain relevant papers that included g-loading estimates for a given cognitive domain. The "g-loading" of a cognitive domain can be thought of as a measure of how strongly a given construct correlates with a hypothesized general factor. In models like those in Figure 1, Panel B, g-loading is represented by the magnitude of the path between a general construct and the specific cognitive domain's latent factor in the structural equation model. For each cognitive domain, we then computed sample-size weighted averages combining available g-loading estimates. Using Cabeza and Nyberg's meta-analysis, we then selected each of the Brodmann

---

[3] Thomson, working over 80 years ago, was not focused on modularity issues, and the particular instantiation of overlapping resources that he considered—in terms of "bonds" in the brain—might conceivably be cached out in a very unstructured view of the mind, in which computational problems were solved anew from a completely shared pool of neural resources. Here, we consider a more structured instantiation of his general viewpoint, in which the neural resources at issue might correspond to larger units (e.g., brain regions or populations of neurons) and be configured in systematically structured ways.

areas that were recruited by at least 50% of the studies in at least two task domains and computed, for each cognitive ability domain, the average number of these overlapping Brodmann areas recruited by each cognitive domain.

We then examined the meta-analytic estimates of *g*-loading for each cognitive domain as a function of these estimates of overlapping neural recruitment. The results of this analysis (Figure 2) suggest that the *g*-loading is strongly related to the number of overlapping Brodmann areas recruited by that domain. To replicate our results with an alternative measure of neural recruitment, we repeated this analysis with estimates of neural extent derived from a relatively recent and more sophisticated meta-analytic technique, the activation likelihood estimation (ALE) method, which pools 3-D coordinates of brain activity from a given set of studies using similar tasks to compute a maximum likelihood estimate of the neural tissue recruited. We searched the BrainMap database for all papers falling into our original cognitive domains and extracted the ALE estimates of volume of recruited neural tissue from all relevant papers (Laird, Lancaster,

& Fox, 2005). Pairing these available estimates with our original estimates of *g*-loading results replicates the pattern found using the Cabeza and Nyberg (2000) meta-analysis (Figure 2). The greater amount of neural substrate recruited by a cognitive domain—whether the amount is quantified at the level of Brodmann areas or sheer volume of activation—the greater the *g*-loading of that cognitive domain, with our measures of neural recruitment accounting for between 80% and 90% of the variance in *g*-loading. As one would expect if the positive manifold resulted from resampling from an overlapping set of neural resources, the more a cognitive ability domain draws on that set of neural resources, the more related that ability domain is to the variance shared across cognitive domains.

Could *g* be a statistical artefact?

To the extent that empirical data suggest that positive manifold derives in large part from neural overlap, an even more radical question must be raised: Given what we know about the neural recruitment of different cognitive

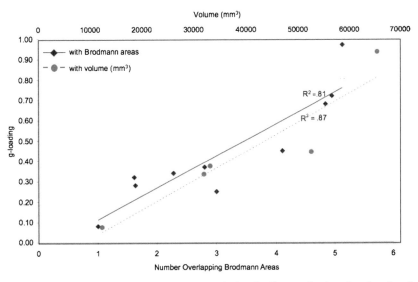

Figure 2. *Average g-loading of ability domains by neural resources recruited. g-Loading as a function of number of overlapping Brodmann areas from Cabeza and Nyberg's (2000) meta-analysis (bottom axis) and as a function of significantly activated brain volume derived from activation likelihood estimation (ALE) meta-analyses (top axis). From "Why are Human Cognitive Abilities Strongly Intercorrelated?", by C. Rabaglia, S. P. Lane, and G. F. Marcus, 2011. Adapted with permission.*

domains, could positive manifold and the appearance of a general factor emerge even when there is no truly general factor at all?

To begin to answer this question, we constructed a simulated data set, consisting of 10,000 individual differences "studies", each comprising data from 200 individuals. Drawing on a meta-analysis of brain regions recruited by different cognitive tasks (Cabeza & Nyberg, 2000), we generated, for each individual in each simulated study, test scores on 15 hypothetical tasks, 3 from each of 5 cognitive domains. There was (by design) no "Spearman-esque" general factor; rather, individual simulated task scores were generated based entirely on separate, uncorrelated differences in each brain region reported to be recruited by the individual tasks' domains.

We then fitted the resulting sets of data with two competing models, as depicted in Figure 2, and compared their respective fits. The first model (Figure 3a) is a traditional *g*-factor model, where correlated individual differences emerge due to a common factor that influences performance on all cognitive domains to some

degree. The second model (Figure 3b) is a simple correlational model. This model is more general than a *g*-factor model in that, while it posits that there will be some correlation between the different cognitive factors, it does not presuppose a common *causal* source—as is explicit in the form of the *g*-factor in the *g*-factor model—to the interrelations between different cognitive tasks; instead, it can be seen as a test of the question of whether the positive manifold—significant correlations between cognitive domains—could in principle emerge as a sheer epiphenomenon of neural reuse.

If what appears to be a general factor can emerge purely from neural overlap found in imaging data, the *g*-factor model should (still) fit the data well. At the same time, if the positive manifold can emerge purely from the pattern of neural recruitment observed in neuroimaging studies alone, then the simulated data should, on average, show relationships between cognitive abilities in different domains, such that a correlational model fits the data well even in the absence of a causal general factor.

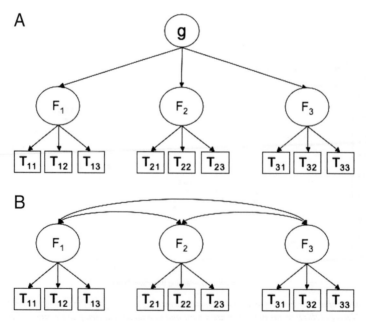

Figure 3. *Structural equation models fit to the data: (A) g-factor model and (B) a correlational model. For simplicity, error terms are not shown, and only three factors are shown.*

Table 1. *Probability of activation and total possible pairs of overlapping areas in a given simulated sample*

Cognitive domain	Simulated Brodmann areas[a]										
	BA6	*BA7*	*BA9*	*BA10*	*BA18*	*BA19*	*BA22*	*BA32*	*BA40*	*BA46*	*BA47*
Problem solving (F1)	.50	—	.50	.56	—	.81	—	—	—	.50	—
Attention (F2)	.30	.40	.80	—	—	—	—	—	.40	.30	—
Imagery (F3)	.43	.86	.29	—	—	.71	—	—	.57	—	—
Language (F4)	.44	—	—	—	.56	.44	.67	—	—	—	.56
Episodic memory (F5)	—	.53	.53	.58	—	—	—	.58	—	.53	—
Possible pairs of overlap (total = 23)	6	3	6	1	0	3	0	0	1	3	0

Note: BA = Brodmann area.
[a]Based on proportion of studies in meta-analysis by Cabeza and Nyberg (2000) that showed significant activation.

Simulation methods: Data generation

The simulated data were constructed based on Cabeza and Nyberg's (2000) meta-analysis, focusing on five cognitive domains taken from their analysis that are also typical domains assessed by individual differences literature—problem solving, attention, imagery, language comprehension, and episodic memory. For each domain, we computed the proportion of studies that reported recruitment of each of the Brodmann areas (BA), resulting in a vector with 31 entries (one for each Brodmann area activated by at least one of the five task domains included in the simulation) for each of the subdomains. These percentages in turn served as seed probabilities that represented, for a given simulated sample, the chance that each Brodmann area would be recruited by the domains in the simulation. For instance, if 50% of the problem-solving studies in Cabeza and Nyberg (2000) reported activation of BA 46, then we used .50 as the probability that BA 46 would be recruited by the problem-solving tasks in a given simulated sample. To simplify the simulations (without loss of generality with respect to the concept of neural overlap), we selected the five Brodmann areas in each domain that simultaneously (a) displayed significant activation in the greatest

proportion of studies and (b) maximized the potential overlap in Brodmann areas between cognitive domains.[4] Table 1 shows the resulting matrix of the five cognitive domains and their respective five areas of maximal activation. The bottom row of Table 1 shows the number of possible overlapping pairs between any two of the five domains.

Beginning with the seed data depicted in Table 1, scores for individual tasks were generated in accordance with the steps depicted in Figure 4. Scores on individual tasks in this simulation thus are equivalent, psychologically, to a state of affairs in which individual differences are completely specific to smaller scale neural mechanisms, which are then recombined in different ways in the service of different types of cognitive tasks. Individuals in this scenario, relative to other individuals, have strengths and weaknesses that are specific to smaller scale neural resources and completely orthogonal to their strengths and weaknesses in other neural resources. It is important to point out that, as can be seen in Table 1, while some of the Brodmann areas are used across more task domains than others, no *single* Brodmann area is used in every cognitive task. This work thus does not simply translate to reconceptualizing of the *general* factor to a specific

---

[4] In some cases, the meta-analysis reported activation of multiple Brodmann areas for the same proportion of studies. When this happened, we chose the Brodmann area that would result in the greatest number of possible overlapping areas for the domains across studies. This served to extend the range of possible overlap and explore a greater number of possible scenarios. Sensitivity analyses were done, selecting these areas at random, and the results did not change (although the range of possible overlapping areas was restricted).

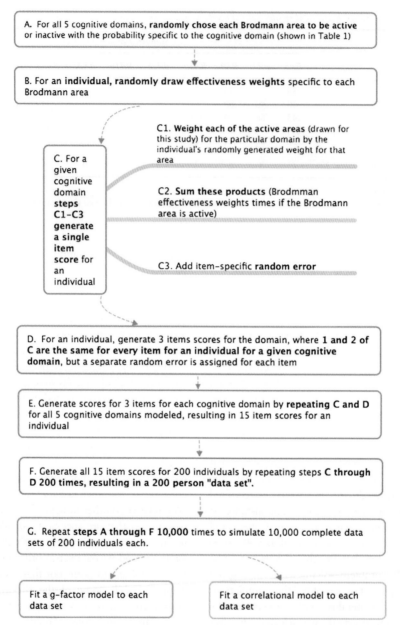

Figure 4. *Data generation steps for the simulation, beginning with the seed probabilities in Table 1. To view a colour version of this figure, please see the online issue of the Journal.*

single brain region or specific set of regions. There is therefore, by the inherent structure of the model, no general individual differences factor (i.e., single dimension common to all cognitive tasks) along which individuals vary.

For each cognitive domain in the simulation (modelled later as a single latent, cognitive factor), we simulated scores for three separate items (each representing a task tapping into a given subdomain). The score for a given individual

k on a item i tapping into a subdomain j can be described by the following equation, where B_{mk} is a random weight assigned to a particular Brodmann area m unique to person k, and A_{mj} is an indicator of whether or not Brodmann area m is active for its corresponding factor j in the sample, and e is a random error unique to the individual and the test item:

$$Item_{ijk} = \left(\sum_{l=1}^{m} B_{mk} A_{mj} \right) + e_{ijk} \qquad (1)$$

Simulations were performed in SAS (SAS Institute, 2008) according to Equation 1. In each sample, each Brodmann area was randomly selected to be active (A_{mj}) with the domain-specific base rate probability given in Table 1. Within each sample, each individual was randomly assigned a weight for each Brodmann area (B_{mk}) from a uniform distribution (with a range from 0 to 1). Random error unique to each individual and task (e_{ijk}) from a normal distribution was then added to each item score.[5]

For a given sample in the simulation, the item scores are thus a function of the summed products of individuals' unique (to that individual and to that Brodmann area) weighting factor for the Brodmann area multiplied by if the Brodmann area is active for that domain in that particular sample, plus error specific to the individual and item. Importantly, if an individual has a particularly "good" weighting score for a Brodmann area, it only matters for the item score if that Brodmann area is recruited by that individual task item in that particular sample. Because a Brodmann area that is "turned on" for a domain in the sample is turned on for every individual in the sample, individual differences in this model reside only in the individuals' separate, independent weighting factors applied to each Brodmann area. Using the empirical meta-analytic brain imaging data concerning

specific Brodmann areas as a kernel, we thus constructed a hypothetical situation in which individual differences across domains are in fact only correlated by virtue of neural overlap, without any causal role for a general factor.

Several indications support the soundness of the emulated data. First, the rank ordering of the average g-factor loadings that emerged from fitting g-factor models to the simulated data (see below) was consistent with what is found in empirical research, with imagery (F3) and problem solving (F1) having the highest loadings and language (F4) and episodic memory (F5) having, relatively, the lower loadings. Further, these loadings directly relate to potential for overlap with other factors via shared Brodmann areas of activation (Table 1) in a way that closely mirrors the relationship inherent in the empirical data (Figure 2). This is most clearly observed in Figure 5, which plots the mean factor loading against the number of overlapping areas in each of the simulated samples. Closely mimicking the meta-analytic results reported in the section on Empirical Results from Brain-based Meta-analyses, there is a strong positive correlation between the number of shared Brodmann areas that are activated and the average g-loading of the cognitive domains ($R^2 = .62$).

Table 2 displays the aggregated results from fitting the two theoretical models to the simulated data. Both models fitted the data very well, suggesting significant positive intercorrelations between cognitive abilities. For the analysis assuming a g-factor model, the average root mean square error of approximation (RMSEA) and goodness of fit index (GFI) and their respective 95% confidence intervals were within what is conventionally considered to be good to excellent.[6]

Further, when we fit the g-factor models to our simulated data sets, a "domain-general" factor

---

[5] The choice of item error variances was selected according to those observed in the literature; however, there is substantial variability in these values. As a result, we fit the same set of models but varied the magnitude of error variances. In all cases, the magnitudes of the parameter estimates and the R-square of the g-factor in the fitted models we present below remained unchanged.

[6] The chi-square value provided somewhat less evidence of good fit to the data; however, the chi-square value is known to be an imperfect indicator of model fit that is especially susceptible to large sample size and large correlations (Kline, 2010), both of which are present in our simulated data.

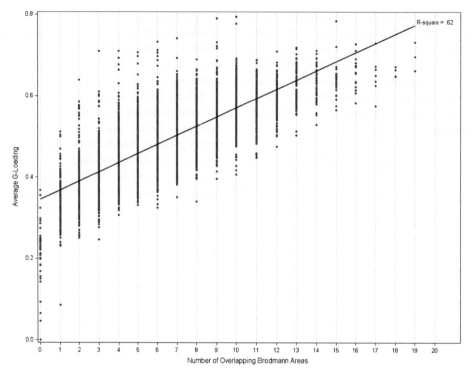

Figure 5. *Average g-factor loadings plotted against the number of overlapping Brodmann areas that were activated for the simulation study. To view a colour version of this figure, please see the online issue of the Journal.*

appears to account for, on average, 34% of the variance in the individual cognitive domains (95% CI 28%, 41%, where CI = confidence interval), a range strikingly consistent with the 40% typically reported in the literature (see Deary et al., 2010). Note that since the only opportunity for relations between the cognitive abilities lies in the individual-specific randomly drawn effectiveness weights for each Brodmann area being reused across domains, similarity between the parameter and r-square estimates in our simulation and those generally found with individual differences data are thus completely determined by the a priori specification of the relationships between the Brodmann areas within and between task domains.

When we then fitted the correlational model to the simulated data, we also observed excellent fit statistics by traditional standards (Table 2). Comparing the results of fitting the g-factor model to the results from the correlational model

(Table 2), in nearly 90% of our generated samples, a correlational model fits the simulated data better than a g-factor model using a chi-square difference test.

From these analyses, we can draw two conclusions. First, it is logically possible to have the appearance of positive manifold—as judged by a pattern of positive intercorrelation between diverse cognitive tasks—even in the absence of any true general factor; second, it is logically possible for a g-factor analysis to fit well and capture a substantial amount of variance under such a scenario.

Discussion of simulations

These results demonstrate that in principle a g-factor model can yield a good fit even when no underlying general factor actually exists. In our simulations, which reflect the combination of neural resource recruitment found in actual neuropsychological imaging data, there is no general

Table 2. *Aggregated simulation results for two different theoretical models for Simulation 1*

	g-Factor model		Correlational model	
	M	SD	M	SD
g-Loading[a]				
F1	.62	.31		
F2	.55	.32		
F3	.57	.32		
F4	.22	.24		
F5	.45	.31		
Factor loading[b]	.86	.12	.86	.12
Chi-square	141.81	47.29	82.40	13.18
GFI	.92	.02	.95	.01
RMSEA	.05	.03	.01	.01
R^2	.65	.04	.75	.05

Note: RMSEA = root mean square error of approximation. GFI = goodness of fit index. Using a chi-square difference test where g-factor model is nested in the correlational model, difference in model fit is 88%: correlational > g-factor.
[a]Average first-order (g) loading across the 15 items averaged over all simulations. [b]Average second-order loading for each of the 3 tests of the 5 factors averaged over all simulations.

factor, yet the overall fit of the *g*-factor model was strong by conventional structural equation modelling standards. Consistent with several recent theories of cognitive and neural architecture (Anderson, 2010; Marcus, 2006), our simulations represent any particular cognitive task in any particular cognitive domain as a function of its own, unique set of recombined neural resources; to test the potential for intercorrelations between cognitive abilities to emerge purely from this neuropsychological organization, only individual differences that are entirely uncorrelated and specific to these smaller scale, recombined neural substrates are present. To the extent that our simulation approximates the underlying empirical realities, it becomes clear that one cannot safely infer a truly general factor in cognition based on extant modelling results.

At the same time, the mere fact that a general factor can in principle be derived from the application of a *g*-factor model to data sets in which

no general factor exists does not mean that there is literally no role for some general factor in understanding human cognitive functioning. In the limit, it is almost certainly the case that environmental factors or system-wide biological considerations, such as neural integrity or white matter volume, must influence functioning across many cognitive domains, and this is probably also the case for variation within the normal population. As mentioned above, a host of generally modest correlations (for a review, see Chabris, 2006) between cognition represented in some general way and variables such as white matter volume suggest, albeit indirectly, that these variables probably do have some role in driving intercorrelations across cognitive domains. Our overall conjecture is thus that one or more of these biologically general factors may indeed contribute to the intercorrelations between individual differences in cognitive abilities, but that their overall contribution is fairly small. Even when taken cumulatively, the data presented here suggest that their contribution to positive manifold is likely to be dwarfed by the effect of neural overlap.

Here we have focused specifically on one modern notion of neural systems' possible contribution to the observed patterns in human cognitive individual differences, and the results clearly demonstrate the potential explanatory power of this pattern of neural overlap alone.

GENERAL DISCUSSION

At the opening of this article, we considered the question: Should modularity theorists be concerned by the abundant literature attesting to the existence of positive manifold? The most candid answer may be "Yes, and no", depending in no small part upon how one conceptualizes what a module is.

The dominant view of positive manifold in the individual differences literature heretofore has been grounded in Spearman's (1904) original general-factor interpretation, which was, essentially, deeply antimodular. The viewpoint that the positive manifold reflects a general factor in the sense of recruitment by all cognitive subdomains is clearly not in the spirit of specialization of function; further, if this general factor is not only present, but—as has been suggested throughout the individual differences literature—accounts for much of the variability in human cognitive life, this lack of specialization of function is not only detectable but a major characteristic of human cognition. Crucially, many modern conceptualizations of the positive manifold, even some that attempt to take modern neurological data into account, share in this viewpoint. Whether the general factor is hypothesized to be instantiated in a particularly fundamental psychological construct such as reasoning ability (Gustafsson, 1984), working memory (Kyllonen, 2002), or the across-the-board recruitment of specific domain-general neural resources such as the prefrontal cortex (Gray, Chabris, & Braver, 2003; Jung & Haier, 2007), all of these theories have a similar flavour to Spearman's original conception. For example, if the frontal lobes are recruited to some degree by all of higher order cognition, then the frontal lobes could be conceptualized as the common or "general" factor influencing nearly every cognitive task; the neural reality would be easily mapped on to Spearman's general factor and would consist of a large portion of the workings of all cognitive tasks being domain general, rather than specific.

Of course, it is not inconceivable that some version of a modularity theory could be rescued even in such a circumstance. Carruthers (2006, p. 289), for example, proposes that the mind is composed of a set of modules that share a common workspace of perception and working memory; if one were to translate this proposition to a structural equation model, such a conceptualization might indeed bear a striking resemblance to a g-factor model (Figure 1b). But, as Ritchie & Carruthers (2010, p. 289) even suggest, in this conception "the sense of module in question is quite weak", in that it abandons core properties of modularity such as information encapsulation; it also implies that at least one core concept in cognitive psychology—working memory—is completely unspecialized for function in that some

shared working memory resource operates on nearly all domains of input (verbal, acoustic, visuospatial, etc.).

To the extent that our data speak against the traditional general-factor perspective, our results are thus good news for those who hold that functional specialization is a hallmark of human cognition, since such a viewpoint could not easily be reconciled with human cognitive function being largely in the hands of a single, domain-general cognitive mechanism.

Our results similarly suggest that any straightforward estimate of a percentage of domain generality—such as the assertion (Deary et al., 2010) that on average 40% of the variance in individual cognitive domains such as memory are accounted for by a domain general factor—is likely to represent a false precision. The simulation presented here shows that, in principle, such numbers can be derived even in the total absence of any truly general factor, and as such it suggests that the notion that a substantial amount of variance can be accounted for by a "general" factor or resource must be interpreted cautiously.

Implications for modularity

Do these problems for the traditional general-factor interpretation entirely rescue modularity theories? Modularity theorists may be out of Spearman's (1904) frying pan—but are they now in a worse fire? Is there, in fact, a coherent version of modularity in which individual cognitive functions are not characterized by unique neural substrates, but rather by unique *constellations* of neural substrates, which, individually, may be recruited in multiple cognitive domains?

Fodor's (1983) famous work points to several candidate criteria for modules: domain specificity; mandatoriness of operation; "limited central access to the mental representations that other [modules] compute"; speed; information encapsulation; "shallow outputs"; fixed neural architecture; characteristic breakdown patterns; and characteristic developmental properties. We would suggest that few, if any, of these criteria are necessarily in conflict with a view of modules as instantiated by configurations of components rather than individual localized elements, and as such sheer overlap by itself does not absolutely militate against some kind of modularity being rescued. Many of these proposed characteristics—mandatoriness of operation, speed, shallow outputs, fixed architecture, characteristic breakdown patterns, and characteristic developmental properties—do not rest in any important theoretical way on how they are neurally instantiated. Others—domain specificity, limited access to the representations other modules compute, and information encapsulation—do seem potentially threatened if certain neural resources are shared across different domains. However, it is theoretically plausible that entire networks remain domain specific even if certain parts are shared across domains and that, via specific and idiosyncratic connection patterns, information encapsulation could remain despite (partially) shared computational resources. There is thus no a priori reason why such neural configurations must necessarily contradict these criteria for modularity (for a similar argument, see Ritchie & Carruthers, 2010).

At the same time, the growing emphasis in neuroscience on the multifunctionality of individual brain regions (Anderson, 2010; Dehaene & Cohen, 2007) might suggest the need to revisit the grain level (e.g., at a high level such as a parser, or at a lower level such as a feature detector) of putative modules. Even if one could show that, for example, the entire language faculty largely consists of a set of neural substrates that also overlap with neural mechanisms that subserve music processing or general reasoning, the most important analysis, for a modularity theorist, might be not on the unique configuration but rather on the specific individual constituents that are shared. While it may not be true that the entire language faculty—a prototypical potentially modular system—is modular or even draws mostly on domain-specific resources, certain aspects of language processing may in fact be. In other words, it is not necessarily true that nature carved the mind at the same joints as psychologists do. Neural reuse is entirely consistent with the idea that particular brain areas could have fairly circumscribed, specialized computational functions, but these functions could turn out to be at smaller grain levels than psychologists typically recognize—not "language" or "music" per se, but hierarchical composition or pattern recognition: repurposable elements that are specialized in their specific computational function but that can also be recombined in the service of other broader cognitive functions, in ways that are either prewired as a product of natural selection or constructed ad hoc as a response to experience.

A related question, which we are not yet in a position to directly address, is the extent to which corresponding patterns of cognitive overlap contribute to the observed intercorrelation patterns in human cognitive individual differences. It has long been recognized in cognitive neuropsychology that no individual task is "process pure" in that no measurable behavioural task can tap solely into an individual psychological construct such as "episodic memory" or even "syntactic parsing". Taken a step further, it is plausible that the typical components of cognitive psychology might themselves be further broken down into finer grained, functionally specialized components that are shared across domains, with an apparent general factor emerging—in a way similar to our neurally grounded simulations—from the recombining of these cognitive processes. Because the underlying units of cognition are not as easily categorized as the activations of brain areas, we are not yet in a position to directly evaluate this conjecture, but we believe it to be an important topic for future research.

In summary, here we suggest a potential way of reconciling a central—arguably *the* most central—finding in human individual differences, both with modern conceptions of neural function and with some forms of modularity and functional specialization in cognitive science. If the general picture we have outlined in this paper is correct, it is unlikely that psychologists will ever be able to directly and uniquely tap into the smaller grain-level modules described above, because any given task will most likely necessarily call upon the operation of multiple hypothesized modules. The best hope of assessing the operation of an individual module may therefore be to explicitly recognize the way in which individual tasks are process impure; on such a view, a careful combination of brain imaging or behavioural work and individual differences structural equation modelling methods—which allow multiple tasks that share specific hypothesized underlying mechanisms to be combined—may be a potential way to get at these finer grained modules. Although individual differences psychology and its associated techniques have remained largely distinct from empirical cognitive science and neuroscience, these considerations thus suggest that valuable theoretical insights could be derived from future collaborations between cognitive scientists, neuroscientists, and individual differences psychologists.

REFERENCES

Anderson, M. (2010). Neural reuse: A fundamental organizational principle of the brain. *Behavioral and Brain Sciences, 33*(4), 245–266.

Barrett, H. C., & Kurzban, R. (2006). Modularity in cognition: Framing the debate. *Psychological Review, 113*(3), 628.

Bartholomew, D., Deary, I., & Lawn, M. (2009). A new lease of life for Thomson's bonds model of intelligence. *Psychological Review, 116*(3), 567.

Beldade, P., & Brakefield, P. M. (2003). Concerted evolution and developmental integration in modular butterfly wing patterns. *Evolution & Development, 5*(2), 169–179.

Borsboom, D., & Dolan, C. V. (2006), Why *g* is not an adaptation: A comment on Kanazawa (2004) *Psychological Review, 113*, 433–437.

Cabeza, R., & Nyberg, L. (2000). Imaging cognition II: An empirical review of 275 PET and fMRI studies. *Journal of Cognitive Neuroscience, 12*(1), 1–47.

Calabretta, R., Ferdinando, A. D., Wagner, G. P., & Parisi, D. (2003). What does it take to evolve behaviorally complex organisms? *Bio Systems, 69*(2–3), 245–262.

Calabretta, R., Nolfi, S., Parisi, D., & Wagner, G. P. (2000). Duplication of modules facilitates the evolution of functional specialization. *Artificial Life, 6*(1), 69–84.

Carroll, J. (1993). *Human cognitive abilities: A survey of factor-analytic studies.* New York, NY: Cambridge University Press.

Carruthers, P. (2006). *The architecture of the mind: Massive modularity and the flexibility of thought.* New York, NY: Oxford University Press.

Carruthers, P., & Chamberlain, A. (2000). *Evolution and the human mind: Modularity, language, and meta-cognition.* New York, NY: Cambridge University Press.

Chabris, C. F. (2006). Cognitive and neurobiological mechanisms of the law of general intelligence. In M. J. Roberts (Ed.), *Integrating the mind: Domain general versus domain specific processes in higher cognition.* Hove, UK: Psychology Press.

Colom, R., Rebollo, I., Palacios, A., Juan-Espinosa, M., & Kyllonen, P. (2004). Working memory is (almost) perfectly predicted by *g. Intelligence, 32*(3), 277–296.

Coltheart, M. (1999). Modularity and cognition. *Trends in Cognitive Sciences, 3*(3), 115–120.

Cosmides, L., & Tooby, J. (1992). Cognitive adaptations for social exchange. In Barkow, L. Cosmides, & J. Tooby (Eds.), *The adapted mind: Evolutionary psychology and the generation of culture* (pp. 163–227). New York, NY: Oxford University Press.

Cosmides, L., & Tooby, J. (1994). Origins of domain specificity: The evolution of functional organization. In. L. A. Hirschfeld & S. A. Gelman (Eds.), *Mapping the mind: Domain specificity in cognition and culture* (pp. 85–116). New York, NY: Cambridge University Press.

Deary, I., Penke, L., & Johnson, W. (2010). The neuroscience of human intelligence differences. *Nature Reviews Neuroscience, 11*(3), 201–211.

Dehaene, S., & Cohen, L. (2007). Cultural recycling of cortical maps. *Neuron, 56*(2), 384–398.

Ferreira, F., & Clifton, C. (1986). The independence of syntactic processing. *Journal of Memory and Language, 25*(3), 348–368.

Fodor, J. (1983). *The modularity of mind: An essay on faculty psychology.* Cambridge, MA: MIT Press.

Gerhart, J., Kirschner, M., & Moderbacher, E. S. (1997). *Cells, embryos, and evolution: Toward a cellular and developmental understanding of phenotypic variation and evolutionary adaptability.* Malden, MA: Blackwell Science.

Gray, J. R., Chabris, C. F., & Braver, T. S. (2003). Neural mechanisms of general fluid intelligence. *Nature Neuroscience, 6*(3), 316–322.

Gustafsson, J. E. (1984). A unifying model for the structure of intellectual abilities. *Intelligence, 8*(3), 179–203.

Jung, R. E., & Haier, R. J. (2007). The parieto-frontal integration theory (P-FIT) of intelligence: Converging neuroimaging evidence. *Behavioral and Brain Sciences, 30*(2), 135–154.

Kanwisher, N. (2000). Domain specificity in face perception. *Nature Neuroscience, 3,* 759–763.

Kline, R. B. (2010). *Principles and practice of structural equation modeling.* New York, NY: The Guilford Press.

Kyllonen, P. C. (2002). *g*: Knowledge, speed, strategies, or working-memory capacity? A systems perspective. In R. J. Stemberg & E. L. Gigorenko (Eds.), *The general factor of intelligence: How general is it?* (pp. 415–445).

Laird A. R., Lancaster J. L., & Fox P. T. (2005). BrainMap: The social evolution of a functional neuroimaging database. *Neuroinformatics 3,* 65–78.

Lee, J. J. (2007). A *g* beyond Homo sapiens? Some hints and suggestions. *Intelligence, 35*(3), 253–265.

Lenneberg, E. H. (1967). *Biological foundations of language.* Oxford, UK: Wiley.

Marcus, G. F. (2006). Cognitive architecture and descent with modification. *Cognition, 101*(2), 443–465.

Marr, D. (1982). *Vision: A computational approach.* San Francisco, CA: Freeman & Co.

Newell, A., Shaw, J. C., & Simon, H. A. (1959). Report on a general problem-solving program. *Proceedings of the International Conference on Information Processing,* 256–264.

Patthy, L. (2003). Modular assembly of genes and the evolution of new functions. *Genetica, 118*(2), 217–231.

Penke, L., Borsboom, D., Johnson, W., Kievit, R. A., Ploeger, A., & Wicherts, J. M. (in press). Evolutionary psychology and intelligence research cannot be integrated the way Kanazawa (2010) suggests. *American Psychologist.*

Peretz, I., & Coltheart, M. (2003). Modularity of music processing. *Nature Neuroscience, 6*(7), 688–691.

Peretz, I., & Zatorre, R. J. (2005). Brain organization for music processing. *Annual Review of Psychology, 56,* 89–114.

Pinker, S. (1997). *How the mind works.* New York, NY: Norton.

Rabaglia, C., Lane, S. P., & Marcus, G. F. (2011), *Why are human cognitive abilities strongly intercorrelated?* Manuscript submitted for publication.

Redies, C., & Puelles, L. (2001). Modularity in vertebrate brain development and evolution. *Bioessays, 23*(12), 1100–1111.

Ritchie, J. B., & Carruthers, P. (2010). Massive modularity is consistent with most forms of neural reuse. *Behavioral and Brain Sciences, 33*(4), 289–290.

SAS Institute (2008). *SAS/STAT 9.2 user's guide.* Cary, NC: Author.

Schlosser, G., & Wagner, G. P. (2004). *Modularity in development and evolution.* Chicago: University of Chicago Press.

Shatil, E., & Share, D. L. (2003). Cognitive antecedents of early reading ability: A test of the modularity hypothesis. *Journal of Experimental Child Psychology, 86*(1), 1–31.

Spearman, C. (1904). "General intelligence," objectively determined and measured. *The American Journal of Psychology, 15*(2), 201–292.

Spivey, M. J., Tanenhaus, M. K., Eberhard, K. M., & Sedivy, J. C. (2002). Eye movements and spoken language comprehension: Effects of visual context on syntactic ambiguity resolution. *Cognitive Psychology, 45*(4), 447–481.

Tanenhaus, M. K., Spivey-Knowlton, M. J., Eberhard, K. M., & Sedivy, J. C. (1995). Integration of visual and linguistic information in spoken language comprehension. *Science, 268*(5217), 1632.

Tarr, M. J., & Gauthier, I. (2000). FFA: A flexible fusiform area for subordinate-level visual processing automatized by expertise. *Nature Neuroscience, 3,* 764–770.

Thomson, G. (1916). A hierarchy without a general factor. *British Journal of Psychology, 8*(3), 271–281.

Van Der Maas, H., Dolan, C., Grasman, R., Wicherts, J., Huizenga, H., & Raijmakers, M. (2006). A dynamical model of general intelligence: The positive manifold of intelligence by mutualism. *Psychological Review, 113*(4), 842–861.

Wagner, G. P., Pavlicev, M., & Cheverud, J. M. (2007). The road to modularity. *Nature Reviews Genetics, 8*(12), 921–931.